Letters from Dorothy

Adventures in the US Foreign Service 1925-1934

Michael Allan Blackledge
Compiler & Narrator

Blackledge Books
14321 Stalgren Court NE
Albuquerque, NM 87123

Manufactured in the United States of America

Library of Congress Cataloging-in-Publication Data

Library of Congress Control Number: 2024915719

Blackledge, Michael Allan
Letters from Dorothy
Adventures in the U.S. Foreign Service 1926-1934
    p.   cm.
Includes bibliographical references and index.

ISBN 978-0-9722704-6-5

Front Cover
 Design: Michael A. Blackledge

Disposition of Letters from Dorothy: A Suggestion for Future Care
This family history has been compiled with the hope that it will be cherished and passed down through generations. To ensure the long-term preservation of this limited-edition compendium, consider donating *Letters from Dorothy* to a library with a genealogy collection, rather than allowing it to be dispersed in an estate sale. Many libraries maintain permanent genealogy and family history collections and would welcome this chronicle.

Contents

Appendices

For Dorothy 1907–1971

Prologue: View from the Roof

"There he is!" Dorothy whispered, peering over the balustrade parapet that crowned the new American Embassy. The Havana sun, even in January, beat down with surprising ferocity, but it was nothing compared to the heat she'd been feeling in her office in the hotel these past six days. Ten-hour days, each one a small victory hard-won, a world away from the life she'd imagined, the life she'd left behind in Ware, Massachusetts. This rooftop vantage point, though, *this* was something else.

> The four-story American Embassy as built in Havana in 1923. Dorothy and her colleagues watched the parade from the roof, looking over the balustrade parapet.

A few years ago, the Embassy itself had been a mere blueprint, a dream of stone and steel. A few years ago, Dorothy was in Massachusetts, an 18-year-old completing her stenography program at Northampton Commercial College, spending her nights in a small attic room. Now she had not only departed Massachusetts – for the first time in her life she was in another country. Staying *and* working at the Sevilla-Biltmore Hotel in a room costing $10 a day. *$10 a day!* What will Arthur think of that?

Dorothy and the US diplomatic mission arrived on Wednesday, checked into the Sevilla-Biltmore, and she'd been working long hours. Her task: typing updates on American views regarding the regulation and promotion of commercial aviation in the Western Hemisphere. Her hometown newspaper misunderstood her role. They assumed she would be taking shorthand during the conference, but those positions were filled by professors from US colleges. Instead, Dorothy's recognized talent was producing polished reports from their dictated notes, much of which were in Spanish and some in Portuguese.

Now it was Sunday, and the delegation had sent a car to bring their clerks from the hotel office to see the President of the United States, driving right up to the Embassy's doorstep. Dorothy held her breath, the humid Havana air thick with anticipation. This was a moment she wouldn't forget. This was an adventure.

From her perch four floors above Calle Obispo, Dorothy had seen the majestic battleship *USS Texas* and its warship escort arrive, the presidential entourage leaving the ships via gangways onto Havana Harbor's piers. The sounds of the parade had intensified for hours, a distant rumble becoming a roar. Finally, it was here. What a day! And now, the main event.

The parade snaked its way down the narrow street, a glittering serpent of polished cars and undulating flags. Dorothy's eyes were fixed on the lead vehicle, a gleaming black convertible. There, in the back seat, sat President Calvin Coolidge himself. She watched as he turned, his face a fleeting glimpse in the bright sunlight, acknowledging the cheers of the crowd. It was dreamlike.

Dorothy's vision for her government job was shifting. *This* was the life, the life she had not even dreamed existed. To be recognized as a valuable part of an important team while stationed in another country. Out of the State Department, into Foreign Service. Yes, Dorothy had to write Mother Kat.

The majestic Hotel Sevilla-Biltmore had been built in 1908; above we see it in 1925, just a few years before Dorothy and the American Delegation moved in for the Sixth Pan-American Conference.

President Calvin Coolidge arrived on Sunday 15 January 1928 aboard the *USS Texas* and provided the keynote address to the Conference on Monday. Lindbergh flew in on 8 February.

THE UNITED STATES PRESIDENT IN CUBA.
President Coolidge driving through Havana, Cuba, on his arrival for the opening of the Conference of the Pan-American Union. Delegates from all the nations of the Western Hemisphere, except Canada, attended the Conference.

Black Diphtheria

requiēscat in pāce

If one American Dream is shattered, is it possible for another to rise from the rubble? To properly appreciate the adventures of Dorothy Forrant in the early 20ᵗʰ century, we need to understand the struggles of her ancestors. Given what her family endured, Dorothy was fortunate even to exist.

Two centuries removed from the horrific experiences of Dorothy's Irish progenitors, it is difficult to comprehend the stressful conditions that most immigrants, especially Irish immigrants, underwent: they felt forced, after years of starvation known as the Great Famine, to acquire the means to get on that ship and come to America.

Though life in Ireland was cruel, emigrating to America was not a joyful event...it was referred to as the American Wake for these people knew they would never see Ireland again. Those who pursued this path did so only because they knew their future in Ireland would only be more poverty, disease, and English oppression. America became their dream. Early immigrant letters described it as a land of abundance and urged others to follow them through the "Golden Door." These letters were read at social events encouraging the young to join them in this wonderful new country. They left in droves on ships that were so crowded, with conditions so terrible, that they were referred to as Coffin Ships.

Even as the boat was docking, these immigrants to America learned that life in America was going to be a battle for survival. Hundreds of runners, usually large greedy men, swarmed aboard the ship grabbing immigrants and their bags trying to force them to their favorite tenement house and then exact an outrageous fee for their services. As the poor immigrant had no means of moving on, they settled in the port of arrival. Almshouses were filled with these Irish immigrants. They begged on every street. One honest immigrant wrote home at the height of the potato famine exodus, "My master is a great tyrant, he treats me as badly as if I was a common Irishman." The writer further added, "Our position in America is one of shame and poverty." No group was considered lower than an Irishman in America during the 1850s.

Free land did not lure them. They rejected the land for the land had rejected them; yet even so they always spoke reverently of the old sod in Ireland. All major cities had their "Irish Town" or "Shanty Town" where the Irish clung together. Our immigrant ancestors were not wanted in America. Ads for employment often were followed by "NO IRISH NEED APPLY." They were forced to live in cellars and shanties, partly because of poverty but also because they were considered bad for the neighborhood...they were unfamiliar with plumbing and running water. These living conditions bred sickness and early death. It was estimated that 80% of all infants born to Irish immigrants in New York City died. Their brogue and dress provoked ridicule; their poverty and illiteracy provoked scorn.

The Chicago Post wrote, "The Irish fill our prisons, our poor houses...Scratch a convict or a pauper, and the chances are that you tickle the skin of an Irish Catholic. Putting them on a boat and sending them home would end crime in this country." [1]

---

[1] "Irish Immigrants in America during the 19th Century," http://www.kinsella.org/history/histira.htm

Dorothy Forrant's ancestors, the Patrick Glancy family of Ware, Massachusetts, were surprisingly well off for first-generation Irish immigrants in the late 1800s. Patrick had been born in Ireland toward the end of the Great Famine[2], in March of 1850 in the County of Roscommon; his spouse Julia Garde was born six years later in Queenstown (now Cobh)[3]. The two had immigrated individually to Massachusetts, where they met and eventually married on 16 February 1879 in Otter River, at ages 29 and 23, respectively.

Soon the family expanded, and about 1892 Patrick applied for a bank loan to obtain farmland outside of Ware, 25 miles south. The loan facilitated the purchase of all the capital equipment required to successfully operate a dairy farm of more than 100 acres. They had several horses, 18 dairy cows, a tractor, a considerable amount of farm machinery, 60 hens — and they soon realized $2,000 a year from their enterprise. It was a true achievement of the American Dream; but it would all change horrifically in the winter of 1895-1896, when five of their seven living children died during what had to have been an unbearable two-month period.

Among Patrick and Julia's seven children at that time, two were boys who both died from diphtheria on Christmas Eve, 1895: Henry Patrick at 8 years of age, and the newest baby, Joseph Francis, at just a few months old. The Glancys boasted two sets of twin daughters: Dorothy's mother Mary was one of a set of twins born on 13 December 1880, and her twin Ellen (known as "Lena") died during that winter, on 4 January 1896, at the age of 15. Celia Catherine Glancy, who would become Dorothy's confidante Aunt Kathie, was also one of a set of twins. Her twin Julia Agnes died that winter (on 4 February 1896) from diphtheria at 11 years of age. A third boy, John Edward, had died the previous week, on 27 January 1896, at age 13.[4] As unimaginably awful as this winter must have been, an even greater tragedy for the family followed in just over a year, as reported rather abruptly in the *Springfield Daily Republican*.

---

[2] Between 1845 and 1852 Ireland suffered a period of starvation and disease that became known as the Great Famine. The potato crop, upon which one-third of Ireland's population was dependent for food, was infected by a crop-destroying disease.

[3] Cove (as in the 'Cove of Cork') was the original name for Cobh, but it changed to Queenstown in 1849 after a visit from Queen Victoria. After the foundation of the Irish Free State in 1922, the town name reverted back to Cobh.

[4] Another boy, Thomas William, had died back in 1892 from "cholera infantum" at 10 months of age. It seems almost superfluous to note that the couple had lost their first born, also named Mary, in July of 1880, at just 8 months old.

HAD HIS NECK BROKEN.
Patrick Glancy, a Farmer, Thrown from his Wagon at Ware.

> WARE, March 9, 1897. Patrick Glancy, age 55[5], a farmer and milkman, while driving a spirited horse on Church street, today, was thrown from his wagon and had his neck broken. He died an hour after. He leaves a widow and two children. Five other children died from diphtheria within a year.

This drastic turnaround in fortune would be memorialized in family lore. In a letter dated May 15, 1942, Dorothy referred to the winter killer as "black diphtheria"[6]: "Diphtheria seems particularly realistic to me because my mother, one of nine children, lost seven brothers and sisters in one year in early childhood. In those days it was called 'black diphtheria'." The death of Patrick Glancy, announced so matter-of-factly in the Springfield newspaper, left Julia as a 40-year-old widow with a graveyard of children, a husband to bury, and two daughters to raise: Dorothy's mother-to-be Mary and Mary's younger sister Kathie.

What was there to do? Julia Glancy had no choice but to sell immediately — at great loss.

Julia held a farm auction, advertised on large (2 ½-by-3 ½-ft) printed posters (reproduced on the following page). The frayed original of this poster was kept by Dorothy and still exists today, now mounted on a poster board backing. The advertisement, dated March of 1897 — just two weeks after her husband's death — provides a considerable amount of detail about the extensive estate, as well as the circumstances leading up to the sale. The sale itself provided relatively little return, although apparently the bank loan had been repaid. The poster presents a poignant account of the couple's accomplishments and the desperate situation of the widow:

> **The late Mr. Glancy bought this place a few years ago, ran into debt for part of it, but he lived to pay for it, laid out on the buildings almost as much as it cost him, raised a large family, and within a year buried five of his children, and at the end of the year by accident died himself, a middle-aged man at that. I say, with all these troubles, mentally, physically, and financially, he owned every dollar's worth of property he left, and several hundred dollars in Savings Bank besides. If this is not the farm to buy at your own price I do not know of one. Mrs. Glancy is left with two minor children, both girls, and no one to see to things, and sees no other way but to sell.**

Patrick Glancy's farm was sold to Joseph Delorme for $4,000. From that amount would be deducted the auctioneer's fee and sale expenses. Julia moved to the small town of Ware and with the net proceeds of the estate sale, purchased a two-story duplex on Eddy Street. One half was rented out, and in the other half Julia lived and raised her two daughters.

Mary was about 16 years of age, and Kathie 12, when the three survivors moved from the family farm to Eddy Street. The sisters would continue their education, both attending Ware High School until they graduated. Then we know that Mary met Joseph Arthur Forrant, and

---

[5] Patrick Glancy would have been 47 years of age, born in 1850.

[6] Diphtheria can cause a gray-to-black, tough, fiber-like covering in the throat called a pseudomembrane. This coating is what French physician Pierre Bretonneau named the disease after in 1826, deriving the word diphthérite from the Greek word diphthera, which means "leather" or "hide."

they married in Salem, Mass., in October 1904. Several years later, Kathie met Roger Crotty, a railroad man, and they married and lived primarily in Waltham, Mass. Kathie and Roger had no children. Mary and Joseph had two: Arthur, born in 1905, and Dorothy Marita, in 1907.

ADMINISTRATRIX SALE
OF
REAL AND PERSONAL
PROPERTY.

Will Be Sold at Public Auction, on

THURSDAY, APRIL 8

AT 9.30 A.M., SHARP,

*[missing]*e of the late Patrick Glancy on the old road leading from Ware
to Gilbertville and near the Asa Breckenridge farm,

the following personal property

*[missing]*ses. all good workers. and one large one; 2 colts, 4-year old, partly broke and 2-year old; 18 cows, all giving *[missing]* 2-year old Heifers. with calf; Yearling Bull. 3 Shoats. 60 to 70 Hens and Roosters. 2 Guinea Roosters. 2-seated Carriage. nearly new. cost $200; single Carriage, 2 Buggies, Express Wagon. good one; 2-horse Wagon, nearly new; 1-horse Wagon, Carriage Pole, low-down Milk Cart nearly new, Tip Cart. Express Sleigh, sleigh. 2-hourse traverse runner Sled, 1-horse Sled, good Buckeye Mowing Machine, horse Rake, Shares Harrow, Cultivator, Cutting Machine. Grindstone, horse Ridger, 1-horse Plough and several Gage Ploughs, 2 Pick Axes, Iron Bars, lot Forks. Binding and Draft Chains. Rakes, Tackle Blocks. 25 Milk Cans. Milk Pails. Milk Tank. several tons Ice. 50 bushels Corn on ear. several Ladders, few Potatoes, some cider. lot of Household Goods. several tons of Good Hay and some Stock Hay. several barrels of hen manure and a few barrels of Ashes. and many other articles too numerous to mention.

At 12 O'Clock the Farm will be sold.

There is a large house with L. also Barn. several small buildings. besides Ice House. Hen House. 100 or more acres of land; 5-acre Lot besides. to be sold separate. The buildings are in good order. Mr. Glancy having laid out more than $1000 on them; all painted and blinded; large light glass windows on house; lots of good spring water at house and barn. The view from the house is just splendid. overlooking the Ware River Valley on the south with Mounts Holyoke, Tom and the Green Mountains in the distance, and the Monadnock Mountain and a large area of scenery in the north. The land is suitably divided into mowing, pasturage, woodland and tillage, the mowing cuts large crops of hay and the pasturage of the best, being able to carry the year round from 20 to 30 head. Plenty of fuel of all kinds and a young orchard 4 years old. There is a first-class milk route connected with the farm which produces yearly nearly $2000 for milk. This is an opportunity seldom offered for someone to purchase a home where everything is already established and all you have to do is turn off the proceeds through your milk route. and take your money every day, no doubts about it. The late Mr. Glancy bought this place a few years ago, ran into debt for a part of it, but he lived to pay for it, laid out on the buildings nearly as much as it cost him, raised a large family, and within a year buried five of his children, and at the end of the year by accident died himself, a middle-aged man at that. I say, with all these troubles, mentally, physically and financially, he owned every dollar's worth of property he left, and hundreds of dollars in Savings Bank besides. If this is not the farm to buy at your own price I do not know of one. Mrs. Glancy is left with two minor children. both girls. and no one to see to things, and sees no other way but to sell. This is no humbug sale. Everything to be sold to highest bidder. Any parties wishing to view the premises before the day of the auction will find Mrs. Glancy on the premises, who will give all the information desired. Come one, come all. Remember the day and the hour. Terms of personal property ninety days with good indorsed note. 6 per cent. interest. Terms of real estate. $100 down at the time of sale. One-half of balance can remain on mortgage at 6 per cent. Insurance goes with sale

MRS. JULIA GLANCY, Administratrix.
B. F. DAVIS, AUCTIONEER.

Ware. March 25. 1897

WA[missing][missing] **PRINT, WARE**

Transcription of the sale announcement poster for the farm estate of Patrick and Julia Glancy, 1897.

Ware

Faber est quisque suae fortunae.

As promised in the advertising poster, the Glancy Dairy Farm was gone with the drop of the auctioneer's hammer at noon on Thursday, 8 April 1897. This event was closely followed by Julia Glancy's purchase of a two-story duplex on Eddy St. in the nearby town of Ware, Massachusetts. Considering her situation, this was a wise decision that provided stability — and potential income — for herself and her two teenage daughters. Mary Viola, known as May, was the oldest by four years of the two and married first, at All Saints Catholic Church in Ware on 25 October 1904. May's sister Kathie served as bridesmaid.

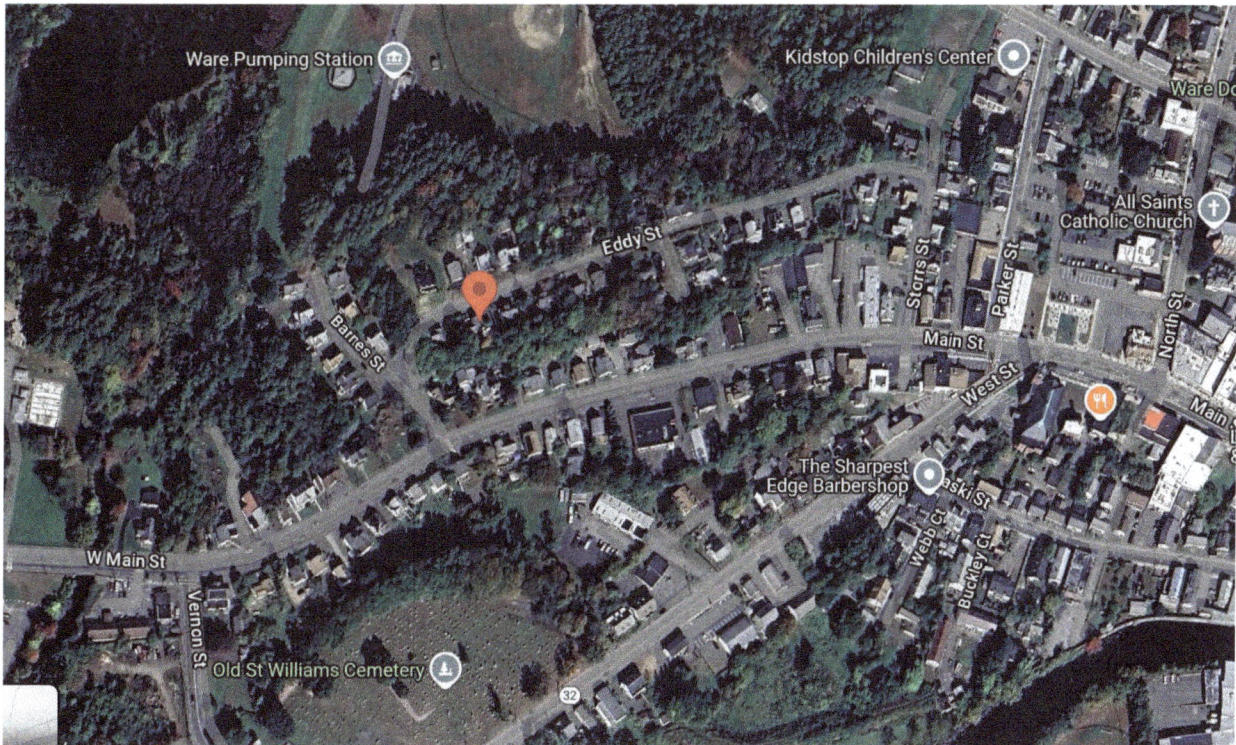

In this current-day drone view of Ware, much of Dorothy's life can be seen within walking distance of "Gran" Julia Glancy's duplex on Eddy St. (red pin). To the north is the Ware Pumping Station, a favorite picnic/park area for May and her children; to the east is All Saints Catholic Church, where Joseph and May Forrant were married in 1904; and to the South is Old St Williams Cemetery, where the Patrick Glancy eight-grave obelisk is the resting place for Julia's husband and her five children, lost to the Black Diphtheria during the winter of 1895-6.

Mary/May Glancy (23) married Joseph Forrant, a 27-year-old butcher from Salem. The Worcester Telegram wrote up the occasion with some fanfare in a lengthy article [see snippet], announcing hundreds of attendees at All Saints Catholic Church, with 60 guests driven after the ceremony to the Wedding Breakfast held at 10 am at the Commercial Hotel, one of the four major hotels in town (along with the Hampshire House, the Mansion House, and the Storrs

House). The couple was to take up residence in Arthur's home town of Salem to start their new life together. May was described as being "among Ware's most popular" and Arthur as "employed in a meat market in Salem."

The article used several column inches to list the wedding gifts received by the couple, and from whom, e.g., $25 from Mrs. Forrant, mother of the groom; silver sugar spoon and marble clock from Miss Katherine Glancy; a Morris chair from shopmates of the bride in the Thomas McBride room of the Otis Company; a wine set from Mrs. Julia Glancy.

The couple moved into Joseph's dwelling in Salem. A son, Arthur, was born to the couple in October 1905; Dorothy was born in February 1907. Sometime around 1913, the little family moved to Ware and took up residence with May's mother in the duplex Mrs. Glancy had purchased with the sale of the family's dairy farm.

Initially Dorothy's was a happy childhood, but after her father died in March of 1921 from what the death certificate lists as General Paralysis of the Insane – syphilis – at just 37 years of age, the family fell into financial straits. At the time that "Pa" died, Dorothy was 14 years old, and Arthur 15. May's mother would die just three years later, in 1924, and May and her sister Kathie inherited the Eddy St duplex. The sisters had been working at the Ware Woolen Mill over the years, and their finances did not improve.

In the early 1900s, the small town of Ware, Massachusetts was home to three major manufacturers: the Otis, Stevens and Gilbert companies, who were noted for their production of textiles, clothing and shoes. The three companies combined employed just over 2,000 workers — quite an impact for a town of 8,800. Their demand for labor brought numerous immigrant families, primarily French, Irish and Polish, to this rich job market. Though jobs were available, living wages were not.

MANY GIFTS FOR BRIDAL COUPLE.

Sixty at Wedding Breakfast at Commercial Hotel, in Ware

JOSEPH A. FORRANT AND MISS MAY V. GLANCY MARRY.

Then They Hie Away Toward Boston Unobserved.

Special to The Telegram

WARE, Oct. 25.—The marriage of Miss Mary Viola, daughter of Mrs. Julia Glancey, Eddy street, to Joseph Arthur Forrant of Salem, formerly of Warren, took place this morning in All Saints church, and was witnessed by hundreds of people.

The church was crowded with relatives and friends of the young couple, Miss Glancey being one of Ware's popular young women. At 9 o'clock the bridal party entered the church and was escorted to the altar by the ushers, in charge of Frank E. Donahue of Worcester, while Miss Nellie G. Carroll, organist, played Mendelssohn's wedding march. Rev Jeremiah A. Riordan, curate, performed the ceremony and officiated at

Above left is the only known photo of Dorothy's "Pa" Joseph Forrant, with Dorothy perched on a wall, and mother Mary/May sporting an umbrella *(June 1913)*. At right is May with son Arthur (somewhat obscured) and Dorothy *(July 1913)*. Perhaps Arthur took the photo at left, and his father took the second. Both photos taken at the Ware Pumping Station, a favorite local outing/picnic area.

Growing up in Ware: *(left)* Dorothy (6) and Arthur (7) on the porch at 46 Eddy St., July 1913. *(at right)* Friend Louise Barry and May Forrant, with Arthur and Dorothy, summer 1914, Eddy St., Ware.

The textile mill was the employer for both men and women. If you look over the 1920 Federal Census sheets of small towns in Massachusetts, you will note (Question 26: "Trade, profession, or particular kind of work done") an occupation response for many of the women, especially the young women: *Operative*. What is an operative?

The Industrial Revolution "transformed economies that had been based on agriculture and handicrafts into economies based on large-scale industry, mechanized manufacturing, and the factory system." (Brittanica.com)

The period spanned from about 1760 to 1840, and in Massachusetts, it made textile manufacturing the dominant industry. The early mills were relatively small, only employing 100 workers or so. However, they gave local mechanics and engineers opportunities to learn rudimentary mill construction, and inspired wealthy merchants in the state to think bigger and develop more sophisticated industrial plans.[1]

One such wealthy merchant was Francis Cabot Lowell, a Newburyport, Massachusetts native who formed the Boston Manufacturing Company (which later became the Boston Associates) and established his first mill in Waltham, Massachusetts in 1813. Lowell's mill used new types of technology, such as a water-driven power loom, and employed young adult women, known as "mill girls," to run the equipment instead of children.

Due to Lowell's success, many new mills and mill towns began to sprout up along rivers across Massachusetts and New England. Around 45 mill towns were established during the Industrial Revolution just in Massachusetts alone. One such town was Ware, with the Ware

---

[1] https://historyofmassachusetts.org/massachusetts-textile-mills/

River providing the power for the looms in such an operation. The "girls" would list their trade as Laborer or Operative, and their industry as Mill – in fact, "cotton mill" was used in the 1920 Census instructions as a sample answer to Question 27 ("Industry, Business, or Establishment in which at work").

Here is how the Hampshire Mills Group of England describes the industry at the time:

> Of all the different industries that the mills of Hampshire were once involved in, these days we only think in terms of producing flour. Back then our watermills were used for pulling wool and working other textile products. Our mills processed fibers of jute, flax, and sheep's wool and these in turn provided industry for many dexterous hands both male and female, whether adult or child, in the matter of spinning and weaving for the cloth trade.

In the states, the employed were predominately female. We see these occupations in the Forrant family going forward – for example, for Richard Forrant's mother Anna as reported in the Worcester Telegram (2011):

> Anna was a spinner for five years at the former Hampshire Woolen Co., retiring in 1979. Previously, she worked many years at the former Ware Knitters, Inc. on E. Main St., Ware.

A spinner operated one of the 'spinning jenny' machines, which had revolutionized the process of spinning yarn by allowing a single operator to spin multiple threads simultaneously. All of the manufacturing occurred under one roof: Raw cotton entered at one end of the factory and finished cloth exited at the other end. This type of manufacturing and labor management later became known as the Lowell System and it completely revolutionized textile manufacturing, making it more efficient and cost effective. It provided employment for hundreds, but the job could be quite tedious for the operatives.

Growing up in Ware: at left, Arthur and Dorothy in their only known formal photograph, circa 1913. At right, Dorothy and Arthur pose at the Eddy St. house with their "Gran," Julia Glancy, circa 1916.

Many of Dorothy's friends who did not marry directly after high school would become mill operatives. In contrast, Dorothy developed a skill that would transform her life — she was a fast and accurate typist.

We know this because of the results of the annual high school typing competitions posted in the local Ware River News, where Dorothy was listed among the winners. The larger typewriter manufacturers of the day, Underwood and Remington, encouraged and sponsored these competitions, providing ribbons and medals for the winners.

Dorothy graduated in a class of 45 — the yearbook profiles only 36; however, the Commencement Program lists 45 – from Ware High School on Friday, 26 June 1925, with the ceremony held in Town Hall. The program divided the 45 grads into Pro Merito (10

Typewriting Awards

The following awards have been made for February in typewriting by the pupils of the Commercial department of the Ware High school, of which Miss Gabrielle E. Lemaitre is teacher: Certificates, 30-word awards: Miss Margaret Garde, Miss Stephanie Sokolowska, Miss Dorothy Forrant, Miss Freda Bloom, Miss Sophie Mettig, Miss Hazel Allen and Maurice Allman; bronze medals, 40-word awards: Miss Florence Siarkiewicz and Miss Carolyn Kristek; 50-word award, Miss Catherine McGrath.

Certificates, 30-word awards: Miss Hazel Allen, Miss Margaret Garde, Miss Helen C. McGrath and Maurice Allman; certificates, 25-word award: Miss Ruth Jacobs and Miss Margaret Malboeuf; 40-word award: Miss Rachel Cummings and Miss Florence Siarkiewicz.

with honors), Classical (total of 9, 6 with honors), Scientific (1 boy), General (16, 1 with honors), and Commercial (9 including Dorothy, and 2 with honors). One one can easily argue that Dorothy Forrant took to heart the Class of 1925 motto: *Faber est quisque suae fortunae.*

This Latin phrase can be found in more than one version:
- *Faber est quisque furtunae suae*
- *Faber est quisque suae fortunae* (Dorothy's class's choice)
- *Faber est suae quisque furtunae*
- *Quisque faber suae fortunae* (from Appius Claudius Caecus, 340 BC – 273 BC)

This Latin idiom in any of the versions translates to *"every man is the architect of his own fortune."* The phrase had been rediscovered and celebrated by humanists during the Renaissance, and conveys the idea that people can succeed through hard work and perseverance — that they should take control of their own lives rather than waiting for others to rescue them. We will see that Dorothy embraced this message throughout her career — and life.

Dorothy Marita Forrant. "Dot". Basketball, I—II—III—IV. Dramatics, III—IV. Asst. Editor of "The Limelight".

"Dot" is the best dispositioned girl in our class. Her sunny disposition makes any class interesting. Practical jokes keep Dot busy. Her vivid imagination was shown in all the compositions that she passed in English IV. Her good looks and charm make them all fall. A dance in Ware or vicinity would not be complete without Dot's presence. Like a duck she is fond of water and cares not when or how. Dot's idea of heaven is not complete without a bowl of chicken chop-suey. She is the center on the basket ball team and took her part with laurels in the Senior Class Play "Getting Acquainted with Madge". Dot is the fastest girl in the class—in typeing. We hope that Dot will never outgrow her honest-to-goodness kiddishness.

Dorothy was active at Ware High School. The class graduated in specialties – what today we might consider majors. In Dorothy's Commercial group were two of her best friends, Albenia

Elliot and Margaret Garde (also her cousin, whom she would visit in 1932). The senior class initiated "The Limelight" as a yearbook, and Albenia and Dorothy served as assistant editors.

The class also reinstituted varsity basketball, and the 5' 7 ½" Dorothy eventually became team captain. Prophetically, the senior class trip was to Washington, D.C. She would return!

EDITORIAL STAFF
Back Row: Dorothy Forrant, Earle Trudeau, Albenia Elliott, Doris Buckley, Margaret Garde, David Kaplan
Front Row: Edmund Jacques, Norbert Lanier, Rose Rohan, Freda Bloom, (Edit. in chief) Chandler Lincoln, Muriel Goodenough.

GIRLS' BASKETBALL TEAM
Back Row: Elizabeth Shea, Genevieve Gura, Jennie Mulvany, Bessie O'Connell, Miss Whitney, (Coach).
Front Row: Madeline Haley, Dorothy Forrant, Rose Rohan, (capt.) Mary Shea, Rose Sjostek.

Washington, D.C.

The Ware High School Class of 1925 fundraised for its Senior Trip to Washington, D.C. The nation's capital, with its bustling energy, offered a stark contrast to the students' familiar surroundings. In Ware, the textile mill dominated the local economy, providing employment for many residents, including Dorothy's mother, brother, and aunt. This trip to Washington, D.C., promised a glimpse into a different world, one dominated by federal government employment rather than the industrial landscape of their hometown. The photo below shows the size of a mill of the time as well as some of the workforce (New Bedford, MA).

The typing competition that propelled Dorothy's State Department career was a semiannual event. The dominant typewriter companies, Underwood and Remington, would hold their contests in January and June at high schools that had a commercial/typing curriculum. Such competitions could extend well beyond high school typing classes, as seen at right at the 'Nationals' for the "World's Champion Typists."

The competition between Underwood and Remington is interesting in itself. In 1874, the Underwood family made only typewriter ribbon and carbon paper; they were among a number of firms that produced these goods for Remington. When Remington decided to start producing ribbons itself, the Underwoods opted to manufacture typewriters. Launched in 1900, the Underwood No. 5 has been described as "the first truly modern typewriter." Two million of these typewriters had been sold by the early 1920s, when Dorothy was in her senior year, and their sales were equal in quantity to all of the other firms in the typewriter industry combined. From the Underwood history[1]:

> During typing competitions, each word is arbitrarily good for five touches. A typist that does 120 words a minute, does 600 theoretical touches a minute. That is ten a second! Stella Willins once typed a repetitive sentence with 264 words a minute. That is 22 touches a second - as fast as you are now reading.

> Is it a coincidence that there are Underwood medals? No it is not, as that manufacturer dominates in all speed competitions since the turn of the century. Not because the Underwood 5 is quicker than an L.C. Smith or a Royal, but because the Underwood has the best 'racing stable' of super typists ... and Charles E. Smith; talent scout in secretary schools, coach, ergonomist and ruthless trainer of 'his' typists in the Underwood training hall at Vesey Street 30, New York.

Pictured below is the Remington 12, the Underwood No. 5, and Underwood medals for 'speed and accuracy' (40 net words) similar to those won by Dorothy and her classmates at Ware High School in 1924 and 1925.

---

[1] https://www.typewriter.be/missspeed.htm (accessed 7 November 2024)

Dorothy's success in high school led her to a one-year secretarial course at the Northampton Commercial College, just 25 miles from Ware. Her transcript shows the range of her training, with one low grade – penmanship. Her success there encouraged her to apply for a clerk/secretarial job with the U.S. Government.

NORTHAMPTON COMMERCIAL COLLEGE, INC
Northampton, Massachusetts

Transcript of Record of

Name Dorothy Forrant Blackledge   Address   2307 Gramercy, Houston 25, Texas

Date of Entrance	Date of Withdrawal	Date of Graduation	Course
9-1-25	6-15-26	6-15-26	Stenographic

Ware High School, Graduated 1925

Subjects	No. of Weeks	Periods per Week	Minutes in Periods	Clock Hours	Grades	Remarks
Accounting I (Elementary)						
Accounting II (Applied Work)						
Accounting III (Intermediate)						
Accounting IV (Advanced)						
Accounting V (Cost)						
Accounting VI (Auditing)						
Accounting VII (Corporation)						
Business Mathematics I	16	5	30	40	B	
Business Mathematics II						
Business Finance						
Business Law I						
Business Law II						
Business Organization						
Business Letter Writing	20	2	60	40	B+	
Economics						
English	20	2	60	40	B+	
Filing	8	5	30	20	A	
Income Tax Procedure						
Marketing						
Office Machines & Appliances	16	5	30	40	A-	
Office Practice, Secretarial	7	5	180	105	A-	
Penmanship	16	5	30	40	C	
Salesmanship						
Shorthand Theory	40	10	60	400	A-	
Shorthand Transcription 120 wds)						
Shorthand Transcription wds)						
Typewriting	40	5	60	200	A	
Word Study	20	5	30	50	A-	

Grading System: A, 93-100; A-, 90-92; B+, 87-89; B, 83-86; B-, 80-82; C+, 77-79
(Lowest certifying grade); C, 73-76; C-, 70-72; D, 60-69.
E, Below 60.

Date   June 9, 1953   Signature   Henry H. Frow
Title   Head of the Accounting Department

During her year at NCC, Dorothy shared an attic room in Northampton with another student; she would take the bus home to Ware on some weekends if she couldn't catch a ride. (Throughout her life, Dorothy never learned to drive but always became skilled in using the local public transportation, wherever she was.) [Because his aunt had gone there, Dorothy's nephew Richard Forrant attended NCC from 1960-1962, right after graduation[2]. Classes were five days per week — usually three on Monday, Wednesday and Friday, and two on Tuesday and Thursday. Unlike his aunt, Richard was a commuter in his baby blue Pontiac Tempest (paid in cash by his mother, Anna Swirk Forrant, with savings garnered over many years from her time at the Hampshire Woolen Mill, which additionally provided Richard with a $200 scholarship).]

Dorothy attended NCC to increase her chances of landing a job other than one in the mill. In the period between World Wars I and II, women made up more than half the work force in the Department of State, with most of their number in lower-ranking clerical jobs. Entry to that world was Dorothy's goal.

And that negotiation process started in 1925 — using the return address of Northampton Commercial College, not her mother's Ware address. Dorothy applied for employment with the State Department in late 1925, but had to decline what she was offered in December of that year until she was ready to move in September 1926. And with that, her world changed overnight: she was now in the Federal Government.

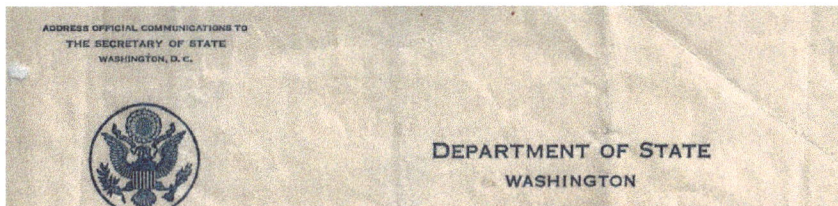

ADDRESS OFFICIAL COMMUNICATIONS TO
THE SECRETARY OF STATE
WASHINGTON, D. C.

DEPARTMENT OF STATE
WASHINGTON

---

[2] Richard recalls: "I did pretty well there, achieving the Dean's List and became Senior Class President. No other colleges were considered by anyone because [Dorothy] went there! I did not research any other schools because it was reasonably close for commuting to keep the cost down and tuition was affordable."

DEPARTMENT OF STATE
WASHINGTON

September 2, 1926.

Miss Dorothy M. Forrant,

    31 Park Street,

        Northampton, Massachusetts.

Madam:

    The Department has been informally notified that you have requested the Civil Service Commission to suspend your name from its registers until September 13, 1926. The records of the Department of State show that on or about December 1, 1925, you were offered a position as Stenographer-Typist at $1320 per annum which was declined by telegraph. Will you please let me know by return mail if you will be in a position to consider an offer of appointment about September 13, 1926 of the same character as that offered before? In any event, please inform me at your earliest convenience of your intentions in the matter.

    I am, Madam,

        Your obedient servant,
        For the Secretary of State:

P. F. Allen

        Assistant to the Chief Clerk
        and Chief, Appointment Section.

Washington, D.C.

Once she accepted a clerk/stenographer job with the U.S. State Department, Dorothy moved to Washington, D.C. and lived in a boardinghouse with three roommates, all of whom were working as clerks/typists/stenographers for the State Department. Dorothy would go swimming at the YWCA during her time in D.C. — she would always enjoy staying physically active during her postings.

August 1927: living in Washington D.C. while employed at State Dept. Dorothy is front at left, with her good friend Bee Comeau at her side.

In the photo above we see Dorothy and her three roommates, one of whom was Bee Comeau; the four young men are also roommates in their lodging at the D.C. boarding house. Even in D.C., Dorothy was reminded of her mother and brother's situation back home. The following recollections were captured in a July 1929 letter to Aunt Kathie:

When I went to high school I used to take the old petticoats [Mother] threw in the ragbag and dye them and make dresses and I am sure nobody showed me anything about sewing, I just did it because I had to. When Arthur and Mother don't have to work in the mill they don't do anything at home. What I mean is, they think I am just having the life of Rielly all the time. They don't realize that ever since I left school I have been studying something or other, either to improve my shorthand or Spanish and if I didn't do that I would take lessons in dress-making or try to learn it by myself. They just say, Dottie's lucky. Well, maybe it is luck to study Spanish every day and to work overtime every chance I get to show them that I want to make good. And then Arthur is thinking of getting married, working

Roommate and good friend Bee Comeau at the Washington D.C. boarding house, c. 1927.

a few days in the mill and still paying for the engagement ring. And then it will be Dottie, lend me some money. They think I am rolling in money, I guess. They think I dress extravagantly. It is no exaggeration to say that I am the poorest dressed girl in the Service and always have been in Washington. All the other girls used to owe money in every store in town and got clothes and money from home too. They don't realize that when you work in a business office you can't dress like you would for a shop or factory. You just can't get away with it, and when you are invited out

```
somewhere you can't refuse and consequently you are
compelled to invite people out yourself once in a while.
Mother's been working about three or four days a week on
the average for about three years now.  Do you think I
would stay hanging on to a job like that when I was able
bodied and knew if I just watched the papers that there are
lots of other chances in other places than Ware. There are
lots of women who make money by canning jellies or making
cakes. It just takes a little ambition that's all. It would
be different if Mother and Arthur were sickly or something
like that. They are just content to drift along and know if
the worse comes to the worse little Dorothy can help them
out.
```

Dorothy would stay close to her roommates from D.C., even after she was posted to Buenos Aires. This is from June 1929:

```
I hear from the girls quite a lot and Bee sent me two
lovely books and a great big thing of soap. One of my
roommates is getting married (in Washington) and the other
one has gone home sick so I guess our room is all broken up
now.
```

We can glean something of Dorothy's life in D.C. from this future observation in a letter from Habana, June 21, 1928:

```
You see there is really too much competition in
Washington to really amount to much but in a consulate or
embassy there is a darn good chance because there are
sometimes only three or four people in the whole consulate
and when I come back to the States I will be able to get a
job almost anywhere.
```

In that letter, we hear echoes of Dorothy's class motto again — "Everyone is the architect of their own life" — in her 'why not?' attitude about going abroad.

Why not, indeed? The opportunity will quickly arise.

Habana

Wait a minute! Is it Habana or Havana? Shouldn't it be Havana, as in Havana cigars?

We need to consider Dorothy's timeline – but first, some historical perspective.

In 1514, Diego Velázquez founded the city *San Cristóbal de la Habana* ("Saint Christopher of the Habana"), the sixth city founded by the Spaniards in Cuba, and the one which later became the capital. **Habana** was the name of the local tribe. When Habana was adapted into English, it became Havana. Theoretically there is a difference, although they are pronounced very similarly.[1]

Since the 1930s, Havana has been the prevailing term in English language dictionaries in reference to the capital of Cuba, but the 'old school' spelling was **Habana**. Use of the spelling *Havana* in literature peaked during the Spanish Civil War (1936-1939), in the years following Dorothy's service with the State Department, and it never changed back. (Yes, Hemingway used *Havana*.) In the first few letters sent to her mother, Dorothy used **Habana** but later switched to **Havana**; the US State Department consistently writes it as **Habana** during this time period.

Sixth International Conference of American States, held at Habana, January 16 to February 20, 1928[2]

More background: The Conferences of American States, commonly referred to as the Pan-American Conferences, were meetings of the Pan-American Union, an international organization for cooperation on trade. Back in the early 1800s, James G. Blaine, a U.S. politician, Secretary of State, and presidential contender, first proposed the establishment of closer ties between the United States and its southern neighbors via an international conference. Blaine hoped that stronger bonds between the United States and its southern counterparts would open Latin American markets to U.S. trade.

On December 2, 1823, President James Monroe had delivered the Monroe Doctrine which would eventually influence then-current Secretary of State Blaine to push for the creation of the Pan-American Conferences. In his speech to Congress, President Monroe stated that any further attempts by the Europeans to colonize the Americas (North, Central and South) would be seen as an act of aggression and would risk intervention by the United States. This doctrine would ensure that the current colonies remained independent but would allow for relationships to slowly develop between the countries.

Through his lobbying of Congress, Blaine succeeded in establishing/hosting/initiating the First International Conference of American States held in Washington, D.C. during 1889-90. Blaine died a few years later, and it was another decade before the second Conference was held, hosted in Mexico. Subsequent conferences followed, although not at a regular interval, until the Sixth was hosted by Cuba in 1928. This was to be 'Dorothy's Conference.' A total of 19 such conferences have been held as of 2024, with the most recent in 2011 (Canada).

---

[1] See https://en.wikipedia.org/wiki/Betacism
[2] See also *Sixth International Conference of American States, Habana, Cuba, January 16, 1928, Special Handbook for the Use of Delegates, prepared by the Pan American Union (Washington, Government Printing Office, 1927);* https://history.state.gov/historicaldocuments/

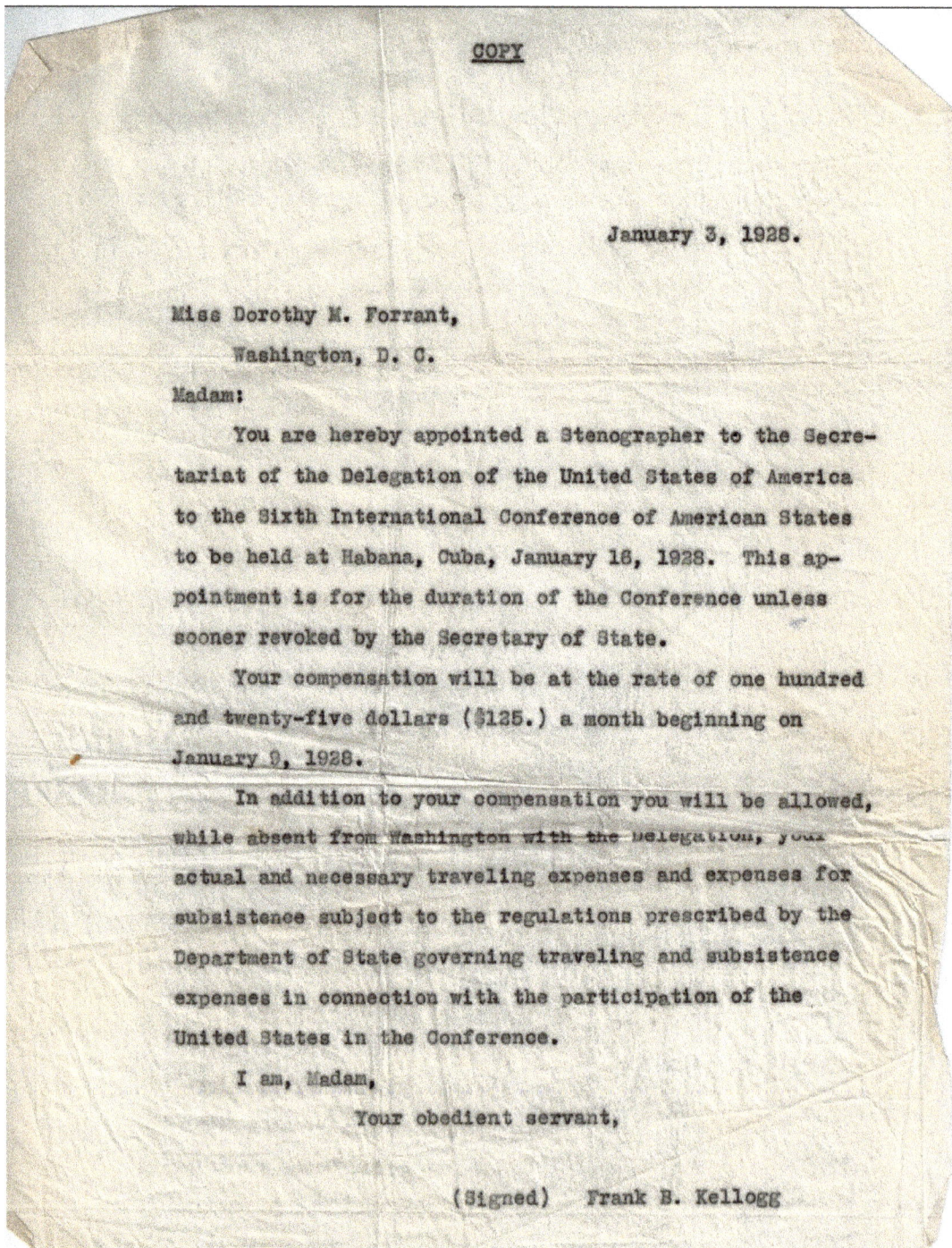

COPY

January 3, 1928.

Miss Dorothy M. Forrant,
    Washington, D. C.
Madam:

    You are hereby appointed a Stenographer to the Secretariat of the Delegation of the United States of America to the Sixth International Conference of American States to be held at Habana, Cuba, January 16, 1928. This appointment is for the duration of the Conference unless sooner revoked by the Secretary of State.

    Your compensation will be at the rate of one hundred and twenty-five dollars ($125.) a month beginning on January 9, 1928.

    In addition to your compensation you will be allowed, while absent from Washington with the Delegation, your actual and necessary traveling expenses and expenses for subsistence subject to the regulations prescribed by the Department of State governing traveling and subsistence expenses in connection with the participation of the United States in the Conference.

    I am, Madam,

      Your obedient servant,

        (Signed) Frank B. Kellogg

COPY

January 3, 1928.

Miss Dorothy M. Forrant,
    Washington, D. C.
Madam:

You are hereby appointed a Stenographer to the Secretariat
of the Delegation of the United States of America to the
Sixth International Conference of American States to be held
at Habana, Cuba, January 16, 1928. This appointment is for
the duration of the Conference unless sooner revoked by the
Secretary of State.

Your compensation will be at the rate of one hundred and
twenty-five dollars ($125.) a month beginning on January 9,
1928.

In addition to your compensation you will be allowed,
while absent from Washington with the Delegation, your actual
and necessary traveling expenses and expenses for subsistence
subject to the regulations prescribed by the Department of
State governing traveling and subsistence expenses in
connection with the participation of the United States in the
Conference.

I am, Madam,

        Your obedient servant,

                (Signed)   Frank B. Kellogg

The timing of the 1928 conference was ideal for Dorothy, who at the age of 21 had worked in D.C. for two years — long enough to impress members of the Department with her skills and diligence. She was invited to be a clerk at the Sixth Conference in Habana, and this adventure served as a catalyst for future promotions and posts.

The conference started on Monday, January 16, 1928. Dorothy had special duty pay starting January 9th and the U.S. delegation arrived several days prior to that opening session. Dorothy would be more consistent in dating letters home later in the Foreign Service portion of her career; however they were undated in Habana. Here is Dorothy's letter prior to January 15th to "Mother Kat," her mother Mary back in Ware:

Dorothy Forrant to Go to Cuba

Miss Dorothy Forrant a secretary in the state department at Washington, D. C., has been chosen as one of the secretaries to accompany the United States delegation to the Pan-American conference this month in Cuba. Miss Forrant is a daughter of Mrs Mary Forrant of Eddy street. She graduated from Ware High school, and Northampton Business college, attaining high honors in her business studies at both schools. She took the civil service examination for government service shortly after her graduation.

1928, January 11: Springfield Republican Daily, "Ware News", page 11.

        Care of the Delegation of the
        United States,
        Hotel Sevilla_Biltmore,
        Room 105,

Dearest Mother:

Well, I have arrived at last. I had a wonderful journey on the boat and was seasick a little but not much. I have a private room with a private bath and a telephone and everything. The only thing is everytime you turn around you have to tip everybody. And talk about your prices in this hotel for eating. This morning I had a glass of milk and two coffee rolls and it cost .50 and I had to tip .15 which made it .65. If you don't tip you don't even get waited on. Well, last night we went to a restaurant and it cost me $2.20 for just a plain dinner. Well, we are allowed $8. a day for food so I guess it will be all right but they sure do charge you.

It is very pretty here with tall, slim palm trees and some of them are cocoanut palms and have big clusters of cocoanuts on them. Everybody where you go you see saloons and the funniest looking people. They go around with shawls on their heads. We went for a ride on a rubbernecked bus last night and saw the whole town, the Casino the big gambling joint and the President's palace. The streets are very narrow and they haven't any traffic rules at all but drive on whatever side of the street they want and dodge in and out all the time and park wherever they want. The President of the United States is coming to Habana Monday and the President of Cuba has proclaimed a leagal [sic] holiday in his honor. They're going to have big bands and everything. The Hotel we are staying at is the most expensive in the city. Even my room is $10. a day without meals. Hot Dog! What does Arthur think of it? It is not so warm as I expected but they say this weather is unusual so I am hoping for some swimming by Sunday.

Did I tell you the girls gave me a surprise party before leaving? They gave me a lovely robe and satin mules. And all went down to the train with me. Another gave me a box of chocolates and another a brassiere. Well, Mother Cat, I will write some more later.

Love, Dorothy. X X

Save this for me Kathryn bring it along when you come

And this was soon followed by another letter:

Dearest Mother:

Thanx for the clippings. Did you get the Havana post I sent you? I know you will be interested to know that I have met a nice English boy here who teaches English in the University of Havana. He is 27, speaks Russian, German, French and Also Spanish like a native, has a college degree and also has a little importing business. He seems to like me very much and is a perfect gentleman. He is blond, very tall and nice looking. Now I suppose you will begin to worry, but if you do I won't tell you anything else because I can take care of myself and know what I am doing by this time.

Well, that old Ware River news ought to be down here if they think I'm not working, seven days a week and until 12 at night sometimes and often until 9:30 or 10. But it is worth it because you see a lot down here.

I have sent to Hoffman's for some pictures and will send you one. Tell Arthur to be sure of himself before he gets too serious with that Sarah Bouvier. I think she is a very nice girl, though. Does he ever hear from Milly? Do you ever see Freda now. Well, Mother Kat, I will write you again later. When you find time drop me a line, too. You don't write as often as you used to, do you?

                                        Love, Dorothy. X X

P.S. The boy's name is Herbert Richer and he has been all around the world to Egypt, France, Germany and used to live in Russia.

The following letter was typed on 16 January, the opening day of the Conference, as Dorothy tells us. Finally she can see a bit of how important this conference is diplomatically, as the President arrives to initiate the proceedings. "It sure is worth it."

                                   Care of Am. Delegation
                                   Hotel Sevilla-Biltmore,
                                   Habana, Cuba.

Dearest Mother:

Why don't you write to me? I am working pretty much so I can't write very much but it seems nice to get a letter once in a while. Yesterday (Sunday) I worked from 9 to 3:30 without anything to eat and then I went out for an hour to see the parade (the President's arrival and then came back and worked until 7:30, so you see I am pretty well tied up and am pretty tired. But it sure is worth it. It was so thrilling yesterday. We were on

THE UNITED STATES PRESIDENT IN CUBA.
President Coolidge driving through Havana, Cuba, on his arrival for the opening of the Conference of the Pan-American Union. Delegates from all the nations of the Western Hemisphere, except Canada, attended the Conference.

the roof of the American Embassy watching the ships come in the harbor with the President. He had about six big ships

escorting him and all you could hear was whistles blowing and
cannons shooting. Then the President came down the street and
all the crowds were lined up and throwing flowers in his path
and we could see fine because we had some field glasses. And
the camera men were turning their cranks a mile a minute.
Just now (this is Monday) they gave us girls tickets for the
opening session of the Conference which is to be held in the
National Theatre. All the men have silk hats on and dress
suits. I went to a Spanish church yesterday and they only
take up a collection from the people who hold their hands out
but there are beggars at the door so you have to give them
some. Gee, Mother, you would think you were rich if you ever
saw the people here. They go around dressed in rags and are
always begging.

   I think I could get a job down here if I wanted to but I
don't think I will stay because the people are so dirty
looking and everything is so expensive. Last night it cost
me $2.40 for dinner and I had only a little kind of a Spanish
stew. So it is a good thing that we get $8.00 a day to eat
on because you have to tip or get kicked out.
Well, Mother, I will write some more later because they are going to take us up to
the Conference in a car now.
                    Love, Dorothy X X Write soon.

Finally, Dorothy received a stack of letters from her mother. We know this was typed on a
Wednesday so most likely it was January 25, 1928.

Dearest Mother:

   I was so glad to get some letters from you. It is too bad
about Violet Wilson, but that is nobody's business but her
own, of course. That was a real nice letter that Emma wrote,
wasn't it? And what she said about Pa was also very nice.
Don't you worry about me dieting I have wonderful meals, even
though they do cost a lot. I am never sick, you know. I
haven't gone swimming yet because I didn't have time at first
but now it is too cold but I hope to go Sunday as it is
getting warmer. You ask me where we are working. The
American Delegation has its offices in the lobby of the Hotel
Sevilla and our rooms are right beside the offices so we have
just to crawl out of bed into the office. But of course we
have to eat breakfast first. Please do not get the idea that
I take shorthand at the Conference. The secretaries, well
known professors from different colleges, do that and then
dictate reports to us. You see a great part of the conference
is in Spanish and some in Portuguese. I don't know where the
Ware River News got all those funny ideas in their heads. Of
course I haven't time to look up the Faneuf's, Mother, and I
don't know where they are. Is Freda still living with her
Mother or is she living in Springfield and working? How is
Arthur's lady friend. Remember me to her. Tell Arthur not to
give her too many presents until he is sure he is in love

with her. I worked Sunday until 11 p.m. at night so Mother
don't think you have to work hard at all. But we got
yesterday afternoon off. (This is Wednesday) I sent Dr.
Barrett his money today.

Wait till I tell you. I went to the Carnival Ball Saturday
night. Tickets were given to all the Delegates (5 bucks each
person) and Mr. Fletcher and Mr. Hughes and their respective
wives couldn't go so we three girls and an older lady went
and some of the newspaper men escorted us and what a sight it
was! It's the big ball of the year. The customs were just
magnificent and just oodles of work on them, all kinds of
flowers and the staircases were covered with great big
butterflies and daises and roses and they threw confetti and
in one part of the ballroom they would be dancing Cuban music
and another American. One of the old newspaper reporters and
I tried to dance the Cuban dance and the Cuban people said
Fine, Fine. That was the only thing they could say in
English. I have picked up quite a bit of Spanish and think I
will study it when I get back. The Cuban Government has been
just grand to us. Most every night we have free tickets to
the theatre, box seats, with the American flag draped over it
and yesterday they offered a big boat ride that lasted all
day to the delegation. I didn't go because I had some important work but I didn't care much about it as I was afraid
I would be seasick. Anyhow they furnished refreshments free,
a big roast dinner and music and everything. Sunday they had
a wonderful parade and like a dumbell I stayed in and washed
and ironed, but when I went out for dinner at six o'clock, I
couldn't get across the street as the parade was just coming
back so I saw pretty nearly all of it. The customs were just
beautiful and all colors and of the lovliest materials and
there was confetti and everything all over the street. You
see there are two weeks of Carnival and they started Saturday
night. I took dictation from Judge O'brien, one of the
delegates, in his suite the other day. And Saturday afternoon
I went up to the University where the Conference is held in
the automobile with Dr. Scott and Dr. Brown, two more of the
delegates and came back with Dr. Wilbur, another Delegate.
Their wives and another girl were also along. But the
speaking was all in Spanish so the girl and I went walking
around the grounds. The University had a very imposing white
marble entrance all long white stairs of marble and there was
a flag of each nation all the way up the walk.

Of course you get the wrong impression from the business
streets because they are very dirty and near together, but
are very quaint. The natives are the most wormiest people I
ever saw. They don't look a bit healthy and the men are
little bits of sawed-offs and the women are very fat but the
young girls are very pretty. But half of the population is
white and half black and there is very little race distinc-
tion among the middle classes anyhow. So many of the Cubans

have intermarried with the negroes that it is hard to tell
the difference.

-4-

Well, Mother Cat, I hope I have told you enough news for
once. Oh, yes, I went to the races yesterday afternoon. I
won $6.70 on the first horse and lost altogether only 4.00
which wasn't much as some of the girls lost about $15. Now
don't get shocked or I won't tell you anything again.
Because you can't come to Cuba without trying to play the
horses. The race track is perfectly beautiful and all around
the grounds are the words "Oriental park Racing track" all
made out of grass and sand and there are beautiful flowers in
the designs of butterflies and words and everything. And
palms all along the way.

Well, I will close for now and write some more later.

Love, Dorothy X X

P.S. I will try and buy you something nice for a souvenir.

Charles Lindbergh arrived in Havana on 8 February 1928 as part of his South American tour.
He flew to each of the capitals, and it was arranged to have him in Havana during the
Conference.

Dearest Mother:

We were all invited to a wonderful reception given by the
American Ambassador, Noble Brandon Judah, in honor of
Lindbergh. I was about 3 inches away from him so I got a good
look at him. They didn't allow him to shake hands though.
Today he is going to take all the Delegates up in his
aeroplane. He is very thin and looks very young and has a
very brillian complexion, and a little taller than I. Herbert
has been showing me a wonderful time. On my birthday he sent
me eighteen dozen roses. The bunch was so big that I had to
give them most all away, because I didn't have any room for
them. The funny part of it was that it was his birthday too.
He was twenty-seven. I am going to give him one of my
pictures. Gee, Mother, I thought you had forgotten all about
my birthday. Thank you very much for the present. You know
you have to pay 30 per cent duty on all things sent from the
State so don't be surprised if I send the things back as I
don't think it would be worth while to pay so much duty and I
can wait ten or twenty more days until I get to Washington to
get them. Do you mind if I tell you that I would very much
rather have step-ins than bloomers? Do you mind changing
them. When I say step-ins I mean the kind that have no top to
them, they are like bloomers but do not have elastic in the
bottom. I never wear bloomers so it would be foolish to keep
them but I need some step_ins very much. Also I haven't seen
the stockings Arthur sent me. It was very very nice of him

but would you mind changing them? For this reason, the last
time you sent me white stockings, size 8 1/2 and I wear size
9 1/2 and would very much rather have gray stockings and I
don't suppose Arthur paid more than a dollar for them so
would you mind putting another dollar to them and get me a
very good pair for best so I can wear them for Easter, as I
hate the kind that have rayon in them which you sent me last
time and would rather pay the difference than to stick them
in my draw, and I know you would rather I would tell you.
Size 9 1/2, either light gray or tan, service weight and be
sure the silk goes well over the knees because it looks awful
when the cotton shows. Thank you very much. I am enclosing
$5. for you, now don't give it to Arthur. I think it is
better to send you it than try to buy anything here as the
cheapest looking things are very expensive. Dresses in most
stores are $3 for the cheapest, etc. So if you pay something
a little more for the stockings or step_ins tell me as it
would be nice to pay a little more and keep them for Easter.
So Arthur is going to get married, well let him. As I told
Kathie, he is the kind of a boy that any girl can wind around
her finger with a few compliments so he might as well marry a
good one rather than the next wild one like Marion he had
last summer. As for me, I will not marry unless it is someone
who can afford to marry me and not make me work like a slave
afterwards, because I enjoy my work now so why marry and be a
slave? I am lucky to have met Herbert. His father has some
kind of a cotton business and as he is getting old he wants
Herbert to take charge of it for him so he has a good future
and besides that he is a Professor, that is he teaches,
political economics, philosophy and English and teaches them
in Spanish and can speak several languages. He is coming to
New York in two or three months so I will see him in
Washington. On our birthdays we went to the Casino and had a
nice time. Last night he took me out to dinner and afterwards
went to lovely open air dance place. Tomorrow, sunday, we and
another couple are going on an auto trip to see the Water
works of Cuba and go through the insane asylum which will be
very interesting as you have to get passes which are very
hard to get.

-3-

I didn't finish telling you about the reception. After
seeing Lindy we went into a beautiful garden in the center of
which was a very long table just covered with cocktails,
sandiwches, almonds, walnuts, all kinds of sweets, coffee
tea, pickles, fruit, and everything imaginable in very great
abundance. And when you wanted anything you just helped
yourself and immediately they would fill all the plates
again. Then in another corner they had a wonderful Cuban
orchestra that was playing tunes made up about Lindbergh and
singing Cuban music. All the time we get free tickets to the
movies and to football games and everything but we are

usually too tired to use them and besides you can see movies at home.

You tell me to drink a lot of milk down here. Mother dear, milk is .20 for a very small glass which is always sure to be diluted. Often it is .25 or 30 a glass.

I will try to get you some views. I hope you notice that this stamp is a Lindbergh stamp. If you have any friends collecting stamps they will be tickled to have it.

Well, Mother, I will enclose my one week's hotel bill, just for my room, so you can see how much it is. It's good that I don't have to pay it, isn't it?

Keep the good work up of writing. It is very nice to get letters. Marg said she and Bee have bought me a birthday present but keeping it as I would have to pay duty. Kathie also has bought me something and is keeping it. Love, Dorothy X X   Margaret writes to me every day and I hardly write at all. Isn't that nice of her?

(over)

-4-

I don't think I told you that this is Carnival time down here. They have a big parade every Sunday, everybody is dressed up in costumes, they throw confetti and big long streamers and the streets are just mobbed. Herb and I were in the parade last Sunday. It is very interesting. All the people yell at each other how beautiful they are. They say "Que bonitos carne" or something like that which means "What a beautiful piece of meat you are" which is a great complement down here.

They have this carnival every Sunday for a month. In some of the churches they have the statues dressed in evening gowns and the women all wear little scarfs over their heads instead of hats.

This had to be rather heady stuff for a just-turned-21-year-old from the small mill town of Ware, MA. As seen from the (following) beach photos, Dorothy found time to appreciate the Habana environs during the five weeks of the conference. But she was recognized within the delegation and the State Department for her hard work and excellent attitude, as captured in several letters of recognition.

In Cuba, secretary to Sixth Pan American Conference

NOTE: The original of this memorandum is in the
personnel files of the Department of State.

DEPARTMENT OF STATE
Assistant Secretary

To: The Chief Clerk.
From: Mr. White.
Re: Personnel to the Sixth Pan American Conference.

The personnel sent to the Sixth Pan American Conference
could not have been better. All worked under great pressure
of long hours every day and late into the night, and this
included Sundays as well as week days. The work could not
have been better done and I wish to speak most highly of each
and every member of the delegation.--------------------------
----

I wish to speak especially about Miss Forrant. In singling
her out I do not wish to be understood as in any manner
minimizing the work done by the others, which was of the very
highest order, but Miss Forrant's work was so excellent and
so willingly done at all hours, from five thirty in the
morning until late at night, and, in view of the fact that
she was the lowest paid of any on the staff, I desire to
express the hope that her work will be recognized by a
promotion.

Francis White
(Assistant Secretary of State)

Mr. White's recognition was followed by an additional memo by the head of the delegation to his boss, the Secretary of State Francis "Frank" B. Kellogg.

                                                    February 24, 1928.

```
The Honorable
      The Secretary of State,
            Washington, D.C.
Sir:
```

   In assisting in closing the offices of the delegation of the United States of America to the Sixth International Conference of American States, I have the honor to make special mention of the work of Miss D. M. Forrant, who has been continuously attached to the Delegation. Aside from the efficiency of her routine work she has shown an extraordinary spirit of helpfulness and of willingness to remain at her desk not only through the long office hours but as well day after day far into the evening. Her services could not have been more admirably performed and it is therefore respect-fully suggested that appropriate notation be made on her efficiency record.

   I have the honor to be, sir,

         Your obedient servant,

                     Harold L. Williamson,
                     Secretary to the Delegation
                     of the United States.
            Note: Original in Department of State files.

Secretary of State Kellogg completed the appreciation cycle.

                     THE SECRETARY OF STATE

                           WASHINGTON

                                                    March 1, 1928.

```
Dear Miss Forrant:
```

   At the termination of your services with the Delegation of the United States of America to the Sixth International Con-ference of American States which was held in Habana, Cuba, from January 16 to February 20, 1928, I desire to express my sincere appreciation and thanks for the high standard of efficiency of your work while under great pressure of long hours during the entire Conference, including Sundays, and the cheerful attitude which characterized your service.

                  Sincerely yours,

                  Francis B. Kellogg

```
Miss Dorothy M. Forrant,

      Care of the Department of State,
```

Washington, D. C.

Now Dorothy could see the work environment she aspired to, the Foreign Service section of the State Department. How to obtain a posting overseas? It could not hurt, Dorothy evidently thought, to request a letter of recommendation that would appear on the company letterhead if one were to apply, for example, for an overseas Department posting in South America:

ADDRESS OFFICIAL COMMUNICATIONS TO
THE SECRETARY OF STATE
WASHINGTON, D. C.

DEPARTMENT OF STATE
WASHINGTON

April 11, 1928.

TO WHOM IT MAY CONCERN:

I have much pleasure in stating that Miss Dorothy M. Forrant assisted me during the meeting of the Sixth Pan American Conference at Habana. Miss Forrant showed special interest in her work, great industry, and proved herself to be a most competent stenographer, typewriter, and general assistant in the office.

Margaret M. Hanna

Dorothy's boss encouraged her to apply for the Foreign Service. In June, Dorothy explained the process – and the difference – in the first letter we have to her Aunt Kathie, and the only one sent from her Department of State address on Connecticut Ave in D.C. This letter explains how the Foreign Service is different from the Dept of State and Dorothy's resignation from one was required to accept employment in the other. More importantly, we see Dorothy's mindset moving toward the Foreign Service, again using Aunt Kathie as a sounding board for the required two-year commitment in a foreign country, after which a resignation from Foreign Service was required to be reimbursed for the transportation costs home.

DEPARTMENT OF STATE

WASHINGTON

June 21, 1928
1310 Conn. Ave.

Dearest Kathie:

I have saved quite a few silk stockings for you as you suggested and do you want me to send them to you or wait till I come home? I am now trying to get the Cuban negatives as I let one of the girls who was on the trip take them. Mr. Ayers, the Chief Clerk who I am working for now, has taken quite an interest in my going abroad. He took my application in personally to the Foreign Service man and said that Mr. Stewart would take me. When an opening occurred. He said there was an opening in the consulate at Costa Rica right now but another girl had to be offered it first but if she refused it I would get it. He said that he almost sure that I would go before the summer was up, anyway. Now, Kathie, I guess you think that I was not in earnest about going but now that you know that I am, don't you think it is all right to go? You know what Mother will do, set up an awful howl, but Kathie if I were a boy I would be in the Navy long ago or something and she would probably see me very seldom. You see there is really too much competition in Washington to really amount to much but in a consulate or embassy there is a darn good chance because there are sometimes only three or four people in the whole consulate and when I come back to the States I will be able to get a job almost anywhere.

So Kathie I think I will save as much as I can till I go and then maybe you can take me shopping a couple of days in Boston as I will also get my retirement fund on account of I have to resign from the State Department if I go because the Foreign Service is an independent branch. My retirement fund must be about $100 by now. You see I will have to buy a lot of clothes because American made clothes are so high in a foreign country that they are about 45 dollars for a $10 dress. Then when I get there I can save all I earn because I won't have to worry about clothes and at the same time go to a language school and learn the language of the country because it is a cinch to learn a foreign language when you <u>have</u> to speak it. So if I get my appointment about August that will be the time that all the summer clothes are dirt cheap and as I am practically sure of going to a tropical country I can buy all summer clothes and also save money by not having to buy a winter coat as I would have had to do this winter. In the meantime I am trying to wear out all my old clothes so I can throw them away before I go because you know if you are employed in a United States Embassy or Legation you have to do justice to the United States and look nice as they expect it. What do you think about it all? I am having my teeth fixed now (three filled and cleaned) and my face needs about two more treatments but looks fine. You won't know me when you see me. I have had my hair cut almost all off for comfort.

- 3 -

We went to a wonderful reception last Friday that one of the millionaires at the State Department gave to the employees. He has an estate about as big as the park in Ware with a private swimming pool bigger than the Pines in Ware. The pool has electric lights on the bottom and reflects a beautiful green light. The house is on top of a hill and long rows of steps lead down to the pool and there box trees all around. it. The cellar is lined with fur rugs all over the floor and filled with all sorts of curios from China, Mexico, etc. The patio had a Mexican orchestra dressed in native costumes and they sang native songs. He also had another orchestra inside the house where there was a ballroom. And what do you know, Kathie, I shook hands with Elinor Glynn. She's the one who wrote Three Weeks, It, and all those books. She had bright red hair (she must he about 60 because she has grandchildren) her face was all made up with white powder and black eyebrows. There was a roof garden too and they served refreshments from a sort of grill that took up half of the serving or reception room. It was heated by electricity and all the food was kept warm on it. You could have anything you wanted, chicken, ham, roasts, salads, icecream, punch, etc. Just asked for it. Mr. Ayers, the chief clerk, took us girls in his office so we were pretty swell and every time I would go by the kids from the Stenographic Section I would turn my nose up. I sent Mother the money for the yard of cloth as I couldn't match it here as I got it on sale. I thought maybe you might match it for her in Boston. I tried every store in town.

The Secretary of State is giving a reception in the Pan American Union building (the one with all the oriental palms and poll-parrots and fountains) for the Under Secretary and we all are invited so I guess we'll go.

Well, Kathie, I will write you again soon. What do you think of me going away? Don't you think it is a wonderful opportunity? The Government pays all your transportation expenses and if it takes you 21 days to get to the place you are going to those 21 days are counted working days and you are paid for them besides. Isn't that nice? After two years you can come back and the Government pays your transportation back but you have to stay 2 years anyway to get your transportation back.

Of course you have to resign in order to get your transportation back but I guess 2 years is enough to be in a foreign country.

Love, Dorothy X X

Don't forget to remember me to Roger.

How is his eye?

P.S. I am not going on that week's vacation as it would cost too much and if I go abroad that will be plenty of vacation.

Success! Near the end of 1928, Dorothy was offered her first Foreign Service position. The requirements are outlined in this mid-December letter, which included being single:

December 13, 1928.

Miss Dorothy M. Forrant,
    Care of the Department of State,
       Washington, D.C.

Madam:

With reference to your application for a clerical appointment in an American diplomatic mission or consulate, the Department now takes pleasure in offering you the position of clerk in the American Consulate General at Buenos Aires, Argentina, with compensation at the rate of $2200. per annum, beginning on the date of your departure for your post.

You will be allowed your transportation expenses in proceeding to your post form your home in the United States, while actually and necessarily in transit. Your steamer passage will be arranged and paid for by the Department and you will be furnished with transportation requests for your railway and Pullman fare in the United States. Your other expenses for travel and subsistence, such subsistence expenses not to exceed $7.00 in any one day

- 2 -

within the continental limits of the United States and not to exceed an average of $8.00 per day while you are traveling outside of the continental limits of the United States, will be paid after your arrival at your post. An itemized account must be rendered therefor, supported by vouchers. You will also specify the places at which expenditures are incurred. The Department will make no reimbursement for expenses incurred in the transportation of effects other than those carried as personal baggage.

You have been offered this position because of the urgent need for clerical assistance at the post mentioned and the Department, therefore, requires a written acceptance or non-acceptance in accordance with the terms herein stated, within ten days after the receipt of this letter.

If you accept the position offered you, you should immediately make application in person for a "Special" passport to the clerk of the nearest federal court or a state court authorized to naturalize aliens. Passport Agencies of the Department are located in Boston, Chicago, New Orleans, New York City, San Francisco, and Seattle. If you can conveniently visit one of these Agencies, your application should be made there. Applications may also be filed at the Department of State.

- 3 -

It should be understood that the position is offered you on the condition that you are single, it not being found practicable to appoint married persons to clerical positions in the Foreign Service. If you have been married since filing your application or contemplate marriage in the near future, it will be necessary to withdraw this offer. You should say specifically in your reply to this offer whether you are now married or contemplate being married soon.

Appointees are expected to remain in the Service for at least two years, and their transportation expenses in returning to the United States in case of resignation are not payable unless they have served for that period.

The expenses of proceeding to the post are paid by the Government, as above explained, but it is required that in accepting the position offered you an agreement be made by you that you will remain at the post to which you are appointed for a period of at least two years unless the Department shall decide otherwise.

You are requested to indicate in your acceptance whether you now hold a position under the Federal Government in which you are entitled to the benefits of the retirement act of July 3, 1926. If so, it will be necessary for the

- 4 -

Department to deduct 3 1/2 per cent of your compensation for the benefit of the Civil Service Retirement Fund while serving under this appointment. This does not apply to those who do not now hold or have not recently held positions under the Federal Government entitling them to the benefits of the retirement act.

Should you accept the position you should specify in your acceptance the place from which and the earliest date on which you will be prepared to start your post. You should not begin the journey, however, until you are advised by the Department as to the date of sailing.

I am, Madam,

Your obedient servant,

For the Secretary of State:

(Signed)   WILBUR J. CARR,

Assistant Secretary.

From the Archives and History of the Department of State, we again see the fortuitous timing of Dorothy's adventures, culminating with that April 1928 letter signed by Margaret M. Hanna:

The Department of State grew from 91 employees in Washington, D.C., and a budget of $141,000 in 1900, to 708 employees and a budget of $1,400,000 in 1920. World War I set in motion some changes that could not be held back. One of the most important consequences of *the war was the increased employment of women and their rise to places of increasing leadership in the Department of State. Margaret M. Hanna had served as a clerk in the Department for 23 years when she was made Chief of the Correspondence Bureau.[3]*

Before Dorothy was accepted into an overseas Department post, she received an invitation to the December 1928 (League of Nations-related) International Conference of American States on Conciliation and Arbitration[4]:

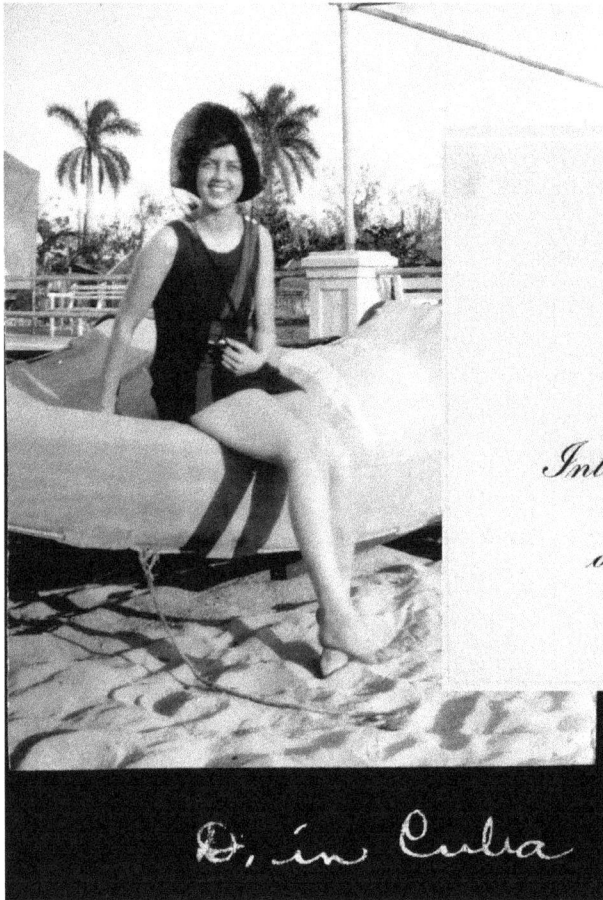

D, in Cuba

But Dorothy did not attend that conference in D.C. She was already packing for her next adventure – in South America.

---

[3]Source: https://1997-2001.state.gov/about_state/history/dephis.html

[4]Washington, D.C. from Monday 10 December 1928 to 5 January 1929. See Wikipedia article for purpose "to end war as a tool of diplomacy."

Buenos Aires

Once the Sixth International Conference concluded, all of the United States Delegation returned by ship to their 'day jobs' at the Department of State in Washington, D.C. However, with the accolades Dorothy had received, and the sense of accomplishment and adventure stimulated by the five-week posting – well, it wasn't long before Dorothy would apply for another position, this time one of greater duration, increased pay, and more adventure. To his credit, her State Department boss in D.C. encouraged her to do so.

Dorothy knew that formal letters of recommendation would enhance any application and started requesting them immediately following her return from Habana. Recall that she had requested and, in April 1928, received such a letter from Margaret M. Hanna relating to her initial work with the Department's Conference in Habana. Why not go all the way back? A glowing letter about her school achievements in Massachusetts certainly couldn't hurt.

NORTHAMPTON COMMERCIAL COLLEGE, INC.
JOSEPH PICKETT, PRINCIPAL
NORTHAMPTON, MASSACHUSETTS

April 26, 1928

To Whom It May Concern:

I am glad to state that Miss Dorothy M. Forrant of Ware, Massachusetts, entered this school in the fall of 1925; earned her way while attending here until she graduated in June, 1926. She maintained high grades in all her commercial studies and was an exceptionally rapid and accurate typist--one of the best we have turned out for a number of years.

In earning her way, she was sent by us to do emergency work for a good many people and to the heads of many departments in Smith College. Her work was so efficiently and pleasantly done, we were regularly asked that she be again supplied. I consider Miss Forrant a very rare and exceptional character. Any corporation, department or individual who secures her, in a stenographic or secretarial capacity, will be fortunate.

Northampton Commercial College, Inc.

John C. Pickett

JCP:HLO

Assistant Principal

The approach was successful: the application was accepted and she was offered the job with the American Consulate in Buenos Aires. Now that it was going to happen, Dorothy had to be ready to move once again – farther away and, of course, by herself.

In the State Department at this time, an employee could apply for any foreign posting, but if you were accepted, the process required you to formally resign your current position in order to accept the new post with the Service. No loose ends.

DEPARTMENT OF STATE

WASHINGTON

```
                                        January 2, 1929.

Miss Dorothy M. Forrant,
   1310 Connecticut Avenue, Northwest,
      Washington, D.C.

Madam:

   Your resignation as a Clerk in Grade three of the Clerical,
Administrative, and Fiscal Service at $1680 per annum,
tendered in your letter dated December 26, 1928, is accepted
to be effective at the close of business January 10, 1929.

   In accepting your resignation, I wish to express the
Department's appreciation of the faithful and efficient
services you have rendered since your appointment September
20, 1926, and extend its best wishes for your future success
in the new position to which you have been appointed.

   I am, Madam,

      Your obedient servant,

         For the Secretary of State:

                  E.J. Ayers
               Chief Clerk and
            Administrative Assistant.
```

A letter dated the same day (but going to Dorothy's permanent address) recognized the acceptance of this exciting new position – and set a start date:

DEPARTMENT OF STATE

WASHINGTON

```
In reply refer to            January 2, 1929.
F.A.

Miss Dorothy M. Forrant,
   46 Eddy Street,
      Ware, Massachusetts.

Madam:

   The Department has received your letter of December 13,
1928, by which you accept the position of clerk in the
American Consulate General at Buenos Aires, Argentina with
compensation at the rate of $2,200 per annum, as offered to
you in a letter of the same date and accordingly hereby
appoints you to that position. Your compensation will begin on
```

the date of your departure from your home for your post.

Government requests are enclosed for your railway and Pullman fare from Ware, Massachusetts, to New York City, and a ticket is enclosed for your transportation on the Steamer Southern Cross of the Munson Steamship Line sailing from New York on January 12, 1929, to Buenos Aires.

- 2 -

You will, of course, after arrival at your post and upon the submission of a proper account, be entitled to reimbursement for actual travel expenses necessarily incurred en route subject to the Travel Regulations, which are enclosed. You are authorized to charge for per diem in lieu of subsistence at the rate of $6.00 while traveling in the United States. No per diem can be authorized for time spent on the steamer, as the price of passage includes meals and berth, but you will be entitled to reimbursement of other expenses of subsistence on the vessel, such as tips and laundry.

In the event of your voluntary resignation after two or more years of service, you will be entitled to the payment of transportation expenses in returning from your post to your home in the United States, subject to then existing appropriations.

When you shall have obtained your special passport, you may proceed to your post without further orders.

I am, Madam,

    Your obedient servant,

        For the Secretary of State:

        Assistant Secretary.

Enclosures:
        Standardized Government Travel Regulations with
  Department of State Supplement.
        Transportation request.
        Steamer ticket. [1]

Oh, my! This was like Habana, only for at least two years — and with a salary, not just an hourly rate!

---

[1] The reviewers have pondered this signature. Lindsay Henderson of State Dept says: "the signature looks like William. The surname isn't legible, though, and doesn't look like Ayers to me, but I could be wrong. It probably would not have been unusual at the time for a job offer to be officially from the Assistant Secretary and go out under his name, but signed by another staff member. Would not have been terribly unusual in an era before the auto pen. Those tasks are usually delegated these days—I doubt we have assistant secretaries signing hiring letters and travel instructions—which makes your letter all the more interesting. Quite an artifact!"

Dorothy had spent the month of September 1928 with her Mother in Ware before returning to D.C. Now that this foreign travel had been finalized, she used the Transportation Request and material provided by the Department to return to Ware before departing the country. Dorothy said goodbye to her mother May in Ware on Saturday, 12 January 1929 and sailed on the *Southern Cross* on Monday 14 January 1929 from Hoboken NJ, as reported in the Springfield Republican of January 15.

The passage from Hoboken to Buenos Aires took about 14 days. Amazingly, we can display a menu from the *Southern Cross* dated Thursday 24 January 1929 so we 'know' what Dorothy ate for that day.[2]

...church lot the privilege of establishing a cemetery on West Main street near the home of Olaf Mattson. The cemetery site, which lies just west of the Mattson place, consists of about 12 acres and was sold to the church organization by Mr Mattson.

Miss Dorothy Forrant of Washington, D. C., left the home of her mother, Mrs Mary Forrant of 46 Eddy street, Saturday for New York and sailed yesterday from Hoboken for Buenos Aires, Argentine Republic, to begin her duties there as clerk in the United States consular office to which she was recently promoted by the state department.

Word has been received by Ben A. Rowe of Highland street that his brother, Freeman Rowe of Tonawanda, N. Y., had passed the crisis of his illness with pneumonia in a Buffalo hospital and was now expected to re-

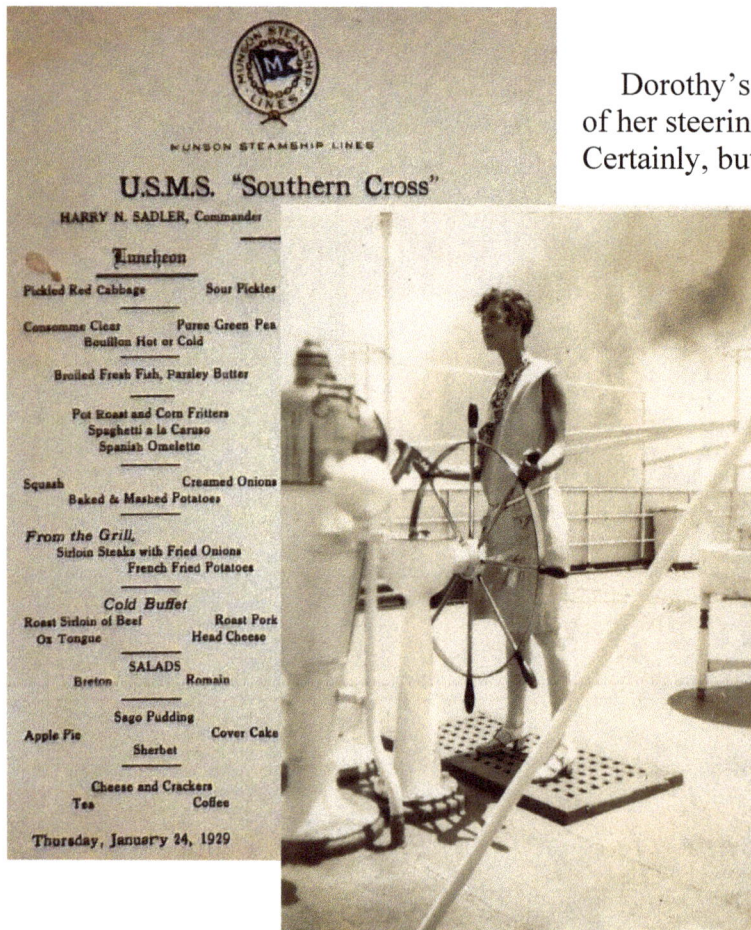

MUNSON STEAMSHIP LINES

U.S.M.S. "Southern Cross"

HARRY N. SADLER, Commander

Luncheon

Pickled Red Cabbage   Sour Pickles

Consomme Clear   Puree Green Pea
Bouillon Hot or Cold

Broiled Fresh Fish, Parsley Butter

Pot Roast and Corn Fritters
Spaghetti a la Caruso
Spanish Omelette

Squash   Creamed Onions
Baked & Mashed Potatoes

From the Grill,
Sirloin Steaks with Fried Onions
French Fried Potatoes

Cold Buffet
Roast Sirloin of Beef   Roast Pork
Ox Tongue   Head Cheese

SALADS
Breton   Romain

Sago Pudding
Apple Pie   Cover Cake
Sherbet

Cheese and Crackers
Tea   Coffee

Thursday, January 24, 1929

Dorothy's collection includes this wonderful photo of her steering the *Southern Cross* – a bit posed? Certainly, but so delightful! What an adventure!

The first letter we have by Dorothy sent from Buenos Aires to her Aunt Kathie is not in Dorothy's collection. It is dated 14 February 1929 and was published in the Ware River News (WRN) under the headline: *Another Letter from Miss Dorothy Forrant.* Those WRN files were lost in the 1938 hurricane /flood, however the letter is transcribed here from a WRN clipping Dorothy or her mother or Aunt Kathie had saved.

"Esmeralda 1072" is Dorothy's new/second address[3] in Buenos Aires after moving out of her original BA quarters at the YWCA. The YW itself was on Sargento St, just a few miles from the Bank of Boston (Consulate) building.

---

[2] From Internet research conducted by W. Michael Young, San Diego, CA, November 2024.
[3] The WRN mistakenly published street address as 1972, but corrected below to Esmeralda 1072, re Dorothy.

Another Letter from
Miss Dorothy Forrant

Esmeralda 1072
Buenos Aires, Argentina.

February 14, 1929.

Ursula Dowd[4] called me up almost the day I arrived and invited me out to her house for the week end so I went Saturday and stayed over Sunday and had a lovely time. They have a great big house in the suburbs, you have to take the train, and a cab and walk. The girl, Victoria is very nice also and so is Mr. Julio. Ursula is coming to the States in about June and is going to call on you. She remembers being at your wedding and told me how nice you looked. They even took my picture in the motion picture camera, which they have and showed me some pictures on a miniature screen they have in the house. They were just like real movies. They live in Belgrano and instead of saving milk in bottles a cow is brought to the door and milked while you wait for it. It is carnival time here just like it was when I was in Cuba this time last year, and even the cows have ribbons and flowers on them. All the streets are lighted up with some kind of lamps made to represent flowers, birds, etc. and it is just like a fairyland and all the people are dressed up in all kinds of costumes and go around throwing confetti and serpentinas.[5]

I have started taking Spanish lessons, one hour a day, from a retired Argentine school teacher who lives in the same house I do. She can't talk any English and I can't speak any Spanish so we get along famously. I am learning a lot though.

I was up to the Consul General's house for dinner, it is very beautiful. There were twelve other people there. Also the Chief Officer I was telling you about took me out to dinner three times on the boat he owns now. Monday and Tuesday of this week was a holiday because of the carnival. You see, we have to observe our holidays and the Argentine ones too so that makes it nice.

I was very lucky because one of the Vice Consuls whose name is Walter Washington took me boating on the Tigre River, which is the great sport in Buenos Aires. He belongs to a very select club and I never would have been able to go unless I was invited. We went in swimming too and had dinner up there. Kathie, thank you very much for the birthday card. I didn't think anyone would think of it, but I got a card from Margaret Myhr, Margaret Swanson and Bee Comeau too, also a valentine from Margaret. I got about two tons of mail today, the first I have had since I came here, and it sure looked good.

---

[4] Ursala Dowd was a Ware girl who lived in Buenos Aires for several years.

[5] streamers

I bought a dictionary for my Spanish and a Spanish book and they cost me 15 pesos which is about 3 dollars. I had an awful time trying to buy a washcloth. It seems they don't use them here but some kind of glove made out of Turkish toweling that was 16 centavos so I bought half a meter of toweling and made my own. Soap

is very expensive and most everything else but just as long as I can get things sent through the pouch I will be all right but you have to buy shoes and things like that yourself. You see, they don't manufacture anything but import things and that is why. So far I have worked for no one but the consul general so that is a pretty good start. He is very nice. We have to work nights though, for [clipping cut]

You see I have moved from the Y.W. They used to cut off all the lights at 11, whether you were in the middle of washing your hair or hadn't come in yet and after banging my head a couple of times I decided I had better move. All the folks at the Consulate are just great and I love my work but I am very tired at night, on account of the heat and working with six others and not eating until late but I will get used to it. I am getting so I wouldn't care for anything to eat except the rolls and coffee that we get here. I can't imagine eating a regular breakfast again.

Well, I have to study my Spanish lessons so I will have to close now but will write soon. I suppose you will get all my letters in a bunch like I did yours. They were great.

Dorothy's mother Mary/May noticed the increased pay as well. We learn more as Dorothy writes letters home, beginning with some hand-written postscripts as to how to allocate the new funds.

$10 is for radio
$3 for May's baby's present
I will try and send $10 more for radio the first
of June.

> Dorothy marked this page from the Bank of Boston brochure to indicate her work location

The FIRST NATIONAL BANK of BOSTON

FLORIDA 99

I work here. We have almost whole

Callao 224   Pueyrredón 175   Alsina 999

Av. Gral. Mitre 301
(Avellaneda)

of second floor, about
15 offices
Mr. allen on first floor

AMERICAN CONSULAR SERVICE
BUENOS AIRES, ARGENTINA.   May 7, 1929.

Dearest Kathie:

It's colder than the dickens here now and awfully damp
and so it goes right through you. The worst of it is the
Argentines don't believe in stoves in the winter so none of
the boarding houses or homes are heated except those of
some of the Americans. So you can just imagine me one big
icicle all winter. It was awful cold in the office too as
they don't start the steam heat in the offices until the
first of June so I see where I will have to wear mittens to
work.

Thank you very much for the book mark. It is an awfully
pretty little Easter greeting. I would have sent you one
but I don't know where they sell them down here, if at all.

Margaret Myhr has gone to London, England on some kind of
a conference like I went on for three months. Isn't she
lucky? I'm awfully glad that she got it because she sure is
a peach. Bee and she sent me a cablegram Easter morning and
last week Bee sent me two lovely books. And I get letters
from the girls all the time but mostly they gave me call
downs for not writing. It seems I spend half my time
writing but somehow I seem never to catch up. I guess it is
because I write too long letters. This is Saturday
afternoon so I thought I had better stay at the

-2-

office and send this letter so that it will go on the next
boat. I hope by this time you and Roger are going to think
seriously of buying your little home. Because I know you
would just love to fix one up.

From the Y. W. I went to a pension that is made up of old
ladies, the next youngest being 65 but it is the cheapest I
could do ($120 or about $55 U.S.) and at that I am rooming
with one of the old ladies. But things are sky high down
here. It is supposed to be on a par with Paris for
expensiveness and about the most expensive city in the
world. Even the Consul General is always complaining that
it costs him more than twice his salary to live down here.
But I don't care because I think the experience I am
getting is worth a lot to me.

Now I am living in Olivos a suburb but just for a month
or two. One of the girls I came down on the boat with
(about 35 years old) was coming to visit a girl friend of
hers who is married to a big manufacturer down here. Mrs.
Nichelson had to go to Cordoba for the childrens health so

Anne didn't want to stay alone in that big house so they
invited me out to stay. But of course I had to put a
deposit on my room and have to pay train fare and lunches
so I am going to come out about even but it is such a nice
change and Anne is so kind that I was only too glad of the
chance. We have a cook for

[Editor's note: This May 7, 1929 letter is missing pages 3-4; it picks up with page 5.]

-5-

I am going to look up some flower seeds for you right
away. Well, I've been here 1/3 of a year already so you
see how the time flies (or it will be when you get this
letter).

Yes they have radio here but electricity is so sky high
that very few people have radios and when you get music it
mostly consists of tangos and stuff like that. Everybody
seems to be dyeing in Ware, don't they? I bet you're glad
you're out of Ware because all your friends are leaving,
aren't they?

I still like my work very much and Mr. Messersmith is
very nice to me.

The girls at the office have asked me to a couple of nice
dances at their homes and some bridge parties.

Don't forget to tell me what you think of my plan for
Arthur and Sallie, will you?

                    Lots of love,

                        Dorothy X X

Thanx for all the letters and I am glad Roger is getting so
nice and fat. Has he got a double chin yet? I have had to
give away four of my dresses because I couldn't fit in them
at all. So I must weight about two tons now because there
is no place to go swimming.
My picture was in the paper by accident so don't forget to
ask Mother to see it.

We will hear several times about Olivos, as Dorothy stayed there longer than she planned. Olivos is a suburb on the Río de la Plata estuary located directly north of the city of Buenos Aires, the *cabecera* (county seat) of the Buenos Aires *provincia* (province).

DEPARTMENT OF STATE

I am going to send a messenger with this letter
to get it on the last boat because I am afraid
it will be too late three weeks from now.

AMERICAN CONSULAR SERVICE

Love, Dorothy X X

American Consulate General
Buenos Aires, Argentina.
June 1, 1929.

Dearest Kathie:

It seems as though I haven't heard from you for about a year. But by the time this letter gets to you you will think you will never hear from me because I am enclosing a check for $20. towards the radio and I am afraid to send it in the open mail and therefore have to wait for a pouch to be going in the Munson steamer that takes mail to the Department because lots of people have had mail opened down here and checks taken out. Especially they open the registered ones.

Well, I am still in Olivos because Mrs. Nichelson is staying in Cordoba another month, so I have given up my room in the boarding house where I was staying and expect to move to an Argentine family's house in Belgrano, another suburb but only ten minutes from the city, in July. So that makes four times I have moved in four months since 1 have been here and get a big kick out of it because I am meeting many people that way. Anne and I are invited to dinner to other peoples houses about three times a week and then we have them come to dinner at our house so I am getting quite a social butterfly. I went to a big party Saturday night at a very wealthy home.

There were about 150 young people there and we had a lovely time. They had everything you could talk of to eat but unfortunately I couldn't eat anything on account of being so excited. I have bought some winter underwear so you can guess how cold it is down here. Outside in the sun it is just like spring but inside they have no fires and no cellars in the houses so it is very, very damp and goes right through you. The house where I am living has steamheat but you would never know it. But it does take the dampness off. Then we have a big fire in the fireplace and a naptha stove and between the three and a bathrobe I manage to keep pretty warm. Just think when you get this letter it will be going on six months that I have been here, not counting the sea trip. Everyone I have met has been so nice to me but I don't think much of teas and things like that and get out of them whenever I can. Did I tell you that I am getting so fat that I had to give away four of my dresses. If I only had some place to swim I would be all right. I haven't been taking any Spanish lessons since living in Olivos because I couldn't get out there in time for dinner but I have just started taking my lunches in an Argentine boarding house so I can hear a little Spanish. The food is awful, mostly fried, but I don't want to eat much anyway because I am getting so fat. But I always have a good dinner at night as Anne tries to cook everything that she thinks is best for me.

- 3 -

Our cook took French leave on us about two days ago so we are struggling along the best we can. She got a nail in her foot and asked if she could go to her aunts house to stay the next day as she didn't walk on it but hasn't come back.

Last night we went out to dinner to a married couples house who have an apartment in town. It is on the <u>17th</u> floor so you can guess how high the buildings are here and it isn't really as wild as it sounds. You have the most beautiful view of the city from it I ever saw and it also looks right over the river. I hear from the girls quite a lot and Bee sent me two lovely books and a great big thing of soap. One of my roommates is getting married (in Washington) and the other one has gone home sick so I guess our room is all broken up now.

One of the pretty things in Buenos Aires is at night from four to about 7 one of the principal streets is closed to traffic and the whole population turn out in their best clothes and walk up and down and see what everyone else has on. It's a big city but very countrified in a way because people walk in the streets just as much as on the sidewalks and the taxi drivers almost run over you every other minute. They all have to keep to the left here and all the wheels on autos are on the opposite side too, which is hard to remember. I went sailing Saturday in the River Plate and last Saturday also. There were other sail boats too and we raced them and also had little cakes and ginger ale in the boat.

Well, Kathie, I will write you a much nicer letter next time as I can't think of anything else before I put this in the pouch. I bet the radio will be a peach and thank you for getting it for me. Please get a good one because I would rather pay a little more as they are something which lasts a lifetime.

Lots of Love, Dorothy X X

This next letter is just three days later, 4 June 1929, and one of the few from Buenos Aires to Dorothy's mother. Dorothy's theme to her mother is often a bit gloomy, to include local expenses, to emphasize that salary does not cover everything.

DEPARTMENT OF STATE

AMERICAN CONSULAR SERVICE

American Consulate General
Buenos Aires, Argentina.

June 4, 1929

Dearest Mother:

Don't forget to send my letters to the above address instead of to 1072 Esmeralda as I pretty nearly didn't get a couple of them. I have bought some winter underwear as it so awfully damp here. It is very nice outdoors but it is awfully damp in the houses and they don't believe in steam heat, although we do have it in the office. I am still living in Olivos which will be for another month because the lady isn't returning till July. Then I am going to move to Belgrano another suburb, about ten minutes ride from town, with an Argentine family. But I have to pay over $50. U.S. for my board without counting my lunch which I will have to have in town, that being about $15. U.S. besides and then I have to buy my ticket as I have to commute so it will cost me about $75. a month for my board and room, not counting anything else. But I have got to learn Spanish and I hear none of it all day in the office so this is the only way. I am taking my lunches in town now at an Argentine boardinghouse which is costing me $12. just for five days a week, but they talk Spanish all the time at the table so I am learning a little bit about it. I am sending Kathie $20. towards the radio. Last time I sent her $10. for it, but I can't send the $20. until the 13th as an American boat doesn't go till then and as I put it in the pouch which takes the Consulate mail I will have to wait till then because it is dangerous to send checks in the open mail, even registering them, as sometimes the clerks open them and take out the checks. I hope you like your radio, and I told Kathie to get a good one.

I went to a big dance Saturday night at one of the girls friends houses who work in the office. There were about 150 young people there, and had an orchestra and a big table full of good things to eat. Everybody here is either awfully poor or awfully rich, and mostly rich, I guess. Anne and I (the girl I am staying with in Olivos) have been invited out quite a lot and have been sailing twice. We are invited out to dinner tonight and it is a good thing because the cook left this morning. So I guess Anne will have to be the cook and me the bottle washer.

I hope Arthur does get married, it will do him good, and I hope Sallie trains him right. I'll be glad to give her any help she needs, just ask me, what?

I am getting so fat you would never know me but I don't have a chance to take any exercise so I will make up 'for it when I came home. Just think, when you get this letter I will have been here almost half a year. So you see it won't be long before I come home again and look all I will have learned. I suppose I will have a couple of nieces or nephews by that time.

Well, Mother cat, I have to get back to work now and mail
this letter so it will get on the next boat, and Kathie can
expect the $20 on the boat that leaves here on the 13th of
June. Tell Arthur to have a swim for me.

                    Lots of Love, Dorothy X X

The place where I went to dinner last night was up on the
17th floor so you can see how high the apartment buildings
are here.

Nine days later, 13 June 1929, again writing to her mother as a follow up on the funds sent
to Aunt Kathie.

DEPARTMENT OF STATE   June 13, 1929.

AMERICAN CONSULAR SERVICE

Dearest Mother:

This is just a short note because the boat is sailing in
half an hour and I want it to get in the mail. I have sent
Kathie $20. more towards the radio and I expect you will
have it very soon. I hope you enjoy it, and I guess you
will all right. I told you I was out in Olivos for another
month, so I am not lonesome at all as Anne is very nice to
me. I'm awfully glad Addie was so kind. Tell the girls that
I'd love to hear from them once on a while if they have
time. Don't forget to write and tell me if any of them get
married or anything. I don't seem to get the Ware River
News but once a month, and if you can, please send it
oftener as I always get a laugh out of it.

I have got a new room to work in that is very nice, a
great big one. They are going to put one more girl in it.
It is twice as big as the parlor, or I should say three
times as big and has a nice carpet and telephone and
everything. When you get this letter I will have been here
almost half a year so you see how time flies. I wonder if
Arthur has gone and got married by this time. He'd better
write and announce it if he wants a wedding present.

I am taking my lunches at an Argentine boarding house
just to hear the language and you ought to see the things
they give me to eat. Awful blood sausages and puchero,
which is a native dish of cabbage and old meat and boiled
potatoes and anything else they happen to think of it. It
is very damp here now and rains almost every day. It is not
so cold. but seems colder than home as the dampness goes
right through you and they don't believe in having fires.

I haven't got my cuffs yet and hope they haven't got lost

in the rush. Well, I haven't had any mail from you for
about a year so I expect you have been sending it to the
wrong address again and I will get all at once like I did
before. Don't forget to send my mail to American Consulate
General, Buenos Aires, Argentina.   I have been working
very hard, till almost seven every night, but like my work
very much. We are getting more stenographers soon thank
goodness.

       Lots, of love, Dorothy X X

P.S. Anne and I went to confession and communion last
Saturday so you don't need to worry about that.

In this next letter, 21 June 1929, we see that the Department has recognized the quality of
Dorothy's work with a small raise, not an easy achievement during these Depression days.

DEPARTMENT OF STATE

AMERICAN CONSULAR SERVICE

     Buenos Aires, Argentina.   June 21, 1929.

   Dearest Kathie:

I didn't get a bit of mail from home on this ship and
none from you for a long time. I hope you aren't sick or
anything. I got two letters from Bee and one from Margaret,
it seemed so funny to get one from Bee in the states and
one from Margaret in London. Margaret is having a grand
time being entertained by Ladies and Duchesses and people
like that and will be back home in July after visiting
Switzerland, France, etc.

It seems awful cold here on account of not having heat in
the houses. I have found an Argentine family to live with
to try to learn the language and I am leaving Olivos the
end of this month. I met lots of nice people out there and
kind of hate to leave. I am going to pay $55. a month for
my rent in this Argentine family, not counting my lunch
which is $15. more in an Argentine boarding house. Then I
have to buy my ticket from Belgrano to Buenos Aires and I
am going to start taking Spanish lessons again, so it sure
costs plenty to live here, but I putting a little in the
bank every payday towards my ticket for coming back. I am
enclosing a check for $15. for a nice sweater and skirt.
Would you mind buying one for me? I hate to bother you but
I have just come back from pricing them here and they
average about $40. for a decent one (All these figures are
in U. S. currency), so I decided it would be better even if
I did have to wait. I would like a slipon sweater with long

sleeves of wool or silk and wool, of one of, if possible,
two shades of blue like the diagrams on the left. I don't
want one that has a high neck, I mean that goes away up
like a man's collar. And if you wouldn't mind getting me a
sweater to go with it of flannel to match with kick pleats,
one, two or three (just in front) I will be tickled to
death. Please spend the whole fifteen dollars on the
sweater and skirt if necessary because I have begun to find
out that it doesn't pay to buy things that are too cheap.
And besides I am going to wear it to the office and for
tennis just as soon as I get it. That is the reason I don't
want too loud, but just enough to be stylish. And I'm
quite fat around the hips so please get about a forty or
else one that is rather loose around the hips. Thank you
very very much.

- 2 -

I have been having a lovely time in Olivos because we
give a dinner party about once or twice a week for about
eight people and have regular courses, from soup to fish,
etc. and have about ten knives and forks at each place, and
then have to wait to see which ones to use at the right
time by watching our guests.

Last Sunday two sailboats of us went sailing all day from
early in the morning and took our lunches with us, even
though we did freeze our toes, it was a lot of fun. One of
the boats had a victrola and it sounded. so nice on the
water, and then we raced each other.

We are having some real nice weather this week, they call
it Indian winter or something like that, as there is always
just one week of it in the middle of the winter and then it
gets as cold as anything.

I was on my way home the other day when a man stepped up
to me and said haven't we met before and it sure was a
strange coincidence because the last time I had seen him
was two years ago when we went to Cuba and he was
representing the Associated Press there. I don't know how
he remembered me. He is representing the Associated Press
here now permanently.

I tried to find out if we could send packages through the
pouch like I receive packages here without duty but they
said that we could only receive packages and not send them.
So I am awfully sorry about not being able to send you any
seeds and besides I am afraid it would have been rather
late when they got to you because I had forgotten that you
are having your warm weather when we are having winter.

I hope Roger and everybody is fine and thank you very

much for buying me the sweater and skirt. I got the cuffs
that Mother sent me but I noticed that she declared the
things on a piece of cardboard for the customs officers.
Now, that isn't necessary at all because the things I get
from home come direct in the department pouch which is a
great big bag that mail is sent in from the Department. So
if you will just make as small a package as possible of the
sweater and skirt and address them to me in Care of the
Department of State, putting on one side "To be forwarded
to Buenos Aires by pouch" and buying postage from Boston,
or whereever you buy it, direct to Buenos Aires, and just
insuring it as far as Washington, I will get it absolutely
safe. If there is any money left from the $15., enough to
buy me a nice white good quality crepe slip, maybe you

- 3 -

wouldn't mind slipping one in the bundle, but if there
isn't enough money, don't buy a cheap one because in a
little while I am going to ask you to get me a few
underclothes and you can save it till I send enough more.
But I would rather you spend the whole $15. for the outfit
rather than skimp because cheap things sure look cheap and
don't last at all.

I got a raise of $100. per annum starting the first of
last May and feel quite nice about it because I was the
only one who got a raise and one of the stenographers who
was getting $2200. per annum got her salary cut to $1400 a
year. I guess I told you I am in a wonderful new office but
there is going to be another new stenographer here with me
before long, but even so it's some office.

Write to me soon won't you Kathie, because it sure feels
good to get letters and find out who's dead or going to
die, etc.

If you are in doubt about the sweater being too loud or
something, just get me a plain powder blue one. If you see
a sweater or skirt that you think are much prettier than
the power blue outfit, you buy that because I know you have
awfully good taste.

Lots of Love, Dorothy X X

This letter was forwarded by Kathie to Dorothy's mother May, and appended a personal note; the reference to *R.* would be Roger, Kathie's husband. This is the only note in the collection from Kathie.

May, be sure and save this letter as you try it on, and, May, Miss S. was in Whites and Chandlers today and, seen some lovely ones look at the 3 piece ones. You know there a coat sweater with it but use your *own judgment. If you could get the sweater and skirt for $2.98. you could get the slip and R. would owe you the extra $.*

The 6 July 1929 letter to Kathie provides a history of hard work and a candid view of Dorothy's resentment regarding the continuous pleading for funds by her mother that will be a theme throughout May's life, right up until her death in 1940. In this letter, Dorothy explicates her lifework philosophy of hard work, doing more than the minimum, plus continual education to get ahead.

DEPARTMENT OF STATE

AMERICAN CONSULAR SERVICE

July 6, 1929.

Dearest Kathie:

   I was so glad to get your letter which came by air mail. You mailed it June 8 and I received it July 5, so that doesn't seem to be any quicker than by boat. But the envelope had "Postage due" on it but I didn't pay any postage so maybe it got held up in the States. You say in your letter that you are sending this letter to the office. Maybe you have sent me others and I haven't got them because this is the first I have received for a long time from you. You see, one time I put my address of the boarding house under the heading at the top of the letter and maybe you thought that was the address of the American Consulate General. Anyhow, I came pretty nearly losing three of Mother's letters that she sent to that wrong address. If you just address them to me American Consulate General, Buenos Aires, Argentina, I will get them sure.

   I'm glad you got my money order. I have sent thirty dollars towards the radio altogether and I can't put any-thing in this letter because the boat goes the 11th and we don't get paid until the 15th, so I'll write one just after I get paid. I don't know what to do about it, Kathie, because I get so discouraged about the letters I get from home. I never get a cheerful one, for instance, I am enclosing what I got in the last letter. Mother says that although she would like a radio she needs two new dresses and isn't working much. Gee, Kathie, I don't think it is fair. She is only working about three days a week and yet she doesn't try to save a little by making over her old clothes, she has a whole shirtwaist boxful in the bedroom and a whole closetfull up stairs, and she could at least make slips and things like that. I know I saw lots of slips that needed just to be sewed a little and a lot of dresses that just needed to be dyed a little and she could make curtains of old dresses and things like that. When I went to high school I used to take the old petticoats she threw

in the ragbag and dye them and make dresses and I am sure
nobody showed me anything about sewing, I just did it
because I had to. When Arthur and Mother don't have to work
in the mill they don't do anything at home. What I mean is,
they think I am just having the life of Rielly all the
time. They don't realize that ever since I left school I
have been studying something or other, either to improve my
shorthand or Spanish and if I didn't do that I would take
lessons in dress-making or try to learn it by myself. They
just say, Dottie's lucky. Well, maybe it is luck to study
Spanish every day and to work overtime every chance I get
to show them that I want to make good. And then Arthur is
thinking of getting married, working a few days in the mill
and still paying for the engagement ring. And then it will
be Dottie, lend me some money. They think I am rolling in
money, I guess. They think I dress extravagantly. It is no
exaggeration to say that I am the poorest dressed girl in
the Service and always have been in Washington. All the
other girls used to owe money in every store in town and
got clothes and money from home too. They don't realize
that when you work in a business office you can't dress
like you would for a shop or factory. You just can't get
away with it, and when you are invited out somewhere you
can't refuse and consequently you are compelled to invite
people out yourself once in a while. Mother's been working
about three or four days a week on the average for about
three years now. Do you think I would stay hanging on to a
job like that when I was able bodied and knew if I just
watched the papers that there are lots of other chances in
other places than Ware. There are lots of women who make
money by canning jellies or making cakes. It just takes a
little ambition that's all. It would be different if Mother
and Arthur were sickly or something like that. They are
just content to drift along and know if the worse comes to
the worse little Dorothy can help them out. At least Mother
could make a home out of that house. It is really awfully
pretty but it certainly looks very far from what it did
when Arthur and I used to come and visit for the summer in
Ware. And then she wonders why I go so far away from home.
Well, I never had a home, a place where I wasn't ashamed to
bring my friends for fear that it might be all messed up or
anyhow Mother would always be yelling at us not to throw
things around or make any noise or to go home early. What a
life !

   Well, I suppose I'll be sorry I wrote this tomorrow but I
don't know what to say. I feel so sorry for Mother but I
don't care, no one has to be so <u>shiftless</u>. You just do
what you want to about the radio, Kathie, because I know it
will be all right. I guess I can have the radio paid for by

the time it is time to buy the heatrola, or whatever it is.
Mother says they are only $145. She thinks she is the most
abused person on earth. What if she had to live in one room
ever since 1925 or maybe a third of room like I had in
Washington or 1/2 an attic room like I had in Northampton.
Doesn't she suppose that I ever get lonesome for a home
like the other girls have? You see, Kathie, I am paying
about $75. American currency a month just to live, and my
Spanish lessons, that is just for food and my little room.
And that is almost twice what I paid in Washington.
Everything down here costs about twice as much.

                              - 3 -

   I have sent $50. to mother since I've been here, and $30.
to you for her plus $10. that I am going to send on the
next boat, which is $90. That is quite a big item when you
consider that I am paying insurance that is $11. per month.
I'm just saying all this so you think I'm being too selfish
with my money. Well, Kathie, I'm enclosing the pay
envelopes and you decide about the radio because you know
more about conditions at home than I do. I just thought a
radio would be a lot of enjoyment for mother and she would
be more content. If you buy the radio I'll try to swing the
heatrola too, but I can't send more money besides, because
I don't have it. All the dresses I bought last summer are
absolutely too small for me. I shouldn't have been so
foolish as to think I could stock up for two years, I
thought I wouldn't grow any more.

   I'm awfully glad you've been working because you can get
some nice new summer things. So Albenia has a daughter,
well, some class to her[6]. They say her husband is awfully
nice. I guess I'd be just out of luck if any one ever fell
for me because he'd just get the scare of his life if I
brought him home and he saw Arthur with his bowl of coffee
and everything on the kitchen table that was there last
year and all the bathrobes and nightgowns hanging on the
walls and the dirty clothes and best clothes everywhere.
They are so used to it all now that they don't see the
difference any more. I would be the same way if I stayed
at home, I suppose, but now I could never stand it.

   I am going to play tennis this afternoon if it doesn't
rain and it would be great if I had my sweater and skirt
but one of the girls at the office is going to lend me one.
I am living in the Argentine family now and they are just

---

[6] Albenia Elliott was a friend and classmate from Ware High School '25. Similar to Dorothy, she attended a Commercial College (Boston) and then took a job as private secretary. Married May 1928; died Dec 1936.

as nice to me as they can be. They were so pleased to know that I was a Catholic and the lady put a picture of the Sacred Heart over the bed. They have six children and I couldn't help think what a contrast it was to our happy family. Every one of those kids is so ambitious. The oldest is a boy twenty-three and works in the Standard Oil Company, the next is a girl 22 who is a school teacher, the next is a boy about 19 who works in the bank, the next is a girl 8 who will be a school teacher next year, the next is a boy who goes to night school, about 17, the next is a boy 15 who is studying electricity. They are awfully nice to me (I only take my dinner and breakfast there) and talk very slowly to me and correct me when I make a mistake. They also told me to come in the parlor anytime I wanted, that I didn't have to stay in my room all the time, the girl twenty-two is very nice and I had quite a long talk with her last night as she was sick and I went in to see her so you see I can talk pretty good now.

- 4 -

And every one of those boys kissed their mother before going out and the house was just as clean as a pin and it was all so homelike and nobody quarreling and the brothers always served their sisters before themselves.

I bought a stove (kerosene), an ironing board on a stand, and a new electric iron. You can't use electrical appliances from the states here because they are entirely different voltage or something like that. The Fourth of July the Ambassador gave a reception so we went to that. They have a lovely home. And then at night there was a big dance at the Plaza Hotel and I went with some of the married people I had met in Olivos. The tickets were over $10. gold each but I didn't have to pay anything, but on account of that there weren't many young folks there.

If Arthur were only like other brothers I have seen, so ambitious and hardworking and kind and unselfish, like I have seen in other girls houses, and not so selfish, grouchy, and lazy, like he is and if Mother could have been like you, well there would have been all the difference in the world in the life of the Forrant's. We might all have moved to Springfield or Washington and taken a little apartment and have been very happy, but as I told you Kathie, last winter, I would rather send every cent of my pay home that I didn't actually have to use for food and get a job at night in a soda fountain than have to live with them. I know that is an awful thing to say, but why be a hyprocrite about it. I would go crazy in a month. If I had stayed home all the time I wouldn't have known the difference but now that I have met other folks and can draw comparisons, well, it would be impossible.

Well, Kathie, I hope that by the Spring you and Roger will be planning to have a home of your own. I don't think it would cost so very much more than boarding out, do you? But Miss Shaugnennsy would sure miss you and it really is like a home of your own where you are, isn't it? Well, by the time you get this letter it will be more than 1/2 year that I have been here so it won't be long before I'll be seeing you all again, So you buy the radio, unless you think Mother needs the dresses more, and I will buy the heatrola afterwards.

Lots of love, to you and Roger,

Dorothy x x

Before the end of July, Dorothy received word that her brother Arthur has made the decision to marry. A paradigm shift occurs from her previous advice against marriage.

DEPARTMENT OF STATE

AMERICAN CONSULAR SERVICE
July 24, 1929.

Dearest Kathie:

I just got word from Arthur that he and Sallie are going to be married Labor Day, and after thinking it all over I think it is the best thing in the world, because Arthur needs someone to wake him. Nannie used to say that he had to be led but I think he has to be <u>pushed</u>. And you know how easy it is for the girls to pull the wool over Arthur's eyes, for example, Milly DeWitt and the other one in Ware that ran away with the baker. I think we all ought to be so glad to see him safely landed at last and a nice homeloving girl for his wife. When Sally starts living up at 46 Eddy Street she might take sort of an interest in the house and make it look like it very seldom looks. That's why I think Mother ought to move upstarts entirely, as I suggested to her, and let them have the down stairs rent free in exchange for her meals and the use of the furniture. Because then they would be responsible for the fires and the coal, and she could have the heatrola up stairs and the radio and be very comfortable, like Nannie had it for a while. Then Sallie and Arthur would take more of an interest in making things look nice and there wouldn't be so much friction (mother-in-law I mean). Because they could all be very happy and much more comfortable if they tried this arrangement. I wrote to mother and told her not to worry if the house <u>did</u> burn down because it was much better to have it burn down than to make everybody's life miserable by jumping downstairs and looking at the fire

every other hour and keeping the house so cold that
everybody froze to death. Let them have all the
responsibility and they will be much happier and so will
she. It is an awful good thing that they are all going to
live together in a way, because Arthur certainly hasn't any
money to buy furniture or anything and Mother of course
hates to stay alone, Let Arthur worry a bit about himself
instead of us worrying because he hasn't got a cent and yet
insists on getting married. Perhaps it will work out
better in the end because he is up there every night so he
might as well get married and stay home.

    I wrote him that I was sending a check for $25. to them
for a wedding present. I'd like to send more but with the
radio, etc. It's about the best I can do. I can't send it
till the fifteenth though of August, because on the first I
have to pay a month's rent ahead.

    Write and tell me all about it, Kathie, because I'm not
going to worry any more because as you said, let them lead
their own lives. If you have bought the heatrola instead of
the radio, it's o.k. with me. Whatever you think best.

                        Lots of Love, Dorothy X X

I am enclosing $10. towards the radio or whatever it is you
have bought. Thank you very much for bothering with it.

The collection holds but one letter in August 1929, on the 20th and again we find how living with 'her' Argentine family provides an intimate look at another culture.

DEPARTMENT OF STATE   *Are you saving stamps for anybody?*

                                AMERICAN CONSULAR SERVICE

                                August 20, 1929.

Dearest Kathie:

    I expect you are just about roasting to death today
and thank goodness the winter is almost over here. That was
certainly a nice letter you wrote me and I am tickled to
death about the radio. I am enclosing $10. towards it and
I think that makes $50. that I have paid on it so it won't
be long before it will be all paid for. Gee, what a bargain
! I certainly appreciate all the trouble you and Roger
have gone to about it. It doesn't seem possible that you

could have got it so cheap. I can hardly wait to get home
to try it. I'd be glad to stay in myself every night if I
had a radio like that. Thank you ever so much.

I wonder if you got the $15. I sent for a sweater and
skirt? I've been sort of mixing up your old address with
your present one and hope I sent it to the right place. But
I guess you have it by now.

It's certainly helping my Spanish heaps to live with this
family. They are so interested and always correct me when I
say anything wrong and I can understand about everything
they say now. Sunday at church I understood almost all the
sermon and have been taking one or two letters every once
in a while in Spanish, but we don't have many to write in
Spanish.

Every Saturday night we go in the parlor and they play
the victrola and try to teach me the tango and I teach them
the foxtrot. The thirtieth of this month is a big feast day
or holiday here and they have invited some of their friends
to come to help celebrate so we are going to put on a
little show or mock marriage or something.

Last Saturday I went to a tea dance on the Eastern
Prince, one of the ships, and Sunday went to play deck golf
on another, I also met a nice American boy, Mark Harris,
who has an office of his own, who took me to lunch and has
invited me to go to see Show Boat. He isn't good looking
but very nice. Yesterday we got off early to go to a
reception that the Ambassador's wife had and ate so much we
could hardly walk. I filled my pockets with candy and took
it home to the family and they were tickled pink. We just
got invitations today from Mr. Messersmith (the Consul
General) to a reception they are having on the 9th for a
new Consul who is coming from Germany. It's just like
spring here today so I'm sure we will have some warm
weather next month. It very seldom ever rains except one or
two months at the beginning of winter, but I guess we've
had unusually good weather this year. It's a dangerous
climate for reumatism, though, as it is always so damp,
especially in the winter.

I still take Spanish lessons but now I take them from
Maria Rosa *one of the Argentine family*, just my age and her
birthday is the very same day as mine too. She is a school
teacher and I have three lessons a week for about $9. U.S.
currency per month, which is cheaper than you could get
them from home as private lessons are very expensive.

Sunday I went to visit Recoleta Cemetery which is very
interesting. Only the rich people are buried there and it
costs about $100. for an inch of land. The coffins of each

family are in beautiful houses of black marble or whatever
kind of lovely stone, and you see them through the windows
on shelfs and over them are the pictures of the persons who
are buried inside and they have a little alter and it is
like a regular chapel and every once in a while the
relatives come and go inside and pray and bring flowers and
there are little alters all covered with beautiful, hand
embroidered cloths and silver candlesticks. I'll try to get
some pictures of it for you as it is a regular city by
itself.

I sent Arthur his $25. for a present by this mail and I
suppose by this time you get this letter he will be a happy
married man.[7] I don't see how he could have had the courage
to ask anyone to marry him without having paid for the
diamond yet, at least I suppose he hasn't. And no wedding
trip or anything or a stick of furniture. Well, I hope it
will change him because it will make Sally's life miserable
if he is a crank around the house all the time like he is
now. But maybe he will get interested in keeping the lawn
cut and things like that.

Well, Kathie, I meant to write you a much longer letter
than this but they tell me they are closing the pouch and I
don't dare to send this check by open mail so I'll have to
enclose it now.

Write soon.

                    Lots of Love, Dorothy.

Thank Roger very much for me for putting up the attanae
(how do you spell it) for the radio.

The following month, the culture and social immersion continues – with a side job!

DEPARTMENT OF STATE

AMERICAN CONSULAR SERVICE

September 5, 1929.

Dearest Kathie:

I just got your box today and I'm just tickled to death
with the sweaters and skirt. I couldn't have found anything
half so pretty myself anywhere and they are just exactly

---

[7] Arthur and Sallie Bouvier planned to marry Labor Day (Monday 2 September 1929); the marriage was
entered into the Marriage Records of Ware by the Town Clerk as of 1 Oct 1929. It was not a successful union
as we will begin to learn in June 1930. It ended in divorce and later, annulment. No children came of this
marriage.

what I wanted. I can hardly believe that the whole outfit
only came to $12.75 but I see the tickets. All the girls in
the office think it is the prettiest outfit they have seen
for a long time and it would easily have cost me $50. or
over for it here, I'm sure over $50.   It was so good to
wear something light, because I've been wearing black
dresses all the winter because they don't show the dirt so
much and I was so tired of them. The little panties are
just as cute as they can be and the cleaner I needed so
badly because I never think of taking out a spot because I
always make it worse and now I can save lots of cleaning
bills. and you can't buy neverslips down here so I had to
explain than to the girls. The slip is just wonderful and
it doesn't seem possible that it was only $2.00. May was a
peach to help get them and I might know that between you
both everything would be half price and in the best taste
in the world. Everything just fits exactly and I'm going to
wear the open sweater as another dress with a white blouse
that I have under it. So now I'm all set.

The girls (Marg and Bee) also sent me a box but it was a
surprise because I didn't ask for it. They put in talcum
powder, face powder, wash cloths, toothbrush, and all
things like that and a nice book "Dancing Daughters". I
thought by this time they would have surely forgotten me
and I surely appreciate their thoughtfulness. They also
sent me some peachy snaps of the girls.

I'm still living with my Argentine family and although
there are lot of things I don't like, for instance, they
fry most of their food which is very bad for you, but they
always have some very good soup and fruit for dessert. And
they are very nice to me. Being in the suburbs sort of
cuts me off from making friends though because I can't
accept invitations as I would have to come home alone at
night and you can't do that in this country. But I have
been very lucky. Saturday night I went to see Show Boat and
had dinner with an American boy down here and he is also
taking me to see Broadway Melody and have dinner this
Saturday. The 10th of this month we are invited

- 2 -

to a reception for the new Consul at the home of Mr. and
Mrs. Messersmith.

Mother says she has been praying to St. Anthony for
someone to send her money for coal and that it is $16.75 a
ton so Kathie, I can't be hardhearted enough to refuse her
anything like coal when she isn't working hardly any, so
the fifteenth of this month I will send you $10. for the
radio and $17. for the coal. Will you see that she gives

it to the coal man and not buy something for Arthur's
wedding? I have three month's insurance to pay this payday
which will be $33. but pretty soon I have got to think of
putting some money in the bank or I'll have to work my way
home on a freighter. That would be lots of fun though. Say
Kathie, I was going to send you money on the fifteen for
two more slips, two lace brassiers (that coarse kind of
lace because they are nice and cool in the summer, size 34
or 36) and a pair of pajamas (calico ones that don't show
the dirt) but on account of sending the. money for the coal
I won't be able to until the 30th of September. Now will it
be too much to ask you to get these things for me and put
them on your charge account and on the 30th I will send you
a check for $10. without fail? I wouldn't ask you but it
takes so long for things to get here that summer will be
over and I will have to buy slips here and pay an outrageous price for them. Thank you very much. This will be
the last time I will bother you for a while.

Thank you for your nice letters. It sure is a big help to
know that you and Roger are so sympathetic and kind. Mother
says that Arthur has a job in the foundry so that's nice.
But he ought to pay rent at home to her instead of to
Sallie's folks when we have such a big house and nobody in
it but Mother. Thank you for all the news about Kathryn
Rielly and the poor Kennedy girl. A lot of changes can
happen in a few months, can't they?

I just love that slip and everything is such a perfect
fit. Believe me, I appreciate your trouble more than I can
say. I am going to join a club this month as it is the only
way I will be able to get out in the open air as I can go
there on Saturday afternoons and Sundays instead .of moping
inside all the time as I do now. Everything is so darned
expensive though but I know I've got to get some kind of
exercise if I want to keep my health and when I get out of
work at night at 6:00 there is no place to take a swim like
I used to in Washington. All the clubs are way out, about
an hour's ride, but it will be a little change at the end
of the week.

-3-

Mr. Messersmith is going home to the States for five
months leave at the end of this month and he is so nice we
all hate to see him go.

It is so nice to begin to have warm weather but it still
damp at night and I have to light my little oil stove. I
have been getting just loads of letters from the girls and
I am sure surprised to be still getting them, especially as
I don't write very often myself. I eat at the Y.W. every

noontime and so have lots of nice vegetables and fruit so I don't mind my dinners at night so much. Some nights they aren't a bit greasy but other nights, you get a fried egg, a fried piece of meat and fried potatoes and some kind of greasy oily sauce over all.

I now have a pupil, an old man who wants to learn English. He is the chief architect of some company down here and his wife is very well known in Buenos Aires as she is a wonderful musician. We are neighbors and all I have to do is to listen to him talk in English on the way to work as we both take the same train in the morning and his office is in the same direction as mine. He pays me $9. U.S. per month which is just what I pay for my Spanish lessons so that balances. He also gives me tickets for concerts and Saturday night he says he thinks he can get me tickets for some Russian opera here so after the show maybe I will go and take the American friend along. But I would rather be getting some exercise than to go to concerts as I don't have much time in the open air. I didn't tell Mother because she would be sure he was trying to kidnap me but as I have met his wife and he is very well known in musical circles here it's all right. But isn't any work at all as I have to go to work the same way he does and he really speaks English quite well.

Well, Kathie, I guess I have raved enough. Thanking you again for getting the things and May and tell her I am really going to write to her very soon. Thank Roger for being so interested in my happiness because I appreciate it just heaps.

Lots of love, Dorothy.

P.S. Say Kathie, I just thought. Would you put in some hair clippers in the bundle as I have to pay so much just for a neck clip and I could do it myself and also if it wouldn't be too much trouble *could you put in a cheap glasses case? Thank you very much. The box to me can't weigh more than 5 pounds.*

DEPARTMENT OF STATE

AMERICAN CONSULAR SERVICE
October 2, 1929.

Dearest Kathie:

I am enclosing $12. for the slips and things I asked you to get and probably it won't be enough, because I want you to be sure to take out the money for postage for this time and for last time also. But you tell me if you need more and I will send it. I'm a little short this payday because this is the day I pay my rent.

Thank you and May very much for the cards you sent me and also for the one from Plymouth Rock. The water looked so good to me I'm afraid I'll have forgotten how to swim by the time I come back and anyhow I'll be so fat that I'll not dare to appear in a bathing suit.

I was invited to a big dance at the home of some rich Argentine people here last night and as all the girls from the office went we had a lovely time and everybody was quite surprised to hear me talking Spanish. Anyhow, I can make myself understood and can understand so that's better than nothing.

We're just starting having nice Spring weather now so I'm in my glory all right. The Argentine family I live with have invited me to a party Sunday so I'll learn some more Spanish then.

I'ts sure nice of Roger to fix up the house all the time and he must be awfully tired of it. I wonder if Arthur is married yet. I can't imagine him married, somehow. I'll be getting my vacation pretty soon, but we only get two weeks here because they need all the help they can get at the office, and for this reason we have to work until six every night because we are only supposed to work till five.

This really is a beautiful city and they are sure putting up some wonderful buildings here now. And all the parks are kept right in order and are filled with all kinds of imported trees. The peach blossoms are out too and you can see them when you're on the train.

I sprained my ankle last week at the Y. playing volley ball so was laid up for a couple of days but it doesn't hurt a bit now and wasn't serious.

Well, Kathie, I'm afraid I'll have to close now as the pouch is going any minute and I want you to be sure to get this check but I'll write a long one next time because you write me such nice, newsy letters. It seems like everybody's dying or getting married in Ware, doesn't it?

                    Lots of love, Dorothy.

P.S. Thank you very much for getting me the slips and things.

Dorothy's letter of 16 October is almost prophetic in that she mentions the cost of a doctor. Within a year, she will be stricken with appendicitis, which her German doctor will misdiagnose as "fallen intestines." In this letter, the 'consulate doctor' is Dr. Vance Murray who in a few months will be shipwrecked with Dorothy at the 'bottom of the world'.

    Does this make $70 for the radio?
            I will write a big long letter next time.

DEPARTMENT OF STATE

AMERICAN CONSULAR SERVICE

Buenos Aires, Argentina.   October 16, 1929.

Dearest Kathie:

Well, we are just starting to have some fine weather down here and it feels just great. I just got a letter from Mother and she seems set on the heatrola so I will try to send you enough money on the fifteenth of Nov. to get it for her Christmas. Would you mind finding out about them? You will know whether it is a foolish thing or not Kathie and you talk to Mother and if you think she would be better off with one I would be only too glad to get it for her. The only thing is I hope I don't get sick or anything with all these bills on my hands because it costs about $10. for a doctor down here. My ankles have been swelling up lately and I asked the Consulate doctor and he said it was either heart trouble or kidney trouble or anemia anyhow, he is going to examine my urine and let me know. He is very nice because it would have cost me plenty to have it done by someone else. I wish I could think of some way that Mother could rent the upstairs part of the house. She could easily if she only tried to think things out a little like Nannie did. It makes me kind of discouraged sometimes, because I thought the heatrola was electric and she wouldn't need to burn coal in it, but it's going to be kind of hart to pay for the radio, the coal and the heatrola all at once and she also says "any time you have green backs or yellow backs I will be glad to get them". Now, Kathie, I hate to bother you so much but if you would please see about getting a heatrola, I mean, find out how much they are and if they are worth the money, I will be only too glad to send it to Mother for Christmas.

I just got the letter telling me about Roger's hard luck and I sure am sorry. I am glad that it isn't going to be anything serious and tell him to take care of himself, won't you? I have been invited to a nice dance by the girls in the office Saturday night and to an Argentine fiesta Sunday, which is the enthronization of the Sacred Heart or something like that so they are going to celebrate it with lots of things to eat and dancing. Then next week end I'm invited to a house party in Campana, which is about two hours ride from here. I went there once before and had a lovely time as they have a great big house and lots of young people.

Margaret Myhr is deeply in love and says she will get married in a year. He is a young engineer in Lowell, her hometown. I haven't seen Ursual since she came back. I just met two young American girls who came down here without work but had a few friends and they have got jobs and are

having the time of their lives. I wish they would stay
because I sure miss not having any girls my own age to chum
around with.

The pouch is going so I have to close now, Love, Dorothy.

In this letter to Kathie in late October 1929, Dorothy describes a whirlwind of experiences
that lead to a most heart-wrenching soul searching as she seeks her aunt's counsel.

DEPARTMENT OF STATE

AMERICAN CONSULAR SERVICE

October 30, 1929.

Dearest Kathie:

It hasn't started to get hot here yet although I
blossomed forth in a short sleeve dress Monday because I
was so tired of wearing winter clothes. But now I have my
sweater back on again. The weather changes so quickly here.

I had a marvellous time over the weekend. Another girl
and I from the Consulate were invited to Campana to a
weekend party at a wonderful country house. Saturday night
we had a big dance. and Sunday we went swimming in the back
yard. It wasn't really a swimming pool, just a big well,
but did very nicely. Then we had an asado, which is
roasting half a lamb or cow outdoors and everybody eats the
meat in their hands. But there other things to eat too.
They also have a tennis court and we had the victrola
outdoors and danced on the tennis court. In the afternoon
we went in a big launch up the river for about six hours
and so spent a wonderful day. It was a nice warm day, too.

This Sunday coming I am going to Lujan with my Argentine
family. Lujan is a shrine of the Blessed Virgin like St.
Anne's in Canada. It is a pilgrimage and every Argentine
from far and wide will be there so I will have plenty of
chance to practice my Spanish. We are going to take our
lunch and so will make a day of it.

- 2 -

Friday (the 1st of November) is a holiday and as I have
joined a Club on the Tigre River I am going out there with
a girl and her husband who works in my office to play
tennis and have lunch and then in the afternoon we will
take a boat out. After you have joined you can take boats
out and play tennis and swim for nothing, just have to pay
about $1. a month to keep up membership. The doctor told me
I had to get out in the sun more so I am trying to. Besides
I love to swim. He said I was a little anemic so I am

taking Blaud's pills[8] like you gave me a long time ago, which he said were very good but they cost me about $1.70 for a little tiny bottle. I also take a spoon of sulphur and cream of tartar every morning to clear my blood up. So I will be all right in a little while.

On Nov. 9 I am invited to a big Am. Legion dance and on the 11th which is Armistice day, all the Americans are getting together at the Swift Golf Club and have a picnic. On the 16th of November one of the girls I work with who has piles of money is having a big dance at her wonderful house. They are going to have an orchestra also. But they are very nice and you would never guess they had a cent.

- 3 -

I am enclosing a letter I just got today, from Mother. Kathie, I wonder if you will have Roger read it and ask him to please give me some advice. Should I send Mother a certain amount of money every month or buy her things like the heatrola and ~~victrola~~ radio? I will send you money to start buying the heatrola next payday (the 15th) as she seems to be set on it. Honest, Kathie, I don't know just what to do. I am meeting some awfully nice people, every boy I know so far has a college education and a good future, and I have to try to look nicer than the girls that work in the bakery shops. I'd like to get married myself someday and I have to look half—way decent so people won't be ashamed to be seen with me. There are lots of American boys down here and very few American girls so I'm sure of getting the right kind of husband but what am I going to do about Mother? I've worked myself up so far and I can't go back to Ware and work for $15. a week and travel around with mill boys and yet how am I going to support us both? I wouldn't have gone to the expense of joining a club except I had to get out in the air more and there is no other way as we work until six every night. Right now it is about seven o'clock. And every time I get a letter from Mother it makes me feel like I'm the most selfish girl in the world. What will I do? I guess I'll just have to give up any idea of ever getting married because I can't tell anybody that he will have to support my Mother too and I can't leave her without enough money, and yet I would always feel bitter towards her if I was cheated out of the kind of happiness that you and Roger know.

- 4 -

---

[8] P. Blaud de Beaucaire was a French doctor of medicine who in 1832 introduced Blaud's pills or iron pills as a medication for patients with anemia.

I'll be 23 in a couple of months and I'm not in love at
all but I just wanted to know what to do. That American
boy, Mark Harris, has fallen head over heels in love with
me but as yet I'm not a bit in love although I wish I were
because he couldn't be any nicer to me and has a wonderful
future as he expects to go into business (exporting),
himself before many years. *His brother is an Army Officer and his father
was President of the School Board in his home town.* Well, I sure would
appreciate Roger's advice about how much money to send home
and whether things are as bad as Mother's letter makes me
feel they are. I get sick to my stomach when I stop to
think of it, of her being all alone, and everything, but
I'm alone too and in a strange country.

Kathie, please don't send me any Christmas presents but I
would appreciate your sending me a very large bottle of
ponds cold cream or two of them and blaud's pills too. Also
could you buy some Kleenex, it's 25 cents a package, for
taking off the cold cream afterwards and is very
convenient. You could get quite a few packages and undo
them and make them real flat. It mustn't weigh more than
five pounds though. I will send you a check on the next
boat. I sure appreciate it.

Cold cream is awfully expensive here and you can't get
Kleenex. Well, I guess this letter is rather a mess but I
haven't anybody else to give me advice and I know Roger's
is gold. So thanking you both very much,

All my love, Dorothy X X.

Dorothy had been at her Buenos Aires post for less than ten months when she felt
compelled to speak up for a cause on behalf of her and her fellow employees: They had lost
the perk of using the diplomatic pouch mail to mail personal items back home. Dorothy
mentioned the situation to the Consul as reported in this 23 November letter back home:

DEPARTMENT OF STATE

AMERICAN CONSULAR SERVICE
November 23, 1929.

Dearest Kathie:

Thank you very much for the enlargement of the picture of
us. It's a shame that you letter was delayed since last
April but I bet lots of them have been lost the same way.
The trouble down here is that the Argentine government
doesn't pay it's government officials regularly and so they
are very careless with their work to make up for it.

Kathie, I sure feel bad about the work that I caused you
and Mae Higgins. You must be all sick and tired of it. They
made that new ruling about not sending things in the pouch
without telling us at all and it's just because they're too

darned lazy to send packages on to us down in the mail
room. I showed your letter that Mae received from Mr.
Clarke to Mr. Reed, the Consul, and he thought it was a
darned shame and told all we girls to write letters of
protest to him. I am enclosing mine. He sent them all on
to washington with the enclosed dispatch. Don't let the
people in Washington know that I enclosed these two letters
to you or they would have cat fits. Thank you very much for
sending on the package in the open mails. Maybe I'll have
to return it to you after all if the duty is too high
because they have an enormous tax on silk down here but if
possible I will keep it. Anyhow, I am pretty sure that
after they read our letters they will make special
consideration for the folks in Buenos Aires. I had just
sent to Margaret Myhr asking her to buy me some hose which
I need badly so I'm as sore as a crab about it. Mae sure
wrote them a good letter and thank her won't you, Kathie,
for me. I'm going to write a nice long letter to her very
soon. I am sending Mother a check in this mail for
Christmas and altogether it amounts to $47. -- $20. for
herself to buy a heater or anything, as I am going to try
to send her $20. every month an I hate to think of her
starving to death or anything like that as I worry very
much about it. $10. for the radio, $5. for Arthur and
Sally and $5. for you to be so kind as to get Bee and Marg,
something for Christmas and a little for Mae Higgins. But
there's no use to say it all over again as I have made an
itemized list in the letter to mother. I sure would
appreciate you doing this for me, Kathie, as next year I
will be coming home and won't have to bother you.

I just came back from a week's vacation. I'm afraid I
won't get any more as we are very busy. I wouldn't have
expected to take a real one as it costs so darned much here
but the Dr. at the consulate had to make an official trip
to Cordoba and so invited two of we stenographers to go
along too. As we went by auto we didn't have to pay a cent
for transportation and we traveled all together 1250 miles.
Some trip. We traveled about 8 hours every day, and didn't
stay in the same hotel twice in order to keep within or
schedule. And what roads! All full of six feet ruts and
water up to your neck. We had to go across corn fields in
order to avoid the big holes in the roads, but it was all
very interesting. and we sure

- 3 -

got a good idea of real Argentine country. Cordoba, where
we went, is the place where the only hills in the whole
Republic are and they call them mountains but really they
are no bigger than the hills around Ware. But it was very
pretty as the road of the hills wound around and around and

the scenery was beautiful. We took some pictures and if
they come out good I'll send you some. I am invited to a
dinner dance Sat. night, a tea Friday and Thursday,
Thaksgiving day, we all are invited to have Thanksgiving
dinner with the Ambassador and his wife. That's one nice
thing about down here, someone is always asking you
somewhere.

Well, Kathie, will you please excuse me now as it is
about 7:30 p.m. and I am in the office and very tired. I
also have to go to the dressmaker and the shoemaker before
I go home and as I live out of town I will have to hurry.

Thanking you again for all the trouble I caused you,

Love, Dorothy.

P.S. I think I asked you to send me some other things in
another letter but don't pay any attention to it until they
let us send things through the pouch again. Please send me
an itemized account of how much I owe you. I'm getting
absent minded and don't remember half the time when I paid
you and when I didn't. I have been sending the money for
the radio regularly though, and when you don't get it
please let me know as I keep all my money order receipts.

As Dorothy had shown Kathie, she petitioned the State Department officer in charge of the Consulate – but not on Consulate letterhead:

Buenos Aires, Argentina.   November 25, 1929.

Leslie E. Reed, Esquire,

American Consul in Charge,

Buenos Aires, Argentina.

Dear Mr. Reed:

A short while ago I wrote to my mother asking her to send
me some much needed articles of clothing. The box was sent
back by the Department with a letter stating that a new
ruling had come into effect curtailing the former privilege
of sending in its diplomatic pouches articles of personal
merchandise to consular employees abroad. I was assured in
the Department before leaving the States that I would be
entitled to receive any personal effects through the pouch.
I will now be forced to pay an extremely high duty on the
box which is coming through the open mail, a duty which
will undoubtedly be 4 times the value of the articles in
question. As you know, silk is especially high in Buenos
Aires as it has to bear an enormous tax and, for this

reason, necessities like hosiery which may be purchased at home for $1.50 a pair is sold here from $4. to $5. a pair and one may buy a silk dress here for $85. that could be bought at home for $15.

As of course this will be out of the question for me.

-2

I feel that I am obliged to tell you that if this curtailment of the former privilege of sending personal effects through the pouch applies to this Consulate General, I shall be obliged to consider looking for work somewhere else. It is common knowledge that in Buenos Aires private concerns pay stenographers far in excess of what is paid consular employees and as I have now a speaking and understanding knowledge of the Spanish language I know that I would have little trouble in obtaining a more remunerative position. Needless to say, I would only resort to this means if it was absolutely necessary, but, as you know, living conditions are so fantastically high in Buenos Aires that the added burden of buying clothing here would make my current salary impossible.

I am very sorry to have to bother you about anything so entirely not your fault but I am sure if the Department only realized the exorbitant prices exacted down here it would readily consent to give this Consulate General special consideration in regard to sending clothing through the pouch.

                        Very respectfully yours,

                                Dorothy M. Forrant.

To increase their chances of success, Dorothy also included this letter she had drafted for Mr. Reed to forward along with her letter and the letters of two of her colleagues to the Secretary of State:

AMERICAN CONSULAR GENERAL.

Buenos Aires, Argentina.   November 26, 1929.

SUBJECT: Right of American clerks to receive articles in pouch.

THE HONORABLE

    THE SECRETARY OF STATE

        WASHINGTON

SIR:

I have the honor to report that the recent action of the

Department in refusing to accept parcels of merchandise for American clerks at this Consulate General has caused much concern to the American members of this staff. Several of them when accepting positions here understood from persons in the Department that they would have the privilege of receiving occasional articles in the pouch and felt that this privilege would tend to offset the high cost of living in Buenos Aires and the impossibility of obtaining certain American articles here.

The Department is no doubt fully informed as to the high cost of living at this post and is aware that practically everything is imported. The high level of prices may be mentioned when it is stated that by far the largest source of revenue of the Argentine Republic is the duty on imports. In the year 1927, the last for which figures are available, the import duties constituted practically 50% of the entire revenues of the Argentine Republic.

-2-

It is hoped that it may eventually be possible for the Department to secure for American officers and clerks in the Argentine the same privileges which they are granted in Germany but in the meantime it is strongly recommended that the pouch service be opened to all American officers and employees stationed in this country. There are transmitted here with letters which have been addressed to me by three American stenographers in this Consulate General.

I have the honor to be, Sir,

Your obedient servant,

Leslie E. Reed,
American Consul in Charge.

Enclosure:

Letters from
        Winifred A. Hunter:
        Georgette A. Curry:
        Dorothy M. Forrant.

624.1
LER:DF

But once that duty was accomplished, the social world beckoned again:

AMERICAN CONSULAR SERVICE
Buenos Aires, Argentina.   December 13, 1929.

Dearest Kathie:

I'm so hot that this letter may sound a little groggy but I want to thank you very, very much for the wonderful things you sent me in the box. It doesn't seem right that you could get all those things so cheap when everything costs so much down here. I went swimming Saturday and invited the girl I was going with to come to lunch with me to pay her back for the times I had been invited to her house, but there's no use even trying to pay back down here because we only had a salad and snails and dessert and it cost me $6. U.S. So that's the first and last time I'm going to try to pay anybody back. If they want to ask me they can but I can't afford to invite people and pay that much.

But Kathie, I was just delighted with everything in the box. The pajamas are wonderful, and usually I can never get them long enough and the silk ones are beauties. That sure was nice of you to send me your glasses case and my glasses just fit and the hair clipper is a peach. The slips are wonderful and thank you so much for the little box of dye and the lovely flower. I showed all the things to the girls and they were amazed at how cheap you could things from the States. Pajamas are about $8. down here for just plain cotton ones so you can imagine how much silk ones are. Well, anyhow, I

-2-

sure was lucky at the customhouse. You have to go through more red tape, from one building to another and then back again. First you have to pay $1. (I always mean U.S. unless I say pesos) and then you get and wait in line for your bundle. Well, I though I would have to pay about $25. duty at least because silk things are taxed especially high, But they were very nice to me because I explained in my best Spanish how I expected to get them in without duty on account of working for the government so I didn't have to pay a cent. Do you know there is a duty of $13.80 on just a plain silk dress? Well, I guess now I have enough things to last me for some time but I do need stockings and the other day when Mrs. Julia called me up to get the things you and Mother sent me I sure was tickled to death because I'm about out of stockings. I sent for some by Margaret Myhr but now I guess I won't be able to receive them on account of the new ruling. All the girls thought the stockings you gave me were lovely and they all wanted to know where I got them. I sure thank you very much for them.

-3-

I had a lovely time the other weekend. I was invited on

board a yacht and the boy who invited me is the son of
Uruguayan Ambassador to England (he is resigned now). His
mother is English and he looks and speaks english like an
American. We had tea on board and then all went swimming
and afterwards we had supper on board and played the
phonograph and danced. Of course, only two couples could
dance at a time because it wasn't a great big yacht but
plenty big enough to hold about 6 couples. I hope I get
invited again. Then last weekend I was invited out to
Olivos by a girl I met when I lived there. She has a car
and doesn't have to work, is Irish and was educated in
Europe but isn't a bit highat and is a Catholic. Everybody
down here seems to have tons of money but you'd never know
it because they are so nice. Well, I went to a dance with
her at her club Saturday night and then slept with her and
we got up early Sunday morning and went to church and then
went rowing in the river and then swimming and then to her
house for lunch and then back to the club for tea. So it
was a lovely weekend.

The Argentine girls down here dress like a million
dollars; they are so darned fussy about how they look that
they wouldn't think of wearing a hat that didn't match
their dress. They sure are pretty, though.

I sent Mother the money for the radio on the last boat so
I suppose you have got it by now. There is no pouch until
the 26th of December but on that boat I am sending a check
for $10. for Mother and $10. for the radio. I couldn't
quite make $30. instead of 20. because I had to pay $35.10
for insurance but will try to make it next pay day.

-4-

The peso has just began to drop in value here so the
Consul advised me if I had any money in the bank(we have to
deposit money in pesos) to use it to pay my board, drawing
it as I needed it and to send my whole pay home, running
right down to the bank when I got paid and changing it into
dollars, so I will do that and will you please start an
account for me in Marlboro, because otherwise when I want
to come home and go to change my pesos into dollars the
peso might be so low in value that I would probably lose
about $50. gold. Anyhow, it is better to play safe. I will
see how the peso is coming along next payday and then see
what to do about it.

Thank you very much for the advice about not buying the
heatrola[9]. I could buy it very easily like I am paying for

---

[9] The Heatrola was a coal-burning stove that produced warm air. The Estate Stove Company in Hamilton, Ohio
advertised the Heatrola in the 1920s.

the radio if I didn't have to send money besides for coal
and food bills. So I think the best solution is to send
$20. a month to mother and let her do what she wants with
it and then I will know just where I stand and won't feel
everytime I spend a little bit that I am depriving her of a
meal. I have a little bank account but haven't put anything
in it since July 15 so it isn't growing much.

   I'm so glad Roger has a new job and likes it. Won't it be
great when you can start housekeeping? I sure would like to
come to visit you sometime.

   Well, Kathie, as the next pouch doesn't go till next week
I thought I would just send this little note and will write
another next week.

                    Love, Dorothy X X

   Thank you a thousand times for the box. Everything is just
                              wonderful.

The Shipwreck

Buenos Aires was Dorothy's first overseas 'permanent' posting, as the Conference was a temporary-duty type of job. As adventures go, it was dominated by the shipwreck of mid-January 1930.

In early January 1930, Dorothy's letter to Kathie shows her looking forward to a two-week vacation cruise to the 'end of the World.' Plus, Roger had provided some advice.

P.S. I will send you a check for what I owe you for the
pills and things just as soon as you let me know how much
it is.

AMERICAN CONSULAR SERVICE   Please let me
                                  know right away,
                                  won't you
                                  Kathie. And also
                                  the postage.

            January 13, 1930.

Dearest Kathie:

   I'm very sorry that I haven't been writing as often as I
should but we've been just swamped with work here on
account of a couple of the girls being sick and it's been
so hot that I just go home and feel like going to bed after
work, but now we are having some nice weather.   Kathie,
you can't imagine how pleased I was to get that box and for
all the lovely thoughtful things you put in it. You can't
imagine how handy every little thing is and, I think it was
you who sent me that lovely stepin for christmas. If I
should thank May please tell me but I think it was you and
I just loved the stockings. And I was sure lucky, because I

didn't have to pay any duty, just $1.75 on the two boxes
which you have to pay for two boxes no matter if there is
nothing in them.   But I hadn't better take any more
chances because surely the next time they will make me pay.
The things were just lovely and thank you a million times.

Gee, I sure appreciated the letter from Roger. It took
about ten years off my shoulders. I am sending Mother $20.
for herself on this mail (it doesn't go till the 23rd) and
$10. for the radio. I'll be glad when it is paid for
because $30. plus $10. for insurance every month sure makes
quite a hole.

Well, Kathie, I am getting two weeks vacation. This is
next year's vacation (1930) and I am very excited because I
am going to take a two weeks ship journey to Tierra del
Fuego, which if you look on the map you will find at the
very end of South America. It is very freezing cold down
there, the mountains are covered with snow, the sun shines
all night and there are many strange birds and beasts. I am
enclosing a couple of things I will see. We are going to
get off the ship and into the little life boats just as the
picture indicates. There are over a thousand people going
and of course it will be anything but comfortable but it is
quite cheap and everybody says you should never leave South
America without seeing it. As this time next year I will
getting ready to come back (it doesn't seem possible) I
thought I had better see it now. There is an officer going
from the Consulate[10] so I won't be entirely alone. I am
going to try to take some pictures and will send you some.

I am moving so as I won't have to pay rent for those two
weeks so you see it isn't going to cost so much after all.

Well, Kathie, please excuse me but I'm not ready to go at
all and have to get both winter and summer clothes. Will
write to you on board ship and tell Roger I'm going to
write him a long letter and tell him how much I appreciate
his kindness in writing me.

Love, Dorothy

Then nothing — no letter for several weeks. Finally, this three-page letter in mid-February 1930, typed single-sided, provides firsthand details.

DEPARTMENT OF STATE

AMERICAN CONSULAR SERVICE

February 16, 1930.

---

[10] Dr. Vance Murray, pictured with Dorothy in the Wikipedia article on *MV Monte Cervantes*.

Dearest Kathie:

　　I guess by this time you must think I've been strayed, lost or stolen. Well, I've got an awfully good excuse for not writing this time and it's this. I've been shipwrecked! I'm writing Mother all about it on this boat too, and I hope you don't mind if both the letters are pretty much the same as I know you will want to know all there is to know and Mother also. You remember I wrote you that I was going on a two week's vacation on a ship that took you sightseeing to the city fartherest south in the world. This big excursion ship, the MONTE CERVANTES, had 1,200 passengers and about 300 crew, and was about twice as big as a Munson liner. The trip down was great but on the way home after leaving Ushuai the Captain thought he'd take a short cut and save a half hour but the short cut was full of rocks and we struck a big one. We would have gone down in seven minutes it made such a big tear in the ship if the Captain hadn't sort of balanced it some way or other on the rock. When we struck I was in my stateroom. We were way over on the side and it made an awful noise. I didn't stop to put on my coat or anything because I knew I couldn't swim with it and I also took my shoes off. But when I got on deck things didn't look so bad because the ship was almost level again but of course wasn't moving.

　　I walked around and watched the people scrambling for the lifeboats and climbed up on a rail so I could see better. Then I met a friend who had a camera and we took some pictures of the people getting in the lifeboats. But finally an officer made me get into a boat although I hated to because I really felt much safer on the ship. One of the lifeboats fell into the water from the top deck and a sailor fell with it and it cut his head but he sort of swam around unconsciously until somebody picked him up but it made us feel kind of creepy when they were lowering ours because we got kind of stuck in midair with one part way down low and there was about 5 inches of water in the lifeboat and everybody thought we had picked a leaky one.

　　One little boy who washed the plates had a lifebelt he was just putting on and an old man tried to take it away from him--but he didn't get it. We didn't get picked up for four hours and I was freezing to death. A man gave me his raincoat but I didn't dare put my shoes on ---besides an old man next to me was vomiting all over my legs so I couldn't get them on. It's a good thing we got picked up because the people in our boat couldn't row and as it was a German ship, half of the people gave orders in German, half in Spanish, and the rest in English and so everybody rowed in opposite directions and everybody was seasick, even the

big strong men who were rowing. I was lucky because I
wasn't sick a bit.

There were lots of babies, one woman having six, and
several people who were cripples, so I think they didn't do
bad not to lose a single passenger. But the poor Captain
went down with the ship. He did try to save himself (the
ship didn't finally disappear for two days and he stayed on
board till the last moment) but he jumped short and instead
of landing in the water, landed on deck and was sucked in
by the water. The ship that picked us up carried us back to
Ushuai. It was just a little town of about 800 inhabitants
where the worst prisoners are sent as the Argentines don't
believe in capital punishment. They (the prisoners) gave us
half their food and we used to go up to the prison to eat
sometimes and sometimes ate other places. We slept the
first night in a billard room, some of us, about 150, and
it was sure funny to see the fat old ladies snoring beside
the waiters. I was so excited, I couldn't go to sleep but
walked round and round looking everybody over. Some of the
women didn't know where their children were and were nearly
crazy with anxiety.

Ushuai is a teeny little town with about three general
stores and cold as the dickens, all surrounded by snow
covered mountains and all the people are poor as church
mice. We had to wait there about a week for a ship take us
back to Buenos Aires and it was sure a funny experience.
Most of the people didn't have any clothes but what they
had on, and people had made hats out of the cloth cut from
lifebelts and coats out of blankets. And we used to sleep
on the floor in our clothes to keep warm at night.

They managed to save some of the baggage but it seems
that lots of the people stole and although a friend of mine
saved my pocketbook, my purse had been stolen out of it. I
saved my two suitcases but one was entirely empty and the
other only half full. I lost lots of things, but the only
thing I felt real bad about was my winter coat, that nice
black one I bought just before coming away, but I'd lose it
a million times over rather than miss the experience. I put
in a claim but there's so many people who said they lost
millions of pesos that I don't expect to

- 3 -

get anything. When I landed in Buenos Aires I went to work
but had to come home that afternoon with a fever and cold
and guess I had the flu because I was in bed almost two
weeks. The doctor at the consulate came to see me twice a
day so it didn't cost me a thing and he almost bought me
medicine for nothing.

Thank you for your nice birthday card and I hope you will excuse my not writing as you see how things are. I am now looking for a boarding house as I am tired of commuting so will be pretty busy this week, also have to buy underwear and stuff that I lost. One girl who was in the wreck of the VESTRIS last year[11] sent me a lovely dress that had grown too small for her and some underwear. And I just received a lovely pocketbook from a man who came on the Southern Cross when I did last year[12] as an anniversary present.

Well Kathie, I will write again and send you some very interesting pictures in my next letter. I have sent Mother a newspaper with an account of the accident and she will show it to you. I am enclosing a draft for $91. and will you please finish paying for the radio, Mother $20. and pay 13 weeks on my insurance which will be $35.10, but they say to subtract .30 so that will be a money order for $34.80 payable to the Prudential Insurance Company of America, Newark, New Jersey.

Will you please put the balance in my new bank account (if there is anything left) subtracting any money I owe you for postage and for sending the money order. I am very sorry to bother you like this Kathie, but the peso is steadily going downhill and if I send an Express Money order it will cost an awful lot on account of the depreciation of the peso. Will you explain this to Mother because she wanted me to send the money to her direct so she wouldn't have to wait. She says she fell down the shortcut and it made her sick. Thank you very much.

Give my love to Roger and I'll be seeing you all in about 10 more months. I'm going to try and have my summer coat interlined for the winter as it would cost me more than I can earn to have a new winter coat.

Lots of love, Dorothy X X

Then, this letter directly to Kathie, two days prior to her following up with her mother:

DEPARTMENT OF STATE

AMERICAN CONSULAR SERVICE
March 5, 1930.

Dearest Kathie:

---

[11] The *SS Vestris* was a steamship with a regular route from New York to Buenos Aires that sank off the coast of Virginia on 12 November 1928. The disaster killed more than 100 people and caused a national scandal over the readiness of the vessel and crew.

[12] Recall that Dorothy had traveled to Buenos Aires on the steamer *Southern Cross* of the Munson Steamship Line sailing from New York on January 12, 1929.

I suppose by this time you have my letter about the shipwreck and I am enclosing in this letter a few snaps. I'm sending a lot on to Mother to put in my box and if you see any that you would like just tell me because I think I can still get the negatives. I am enclosing a draft for $92.45. Will you please send $20. to Mother? If I owe any money on the radio or to you for postage or for the cold cream you sent me please take it out. Kathie, I'm so confused since the shipwreck that I can't remember if I thanked you for the lovely box you sent me with the stockings and everything I asked you for. I got lovely letters from Marg and Bee and they were so tickled with the lovely Christmas gifts that you picked out for them. Thank you very much. I don't see how you got such pretty things for that little bit of money. And I'm glad you got May such nice stockings.

I just read what you said about sending Mother $20. a month and Kathie I'm going to leave it all to your judgment because I know you're a lot wiser than I am. Just put what you don't spend in the bank. That shipwreck sure put a crimp in my sails when it comes to money. I have to start now getting a winter coat made and I guess it will cost as much to have it made as my black one I lost was, not speaking of the cloth. I've been buying some little things like underwear that I absolutely had to have and tonight I'm going to buy a raincoat. We've been having about two weeks of solid rain, very unusual weather for summertime as it is quite cold.

I left the Argentine family and moved to a boarding house that has nice big glass doors that give on the street but it is costing me over $70. U.S. a month so you can imagine how expensive things are down here as the food isn't very good either and the room is very narrow and no heat. But somebody is telling me about another place and I'm going to see about it. It's in a private family and much cheaper and has central heating which is very scarce down here.

I have sent you three drafts for over $90. (this is the third) and hope you received them all. I was invited to a lovely wedding Saturday night of a girl who used to work in the office. Although she is a Catholic she was married at night and although he is a protestant they were married in the Church just like two Catholics. Everybody eats meat on Friday down here too so you see it is quite a bit different. She had four bridesmaids and everybody dressed in white the bridesmaids carrying deep yellow roses and wearing yellow velvet hats to match. Afterwards they had a wonderful reception, orchestra and everything as they have a lovely home with a big garden.

Thank you for the clippings. Yes, that is Bee. Thank you for sending me the sleeve protectors, Kathie, but unless they can be put in an envelope it is better not to send them as even if they let them buy without duty I would have to pay .90 just to stand in line for the practice and you have to wait an hour and then maybe they will charge you duty besides. So I guess until I go home I had better get along with what I have. However, thank you very much for your kind thought.

Say, Kathie, I just remembered. You don't have to deduct any money for Mother this week as in the last letter I sent you I told you to deduct and it has only been two weeks. So this will be clear to put in the bank, unless I owe you something.

Dear Kathie, the pouch is closing and as I don't dare to send this by open mail I will send it now and send the pictures later when I get them.

Love, Dorothy X X

The letter from 5 March is quickly followed by one on 7 March – a rare one in that it goes directly to Dorothy's mother. Perhaps Aunt Kathie and her mother received copies of the description of the shipwreck, but this one is personal to "Mothercat." Dorothy mentions the 'big fight' for pouch privileges but not her role in that fight.

AMERICAN CONSULAR SERVICE

March 7, 1930.

Dearest Mothercat:

The boat goes today so I came to work early to write to you. Yesterday the pouch went and I sent by it some very interesting snapshots of the shipwreck. You'll be awfully careful of them won't you, because they are very valuable on account of being it and they cost quite a lot too. I'm also sending to Kathie by the pouch some money to put in the bank for me towards coming home. The last pouch had money for you, but as it is only two weeks since I don't have to send money for you for two weeks more, do I? Well, if you need anything very bad tell Kathie to give you the money I'm saving to come home on. I have to see about getting a winter coat made down here on account of losing mine. I never realized I lost so many things, it's the little things that count. I just bought a raincoat yesterday because mine was in the wreck and was all torn and stepped on so I had to leave it behind. I was lucky to get a good raincoat, lined, for about $12. U.S. which is darned cheap down here for imported things, as almost everything you buy here has to be imported. We may get pouch privileges, that is to get things from home without paying duty, as they are putting up a big fight for it.

I hope Arthur and Sally are well. I will write to them when I get a minute's time. I have moved from the Argentine family as I spent all my life getting on and off trains but I stayed with them 8 months. I shall try to find another one in town I think as I am fast forgetting all my Spanish. I think I shall have a dark blue coat made with a gray caracul fur collar and lined with gray. Don't you think that will be pretty? I went to a lovely wedding Saturday night. Although only the girl was a Catholic they were married in the Church and at night. They eat fish on Fridays down here too and if they can why can't we at home? The bride was dressed in a long satin dress with a train a mile wide and long. She is just barely 21 and used to work in the office and was the dumbest stenographer going but certainly knew how to dress so you see that counts an awful lot. The groom was a handsome norwegian boy, very blond and she is very dark. The brides-maids wore long white chiffon dresses with orange velvet hats and carried orange roses, or almost orange.

I guess the girls are making a big hit over in London. One of the girls wrote her idea of the London boys and almost got called back to the Department it was so awful. She said they were saggy from the pants up.

We are having nice Spring weather now, although ordinarily it would still be hot at this time, but this is very unusual weather as it has been pretty cold all summer. I haven't heard anything from my claim in regard to the clothes I lost yet and don't expect to as there was so many people.

Well, mothercat, be good. Mr. Messersmith[13] the Consul General returns April 1 and here's something nice Margaret wrote me he said about me.

Lots of love, Dorothy.

Don't get worried about my not writing much as I am very tired when I get home at night and when we finish dinner it is time to go to bed. Besides that I am looking for another boarding house as I am paying about $85. U.S. a month for this month and the food is pretty poor.

AMERICAN CONSULAR SERVICE

---

[13] George S. Messersmith (1883 –1960) served as U.S. Consul General in Buenos Aires, Argentina, from 1928 to 1930 and thus arrived with Dorothy as her boss. Messersmith also served as head of the consulate in Germany from 1930 to 1934, during the rise of the Nazi Party. As Dorothy relates in her letters, in 1930 Messersmith left his position in Argentina to accept the same position in Berlin and invited Dorothy to transfer as well. She declined, for reasons we will learn.

March 24, 1930.

Dearest Kathie and Roger:

   Well, I guess the old months are slipping by and I'll
have to be thinking of coming home. Since I left my
Argentine family, I am lots happier as I have made quite a
few friends in the pension. Next month I am moving into
another Argentine family, but this time it is more or less
of a pension (boarding house) but they always speak Spanish
at the table. I found the place in the newspaper and I have
persuaded a married couple, Americans, (he is an engineer),
and also a nice American architect about 43 and there are
four radios altogether in the family so we will have plenty
of music. The Señora said that after dinner at night it was
all like a big family as she played the piano and her two
children played the violin and we could dance. There are
three other Argentines living there and one English man. It
is really the Señora's home but her husband abandoned her a
while ago and she has to rent the rooms in order to earn
her living. She seemed awfully nice and said we didn't have
to stay in our rooms but were welcome to all the house,
which doesn't mean much because there's only the big dining
room besides the rooms she rents. But she says she will
make us pay a fine if we talk a word of English, and it is
much cheaper than my pension, about $10. a month cheaper.

   I have taken a chance on a nice little chalet down here
for a peso. It has a fireplace and a lovely bathroom and
nice grounds so I'm hoping to win it. I hear Mr.
Messersmith is going to try to persuade me to stay two
years more. He is coming about the first of April and says
he is bringing numerous packages to me from the Department.
But I don't want to stay here two years more because I
don't like to work until six O'clock when there are so many
other posts where you don't have to work only till 4
o'clock. This place is really too big to make friends in
and I can only play tennis Saturdays and Sundays as we get
out too late to play during the week. I also hear I'm going
to get a raise but I don't know and it wouldn't be until
July any way, as that is the first of the fiscal year.

   Those little things you sent me in the box sure come in
handy. Of course I had to lose the nice silk thread in the
shipwreck and May's lovely stepin and my nice silk kimona
the girls gave me and some dresses I had them send me
before they stopped the pouch privileges. And my nice
winter coat. I'm now trying to see about getting one made
as it is impossible to buy one down here. I thought of
having a dark green with lynx fur, a dark blue with gray
caracul or a dark red with black caracul. Don't send me any
more things now till I come home, please Kathie, as I can't

get them through the customs and the duties are terrific.
They're working at the Department trying to get us pouch
privileges again but it will be quite some time. The lovely
silk pajamas sure came in handy when I was sick.

Yesterday I was invited to the Tigre to see the regattas
which are the boat races between the different Clubs. I
went with a German boy I met on the trip to Tierra del
Fuego. He works in the bank here but doesn't talk English
so we struggle along in Spanish. He is very nice and nice
looking and dresses very American but of course I wouldn't
think of marrying anyone but an American so I only see him
once every two weeks which always gives us something to
quarrel about. But I have no desire to stay down here all
my life and that's what it would mean if I got married here
so I just don't think of it. The regattas were fine, the
German Club which the boy belongs to coming in first twice
and my club coming in last every time. Then afterwards we
had supper at the club. It was very nice. Once a week I am

Back view of me and another
girl on a motor boat in the
Tigre River.

Same motor boat.

p. a -

invited out to a suburb to the home of a lady who is crazy
about tennis and has a tennis court of her own and I am
getting to play a little bit better. I have a new racquet
that the doctor at the Consulate gave me which he didn't
just like the weight of so that saved me quite a bit of
money.

Thanks so much for starting my bank account. I filled in
the little card and sent it in the last mail. I'm going to

try to put a check in this mail. I have the pesos but as the peso is starting to go up I'm waiting till it gets a little higher so as to buy dollars with it and gain a little. I think I can send it in this letter.

Never mind about sending the brassieres, Kathie, thank you just the same as I received four silk ones from the girl who gave the dress to me because I lost my things in the wreck, so I'm all set until I come home. Thank you just the same. Well, I'll write more next time.

Lots of love to you both and thank you for everything.

Dorothy xx

AMERICAN CONSULAR SERVICE

April 1, 1930.

Dearest Kathie:

I got your little note about telling Mother about the piano and not giving my money to Arthur, so I wrote her right away about the money but didn't say anything about the piano as I don't play at all and don't care anything about one and as Mother has the radio and he is so crazy about a piano he is welcome to it as far as I am concerned. But thank you very much for thinking of writing to me about it.

I am moving today to my new Argentine family but won't get there till tonight. The doctor from the Consulate is taking me to play tennis this noon so I won't get there till to-night. I am quite excited about it.

Well, as I told you I had to get a new coat and so am having it made. It's costing me about $125. U.S. so you can imagine how expensive things are down here. It's going to be really stunning if it turns out right though. There are big fur cuffs and fur collar and deep fur around the bottom and it is straight all the way down till it comes to the bottom and kind of flares out. It is dark brown and the fur looks like blue fox but of course it isn't but is some kind of a mongrel because blue fox is awfully expensive, but it is good enough for me. The lady said she wouldn't make another coat for less than $170. U.S. and I had to bargain her down from $148. and finally said I had lunch often at the Embassy and a lot of bunk and so she thought it would be a good way to get American clientle as the coat looks stunning on me on account of being tall. Of course this is only a cloth coat but I have to have one so I might as well get one I will like. I'm going to get a brown felt hat to go with it. Gee, it seems a sin to pay so much when I got my lovely black one for $55. in Washington. So I may not send a check the fifteenth of this month as I will have to pay for the coat so if Mother needs money please draw on the bank. I'm enclosing in this letter a check for $38. On account of the peso going down I lost $4. on exchange as I would ordinarly get $42. U.S. for 100 pesos.

I get awfully nice letters from Marg and Bee and Marg is going to get married in March so I guess I will get there for the wedding. I just heard, I'm not quite sure yet, that our two years starts on the day we leave New York so if that's the case I'll be home a month sooner than I expected, so I'll have to try to start saving my head off, and I need dresses badly on account of having only one for best, which was given to me after the shipwreck. I want to try to go home by the Panama Canal, by the West Coast, as they say it is worth seeing. It will cost me about $120. extra as you have to go across to Chile by the trans-continental train but I might never get down this way again so I might as well do the whole of South America.

I am enclosing the check for $38. and also some wonderful photographs of the trip. I guess you have seen the ones I sent Mother. If you see any that she has that you would like just write and I will send them to you.

I was invited to a wonderful dance Saturday night to the home of the richest people in B.A. They are friends of some of the girls that work in the office. Orchestra and wonderful garden and enormous house. Well, one of the Vice Consuls was supposed to come after me and to call up first to say what train we should take but he called three times and each time the maid told him I'd gone out with somebody else, I guess she thought he said some other name, so I sat all dressed up from 9:30 till 11:30 waiting. Gee, I was mad, but those things will happen.

Well, Kathie, I will write again soon, and lots of love to you and Roger. I hope you like the pictures.

Dorothy X X

AMERICAN CONSULAR SERVICE

Buenos Aires, Argentina.   April 16, 1930.

Dearest Kathie:

I just got the lovely brassiers you sent me and I sure appreciate them. That was an awfully clever way to do it because I didn't have to pay a cent on them for duty. It seems as though I haven't heard from you for ages. But perhaps you have been ill or something. I hope not. Thank you again for the brassiers.

I like my new boarding house fine. We get awfully good food and it is cheaper than the other one. I am getting a lot of invitations lately, just my luck when I have only one best dress to my name. There is another girl coming from the Department getting here next week and I hope she will be nice. Mr. Messersmith is coming back next week. Thursday and Friday are holidays this week on account of holy week. We are sure lucky to get the holidays for both countries. Gee, I hope I can save enough money because if I can I would like to go home by way of Europe. It doesn't cost much more about $150. I guess and I will never get the chance again. There is a girl from the Embassy going about the same time so I will have company.

I was invited out to dinner Saturday, Sunday and Monday, and Wednesday, and also to lunch Wednesday. Bee is still in London and she sure is lucky, isn't she? Did you get my check about the insurance? I notice that at the end of April it is due again so I will send another check the 15th of May. The time sure goes by quickly down here and it will seem strange to go back to Washington and see the girls doing the same thing they did when I left. So many things have happened since I've been here that it seems as though I've been gone fifteen years at least.

Next Saturday I am invited to a tea party and at night a farewell dance. I got my new coat last night and only had to pay $96. for it instead of $125. as I had the fur taken off the bottom. "Only", I say, but that is pretty reasonable for down here. It looks nice, though, has big fur collar and cuffs, looks like blue fox, but is a crossing of a blue fox and tom-cat, I guess, the coat being dark brown. I can't get any shoes down here with short vamps and all the girls in the office are borrowing my old ones to have them copied. And I only paid $5. for them at home. All the shoes down here are long, narrow ones and the heels are always too wide behind.

We are having lovely spring weather now and the first of the month it was almost as cold, as winter. I'm hoping it will get cold quick as I have about two summer dresses left to my name and I have a hard time getting one washed in time to take the other one's place. Isn't that a shame about the girl who was killed in London? I often went swimming with her and she was one of the smartest girls I ever knew. Very athletic and very well liked. She had a cute little boy about 5 years old.

Well, Kathie, I will close now so as to get this in the
pouch and hope to hear from you and Roger soon.

Lots of love, Dorothy.

Only 8 more months after this month before seeing you all.

X X

The girls all thought the brassiers were awfully pretty.

30 April 1929: The 1930 Federal Census of the American Consulate General in Buenos Aires.
It is a rare sight to see a census form with the names typed. However, this is not your typical
census enumeration district – this is the American enclave in Buenos Aires, and is to be counted
as every other community on American soil. For the first time, we can see the familial entities:
Messersmith has his family of three with him, as does Reed, Yates, Miller, all the way down to
the stenographers and clerks, who were not allowed to be married, let alone have their families
with them. Dorothy is listed on Line 71, 23 years of age.

Duty in Chile

1930 was one of the most packed years — in both good and bad ways — of Dorothy's
Foreign Service career, and only tangentially because of the work. Starting the year being
shipwrecked was a large part of that, but her health was another. This letter was written 8
June 1930 and was typed aboard the train to Chile – Dorothy taking her typewriter as we
might take our laptop. The letter provides information on Bill Denker, who was to become
her fiancé for several months and get his photo in the Ware River News. More importantly,
we see the signs of her upcoming appendicitis attack and surgery: "If nothing happens in the
meantime …" Prophetic!

Here is Dorothy's [D.] photo caption to her train stop crossing the Andes with her boss:

Train stop crossing Andes. D. accompanying Consul General George S. Messersmith as secretary on his inspection tour of the Embassy at Santiago & the Consulate at Valparaiso, Chile.

Dearest Kathie:

Well, here I am on my way again. I'm on the transcontinental train to Chile. Mr. Messersmith, the Consul General, had to make some inspections of the Embassy in Santiago and the Consulate General in Valparaiso so I was lucky enough to go along to do the stenographic part.

Well, here's another surprise. Mr. Messersmith has been transferred to Berlin, Germany, and leaves here in a couple of months. He was to inspect Peru too so I've missed out on that as he won't have time now. But -- he told me I could come to Germany to work if I wanted to after I finished here. That means six months more here and then two in the States and then if I wanted to go I can, but I'm not planning too far ahead as so many things happen, but it's nice to know I won't be out of a job when I get home as they say things aren't going so well in the States.

Well, this is a swell train and I have a whole compartment to myself as Mr. Messersmith bought the whole one so it would be more comfortable for me. I have a nice comfy chair in the observation car too. It's a beautiful spring day and it's supposed to be the middle of winter. (I hope you don't mind that I'm writing the same to you as to Mother because I can't think of anything different). This is Sunday, June 8th, and it takes two days by train to get to Chile. Tomorrow morning we cross the Andes which are supposed to be a wonderful sight as they are snow-capped even in the summer. So this saves me coming home by way of Chile which means $200. round trip from B.A. to Chile. And I won't go home by Europe either because of the possibility of going to Germany afterwards.

This nice American chap I know, Bill Denker, also had to go to Chile on a business trip so he left last Thursday and will catch this train tomorrow in Mendoza so won't Mr. Messersmith be surprised. He is an assistant manager in the Dupont company here and from Boston. He has spent three years in turkey and seven years in Europe in general, a graduate of Harvard, but not a bit conceited. He is 30 years old, has a moustache, tall but not good looking but very nice. Well, I seem to be raving about someone else every time I write.

I have a new roommate, a new girl sent down by the Department and she's my own age and very nice. It's sure great to have someone to pal around with. We have joined the same tennis club. Her name is Margaret Drane and she's from Ontario, Oregon.

I got a letter from Arthur and it made me sort of sick to my stomach as he said Mother wasn't speaking to Sally and tried to boss them around. Well, I would rather sell newspapers than live at home again. I couldn't stand everybody quarreling. It would drive me crazy.

Well, Kathie, I hope you will forgive me for not writing oftener. I have been very, very busy. Don't tell Mother but I have been having a pain in my side and went to the doctor and had an ex-ray taken and I have fallen intestines. But as usual I have been very lucky as he has been giving me three electrical massages a week and I pay for my treatments by giving him English lessons as he is a German doctor. The lessons are very interesting as we go to the swellest tea room in town and all I have to do is to talk to him and correct him when he says something wrong. He is a well-known German surgeon here and is opening a sanatorium shortly. I feel much better now but am getting horribly fat as he is making me take half a pint of thick, thick cream and a quarter of a pound of butter every day. There's nothing to worry about as I'm getting along fine now. The only thing is I'm supposed to get all the exercise I can but we work till so late and I'm so tired after the three lessons a week that I don't feel like moving around. I gave up my Spanish lessons as I just didn't have the time to study. However, I know enough to carry on a conversation and understand everything. Poor Margaret doesn't know anything so she can't even go shopping alone.

I sent Mother a check for $20. last week but don't think I will ever get enough to send towards my bank account as there is always something to buy. I have one new wollen dress I had made of light brown with dark brown lines which cost me about $17. for material and everything so that wasn't so much. It is long and flary and quite becoming. I also had a silk dress made and that cost me with a slip about $42. You see silk is so darned expensive down here. But the dressmakers sure know their business and it is a lovely dress, dark brown silk flares, with a little flounce of beige at the neck. It looks nice with my winter coat which is also dark brown and dark brown winter hat which has a little beige in it.

Well, I never needed clothes so much as I did after the shipwreck and the shops will look great at home. I'll never buy so many clothes ahead again, though, as they sure go out of style quickly. I will look Almyer Hatch up in Valparaiso as I see that he will be on a ship stopping there. It would be interesting to meet someone you used to go to school with there.

Love, Dorothy X X

I'll be seeing you soon, as I leave here January 12th if nothing happens in the meantime.

That pain in Dorothy's side won't be cured by butter and cream. We pick up a week later with Dorothy — one of those rare letters sent to both her mother and her aunt— and we now find that the Chilean inspection trip is to take about 10 days. We learn that Dorothy actually gets to stay at the American Embassy — more adventures!

EMBASSY OF THE UNITED STATES OF AMERICA
Santiago, Chile.   June 18, 1930.

Dearest Mother and Kathie:

I shall have to write you one letter together as I have only one Chilean stamp left and I would like to mail this from here. We stayed in Valparaiso about a week and then returned to Santiago. In Valparaiso the Consul General there invited us to lunch and he has a wonderful country house with a private swimming pool and a tennis court and a garden full of all kinds of trees, olives growing right on the trees, and oranges, and strawberry beds, cherry trees, peach trees, etc. And around it all is a beautiful hedge about twice as high as Roger and very thick and inside are arches shaped from the hedge which are so wide that a hole is made through them for a passageway. When the sunset they called us out to see it and it sure was beautiful because the city is in a valley and surrounded by mountains, some of them 20,000 feet high and covered with snow, some of

them and some of them absolutely bare. They looked lovely
in the sunset glow, some of them shining white and some of
them almost red.

When we returned to Santiago, the Ambassador invited me
to live at the Embassy because Mr. Messersmith was living
there and it made it easier for him to have me in the same
building. Well, it is like a palace, the most wonderful
house I ever saw, with long winding staircases and
gorgeously furnished. My room is all done in pale green,
the paper, bedroom set and everything, and there is a
mirror every time you turn around and the pillows are the
softest kind of feathers. The Ambassadress just came in
this minute and asked me if there was anything I wanted and
if everything was all right in my room, so you see I'm well
taken care of. I have dinner and lunch with the Consul
General and the Ambassador and his wife every day and it is
lovely because they have red candles when they have a
centerpiece of red flowers on the table, white candles with
white flowers, etc.

Sunday the Consul General and the Ambassador went to the
races, and I was with them. They have a wonderful race
track here and the Chileans, like the Argentines, sure know
how to dress and all look like beautiful dolls.

Well, I'll say goodbye for now as I must get to work.

                          Love, Dorothy X X

P.S. Just got a raise to $2500 per annum.

And now, after Dorothy's return to Buenos Aires, we learn more about Bill Denker:

June 24, 1930.

Dearest Kathie:

I've been trying to hunt up some stamps for you and this
is all I've been able to find so far. The girls in the
office are saving them for some cousins but said I could
have all they didn't use. So here are a few to start with.
I couldn't get any air mail ones. Kathie, to be frank with
you I think there isn't much chance of winning a prize for
the stamps as we were just swamped here when the air mail
first started from people who have collected stamps all
their lives, that is, they sent envelopes addressed to
themselves just so we would send them back and they would
get the envelopes with the canceled stamps. So they got all
kinds of stamps for first flight letters. But if you just
like to collect them for the fun of it, go ahead, but
otherwise I think you would be disappointed. I'll send you

all I can of foreign countries.

I'm back in B.A. again after my trip to Chile and I sure enjoyed it very much. It's supposed to be the most expensive trip in the world for its length, but it was really beautiful. The mountains were so high and there was the railroad winding in between them. Often times the train is held up because of the snow on the tracks and there are snow sheds built all along the way, but we were very fortunate to have nice weather. Mother wrote and told me she only worked two days last week and I am so worried about everything. I sent her a check for $20. just before I went to Chile and have $20. more for her just as the exchange gets a little better but I lose a lot on it right now as the dollar is sky high.

Well, Kathie, it won't be long before I'll be seeing you again, about 5 months after you get this letter as I would leave here about January 12.

I guess I told you I went both to Valparaiso and Santiago. Valparaiso is on the Pacific Ocean and that's where you take the boat for the States if you go home by the west coast, which I won't have to do now as I have already been across Chile. Well, Valparaiso is rather small, about 200,000, when you think that it is one of the two principle cities of Chile. It is surrounded by hills where the most of the houses are and the people have to go home by little elevators that go right up the hills, which costs about two cents. There are only 40 Americans living there and about 4000 English. There are only 4 lady Vice Consuls in the consular service and one lives there and she is very nice. I guess I told you the Consul General there invited all of us out to his country home and we had a lovely lunch. You know this American boy I told you about who was to meet us in Mendoza and take the train with us to Chile? Well, he met us and Mr. Messersmith went to the Embassy to live and they had booked a room for me at the same hotel that Bill stayed. Well, the next night he said he had to go to Valparaiso by the five o'clock train and Mr. Messersmith and I went also by the same train and again stayed at the same hotel, the three of us having dinner together about every night. So it was quite nice and he and the Consul General got on quite well together (He graduated from Harvard when he was only 20 years old so you see he is quite clever). So after a few days we returned to Santiago, but Bill didn't dare to book the same train again as it looked like too much of a strange coincidence so he took the afternoon train and after that I stayed at the Embassy too but we had dinner together one night and he also came down to see us off at seven o'clock in the morning for

Buenos Aires. He'll be in Chile another month.

Well, Kathie, I'll be closing now as I want to get this letter off on this boat. Lots of love to Roger and write soon. I'll be looking for some more stamps.

Dorothy xx

AMERICAN CONSULAR SERVICE

Buenos Aires, Argentina.   July 1, 1930.

Dearest Kathie:

This is a holiday for us as they are taking the cattle census and I am afraid to venture outside because I'm so fat now I just know they'll count me. But Margaret and I offered to work this morning as Mr. Messersmith is in such a hurry as he leaves for Germany in two months. We had planned to play tennis this afternoon but it would pick out this day to rain. But the fourth of July and the ninth are also holidays so we'll get a chance to play yet.

They sure put it over me on that winter coat of mine. I've had it about two months and the sleeves have just rotted away, the lining I mean. So I had to buy some more yesterday and the fur on the collar looks like somebody chewed it. Well, anyhow it's nice and warm. It's so pleasant being here now that Margaret is here. She is twenty-four, smaller than I, slim and pretty. We have a lot of fun together.

I see I forgot to enclose the stamps that I was going to send you so will put them in this letter. I think we're going to move soon because our room is such a wreck we don't dare invite anybody in for dinner or anything and if you don't repay people at the boarding house you have to take them to a restaurant and it costs you all out-doors. I hope Roger is getting along all right.

We had a big wedding at the boardinghouse the other night and lots of fun. An American architect who was staying there got married. He knew the girl only two months so we're all wondering how it's going to turn out. They went to Montevideo on their honeymoon and we all went down to the ship with them and filled their beds with mothballs and drowned them with rice. We had a picture taken at the boat which I am sending to Mother.

Well, Kathie, nothing special has happened lately but will write again soon. I'm feeling fine now so don't worry about me.

Lots of love,

Dorothy

During the "feeling fine" letter of 1 July and the casual mention in the 26 August letter, Dorothy underwent an appendicitis operation – as reported in the Ware River News.

AMERICAN CONSULAR SERVICE
August 25, 1930.

Dearest Kathie:

I have just received your lovely gift and it will be just ideal for tennis and the club this summer. I am having a couple of white linen dresses made to wear with it for tennis and it looks swell. I certainly appreciate your sending it. All the girls like it too.

I haven't got a letter from you for ages. I think I must be missing some of them. Do you address it to me at "The American Consulate General, Buenos Aires, Argentina"? Perhaps it would be safer to put the street address too: Av. Roque Saenz Peña 567, Edificio Banco de Boston, Consulado norteamericano, Buenos Aires, Argentina. That's quite a mouthful, isn't it. Well, I've had the job of opening the mail for the last few weeks so I've managed to swipe quite a goodly number of interesting stamps. Any you don't want just enclose and send back as we get calls for stamps all the time from people in the States. The only thing is that they are all new stamps as we don't get any old ones.

Well, it's awful not to be able to play tennis yet, but I expect to in a couple more weeks. I'm feeling fine after the operation and can do anything but play tennis as that is too strenuous. Our new boarding house is swell, as it is really the home of an English man and his wife, a very modern apartment with steam heat and we have lovely apple pie (the English serve it with custard, and the crust is different from ours as it is like what we make for strawberry short-cake) and two different puddings every day and everything is home cooked. The lady of the house is very nice. Well, Mr. Messersmith is leaving for Germany this week so we are giving him a lovely cigar box all engraved with our names each written in our own hand-writing. The new man to take his place is very, very nice and I think we will get a month's vacation instead of two weeks when Mr. M. goes. Germany still holds open for me and I don't know just what to do. I'm waiting for a letter from you to find out. My latest checks to Mother are May 19th, July 13, July 28 and I'm sending one next week.

I have a whole office all by myself which looks very imposing, but of course the real reason is that it is to make a good impression on visitors.

We are just starting to have some lovely spring weather but I expect next Month it will rain all the time as it should be raining this month. It's sure good to see summer coming.

They're having quite a lot of trouble here in the telephone company. The men are cutting all the cables and breaking things up generally and it may develop into something serious. There has just been a revolution in Bolivia and now there is one in Peru. I wish we would have one here, just to see what they are like.

Well, Kathie, I'll write again soon as I haven't much news just now.

Lots of love,

Dorothy xx

Tell Roger I've not forgotten him.

A weighty decision Dorothy was wrestling with as a 23-year-old working girl in the Foreign Service: Should she get married? That would end her career under the State Department rules. Or should she go to Germany with Mr. Messersmith? Dorothy was considering both, and one precluded the other. As usual, Aunt Kathie was her sounding board.

AMERICAN CONSULAR SERVICE
Nov. 6, 1930.

Dearest Kathie:

I want to thank you very much for the lovely snapshots you sent me of you in the garden. They look more like a painting than a snapshot and you should have them enlarged. I don't know whether I mentioned the card from Hampton Beach either, but I'm glad you're having such a nice time. I sure would like to see some salt water for a couple of weeks.

The Kaiser's grandson came into the Consulate the other day and I thought he was somebody's chauffeur because he sure didn't look very royal. A very tall skinny guy and very plain but looked something like his grandfather. Thanks also for the little leaflet you enclosed with your letter it was very nice.

That was an awful nice picture you enclosed of the Ambassador's daughter in Chile. Her mother showed me a painting of her in the drawing room and she sure is a lovely girl. They have two daughters in school in Washington, and one of them is lame from infantile paralysis, about 14 years old, but is a beautiful girl also. They have one little girl about 4 years old, who has yellow curls and beautiful blue eyes. They are all lovely children. They were born in Rumania I think.

I am sending either in this letter or separately about a million stamps. I hope you'll be able to use them.

We cannot receive packages through pouch, but don't you worry about that because I'll be home pretty soon and buy all the stuff in the world even if I have to start 8 thousand charge accounts. I've just found out about a new steamship line here, the Garcia Diaz line [cargo boats carrying about 12 passengers], and it only costs $150. gold to go from here to States and so when I get that much saved up I will come home which will probably be about in March, as I wouldn't want to get home for the winter anyhow. I don't want you to send me any of the money I have home if I can help it as I will need it for clothes. I look like a ragbag. If I can get passage for $150. gold I will not resign because you see we get paid while in transit and as I get about $50., a week and it takes over three weeks on this line, my passage will have been paid by my salary by the time I reach New York. Then we are allowed 2 months in the States with salary and are paid in transit on the way back. Therefore, I figure I'll have enough to stock up on some clothes. I especially want to buy a winter coat as the one I have is horrible. I shall try to bring it back so you can get an idea of what you can get for $100. gold down here. I also would like a wardrobe trunk.

If I resign, the Government will pay my way back on a Munson liner, which costs about $3400. gold, but they will not give me any vacation with pay in the States and I'll be without a job when I land, although I am almost sure I can get a job in the State Dept. any time I want. Now Kathie, here is the whole thing in a nutshell. Bill is in love with me. I know he's O.K. and would make a wonderful husband and be awfully good to me. So if I decide that I'm in love before I leave here, or I really can wait until I get home to decide, I won't resign at all, but just take my two month's leave in the States as we are allowed by Government regulations every two years and come back here with some nice clothes for a trousseau. If, when I get to the States, I decide differently, I will still have two months to think it over and if I decide I'm not in love I WILL NOT RETURN TO BUENOS AIRES, but I am sure I can get a transfer to some other post or go to Berlin with Mr. Messersmith, although now that I've spent so much time in a foreign country I'm not so anxious to try it again because believe me it isn't all fun but has been mighty lonesome sometimes. But I know that if, by waiting all this time before going home, instead of going in January as I had planned and told Mr. Messersmith I would, I thereby lose my chance to go to Berlin, I will not feel a bit bad about it, because I have absolutely no desire to go to Europe but would much prefer to go to Honolulu or China or India or someplace like that. So no matter what I do I will come out on top. Another thing, they are trying to get Congress to pass a bill whereby we clerks in the foreign service will get a good percentage of our rent, heat and light paid by the Government, besides out salary. The officers have already had such a bill go through for them and ours is going through sure (unless the Democrats get in at the elections).

Well, you and Roger tell me what you think about it all, because you know how much I think of your advice.

Lots of love,

Dorothy xx

Now comes the shocker: Dorothy got engaged! And she is headed home. The announcement was even published in the ol' Ware River News.

Dear Kathie: I wrote Mr. Donovan & it had been over 100 here lately so please give him these little paper clippings to help him win his bet. I think its 102 today

AMERICAN CONSULAR SERVICE

Buenos Aires, Argentina.   February 28, 1931.

Dearest Kathie:

I suppose you got a surprise when you heard I was engaged. But I may change my mind yet, so don't put too much faith in it. As you say, there are lots of things I would learn by going to Europe, and one is married all the rest of one's life. But Bill knows so much I would learn a lot from him. However, I got a telephone call from him a couple of weeks ago (He has been in Chile 2 months) and he asked me to come over right away and get married as he expects to be there indefinitely and will

MISS DOROTHY FORRANT TO MARRY BOSTON MAN

Will Resign Consular Post at Buenos Aires Before Wedding in Summer

Ware, Feb. 18—Miss Dorothy Forrant, daughter of Mrs Mary Forrant of Eddy street and attached to the United States diplomatic service at Buenos Aires, Argentina, will be married this summer in South America, her engagement to William A. Denker of Boston, representative of the Du-

MISS DOROTHY FORRANT

ness school, entered the diplomatic service at Washington. She will make a trip home before the wedding, sailpont Paint company at Buenos Aires, having been announced today by her mother.

return to the States in a year on leave. But I decided not
to rush into things, especially as Mother would be very
disappointed if I didn't come home first. And who knows I
may change my mind on the boat as I haven't seen him for
two months, one month on the boat will be three and it will
be about 6 months before I see him. I will be going back
to Chile instead of B.A. and so will have to give up my
job.

I went to a lovely dinner dance at the American Club a
couple of nights ago and had a lovely time, but it was just
my luck to have our pictures put in the paper and maybe
Bill won't like it. I have written him about it, however,
and told him what a good time I had, A bunch of us are
going swimming from the office this afternoon as it is
terribly hot and I can't wait to get into the water. Every
Sunday a crowd of us go to our Club where we have a lovely
outdoor swimming pool and dive for coins, etc. I regret
not having a pool on board ship very much. I am sorry you
are disappointed about me not going to Germany, but I may
go yet. I got a nice letter from Mr. Messersmith
congratulating me on my engagement so I suppose he has
given me up for lost. However he has written such good
efficiency reports on me that I am absolutely sure of a job
again in the foreign field if I want one, or if not, in
Washington. But traveling teaches you so many new things I
don't think I would ever work in the States again,
especially as I would get about half of the money I get
now.

If it is a choice between seeing me off and meeting me I
would rather you would see me off as those freight boats
are very indefinite, and may arrive May 3 and maybe a day
later or so. One of the girls at the office who left for
the States last week (her husband is with an american
company down here) says she will meet me at the boat so I
won't be entirely alone. Besides, I'm so used to being
alone now, that nothing bothers me.

I will try to find where the boat docks, but anyhow, it
is the SUD ATLANTICO of the Garcia Diaz Line.

Goodbye, for now, Kathie dear and I'll be seeing you and
Roger soon.

        Love,

Dorothy

And … Dorothy's last letter from Buenos Aires. It includes a frank reflection on how marriage would shape her future.

AMERICAN CONSULAR SERVICE
Buenos Aires, Argentina.   March 12, 1931.

Dearest Kathie:

 I just received your little card, and I'm awfully sorry
about not writing oftener. I have sent two letters before
this one, though, but perhaps you had not received them
when you sent the card. I'm getting ready to go now, but at
the last minute I am thinking of taking a train through
Bolivia and coming home by the West Coast as everyone
assures me it is the most picturesque thing in South
America as the scenery is so varied and you can see the
Inca Indians in Peru. If I do come that way I will try to
get some snaps or buy something from the Indians as
souvenirs. The ships on the West Coast stop at very
interest ports, too, including Columbia, Ecuador, Panama
and Habana. The reason I think of changing my mind is that
my freight boat, instead of stopping 5 days in Cuba is
going to stop 5 days in Philadelphia. What a difference!
and 24 days without a single stop, me being the only
passenger, doesn't appeal much to me. So I think it would
money well invested to come by the West Coast and then I
can say I've been all around South America.

 We will have a lot to talk about when I come home, won't
we?

- 2 -

 If I come by the West Coast I'll send my trunk home by
the East Coast, as you are only allowed a certain number of
pounds, and it will be a good alibi for having no nice
clothes, as I'll say I sent them all home the other way.
I've got a lot of shopping to do when I arrive. I may meet
Bill in Peru, and also I may decide not to get married
right away because what's the use of going all the way back
to South America for just about 8 months as he expects to
come to the States then and it costs so much money. Anyhow
I'll have lots of time to think everything over at home
with my 2 months vacation. Anyhow, I'm not a bit sorry
about Germany because it's as cold as anything there and
it's as big as New York and it is awfully hard getting
acquainted in a big city like that.

 The girls gave me a nice going away tea and have been so
kind about everything. We go swimming every Sunday and I
have a nice tan.

 Well, Kathie, this will probably be my last letter from
B.A. but I will drop you and mother a line on the way home.

Lots of love,

xxxx

Dorothy

No letters were posted 'on the trip home' – Dorothy had earned about two months off, during which she thought about Bill Denker and marriage … and decided that she was not in love – at least not enough to get married and chuck her career. There were so many opportunities in the Foreign Service, and her time off opened an exotic one: Japan.

Life (and vacation time) moved on. Very near the end of her two months, Dorothy presented her talk at the Ware Rotary Club luncheon at noon on Monday June 22, 1931. The Ware River News captured much of this talk in the Thursday edition. The archives are lost to time and the 1938 New England Hurricane, but much of it has been transcribed from a clipped segment, perhaps saved in Dorothy's souvenir box by her mother May.

> Miss *Dorothy Forrant* of *Eddy* street, who recently returned from Buenos Aires, Argentine, South America, will be the speaker at the weekly luncheon of the Ware Rotary club at the Hampshire house Monday noon, Her talk will be "My Experiences in South America."

Miss Forrant Tells of Her

Experiences in So. America

Miss Dorothy Forrant, who is lately back from Buenos Aires and on Saturday starts for Tokio, Japan, was the speaker at the Rotary Club luncheon on Monday.

Although it was the first time that she had ever spoken in public, she was at her ease, and spoke effectively and looked charming, and at the end of her talk answered many questions, ranging from her experiences in the Argentine revolution to how Bill Allen likes it in Buenos Aires.

She told of Buenos Aires, where she has been stationed for two years as secretary of the American Consul General. She said:

"I hope no one here has the misconception I had of Buenos Aires before I went down there two years ago.

When you sort of expect to find feathered Indians, monkeys swinging from tall cocoanut trees, and even boa constrictors, it's rather a shock to come upon such a modern and beautiful city as Buenos Aires. It's the sixth largest city in the world, you know, and very cosmopolitan. We have about 4,000 Americans down there and the British community numbers approximately 60,000.

"It's called the "Little Paris of South America" and the many sidewalk cafes, lining the principal streets give it a distinct Parisian atmosphere. It boasts of at least one huge department store that puts to shame any we have in Boston. It's a real bustling, wide-awake city, vying with us even in traffic

jams, and it has been prophesied by some who look far into the future that in another 50 years, it will eclipse New York, both in magnitude and economic importance.[14]

"Many prominent American firms have branches in Buenos Aires, such as Standard Oil, Swifts, International Harvester, etc., and they are making great headway. The I. T. & T. has bought out all British interests in their line. These companies send down American personnel under 2 and 3 year *[clipping cut]*

"Perhaps you'd like to know a bit about our Consulate General in

---

14 *Ed:* The prophecy was correct in magnitude: In 1980, BA was 9.76 m, NYC was 7 million.

Buenos Aires. It's one of the largest and busiest in the world. There are 13 offices and a staff of about 30. It makes market surveys for firms interested in establishing branch offices down there, looks after Americans and their interests in general, and keeps the Government posted on agricultural, economic, and commercial conditions.

"The Government has recently purchased a marvelous new residence for the home of the American Ambassador and shortly they will begin a new building to house the Embassy, office of the Commercial Attache, and the Consulate General.

"Of course you know there's quite a bit of friendly rivalry between British and American commercial interests in Buenos Aires. The railways, walkways, etc., are owned by British capital and many thousands of pounds have been invested in Argentina by the British. The British Economic Mission, headed by Lord of Aberdeen, made a tour of Argentina, Brazil and Uruguay in 1927 which led to a considerable revival of interest in South America generally. The idea was then conceived of reawakening interest in British products by having an immense trade fair. This fair was held a couple of months ago and was sponsored by the Prince of Wales. The British Trade Fair was a complete success and certainly accomplished the basic purpose of reawakening public interest in British manufactures.

"Perhaps I ought to say a word about the climate in Buenos Aires. The seasons are just the reverse of ours, they are in full winter now, and I can truthfully say I've never been so cold in all my life as I have been in Buenos Aires. It's about the same climate you have in Washington, D.C. except you have the great disadvantage of no means of heating the homes in Argentina. I lived with an Argentine family for almost a year and they would come to the table [clipping cut] the real reason is the fact that coal is imported and, like hosiery, considered a luxury.

"That's why it costs so much to live outside the States. What we consider absolutely necessary they always managed to do without so naturally we pay luxury prices there. Of course the fact that Argentina is so essentially an agricultural country necessitates that all manufactured articles be imported and import duties are very high and thus the cost of living is excessive. I think about Woolworth's more than anything in Argentina and when Argentine women come to the States it's a common complaint of husbands that they can't keep their wives out of the 5 & 10.

"I think the Argentine women are the most beautiful I've ever seen. In fact they are so monotonously perfect of profile, with large black eyes and white skin and perfect teeth – that one rather welcomes the few plain girls encountered occasionally.

"The Argentines are very lovely people. They seem to be more happy than we are, or perhaps I should say guided more by their emotions than their intellect. The family is very central to Argentine life. That of course may be because the girls are never allowed to go out with a boy friend, even for a walk, no matter how long he has been a friend of the family. I do think that Argentine girls envy the frank companionship of American and English boys and girls but they would immediately lose caste if they attempted it.

"They love music and have a keen appreciation of opera and good concert events. Some of the most famous of these may be heard every winter when the Colon, the large opera house, is always well patronized. They object a bit to our noisy foxtrots because they say they all sound alike. They can listen for hours to the slow, sad tangos, though, and leave quite cheerful afterwards.

"If anyone likes sports Buenos Aires is the place for them. There must be over 200 golf and tennis clubs which often include a clubhouse for dancing and a good swimming pool. [clipping cut]

Off to Tokyo and new adventures!

Editor's note: The above transcription was constructed from a blurry image of a mostly complete newspaper clipping from the Ware River News (published weekly) during the week of 22 June 1931, the Monday on which Dorothy presented her talk to the Ware Rotary Club at noon in the Hampshire Hotel.

Heidi Reed, Library Director of the Young Men's Library Association, Ware, MA, confirms that the article almost certainly ran in the Ware River News. "Those clippings don't look like articles from the Springfield papers, at least as compared to other clippings we have from the time period."

However, sadly, Heidi tells us "No one in town has the Ware River News for 1931. Some of the back issues were lost in the 1938 flood."

Photos from Dorothy's Shipwreck Gallery

LAST VIEW OF THE MONTE CERVANTES.

Good view of snow-covered mountains in Ushuai.

At left (top) and bottom (right) are two photos taken from the relief ship *M.V. Sarmiento* as Dorothy and the other 1200 passengers are transported back from Ushuaia to Buenos Aires after an unplanned stay of six days.

At left (middle) is the 'original' rescue, 22 January 1930, using the lifeboats from the *M.V. Monte Cervantes* to ferry the passengers to Ushuaia.

Dorothy and her friend E.N. Jones took a number of photos and had them developed at B. Aires.

Dorothy typed her captions at the top (front) of the photos, which can be seen faintly:

LAST VIEW OF THE MONTE CERVANTES.

Good view of snow-covered mountains in Ushuai.

BEAUTIFUL VIEW OF MONTE SARMIENTO.

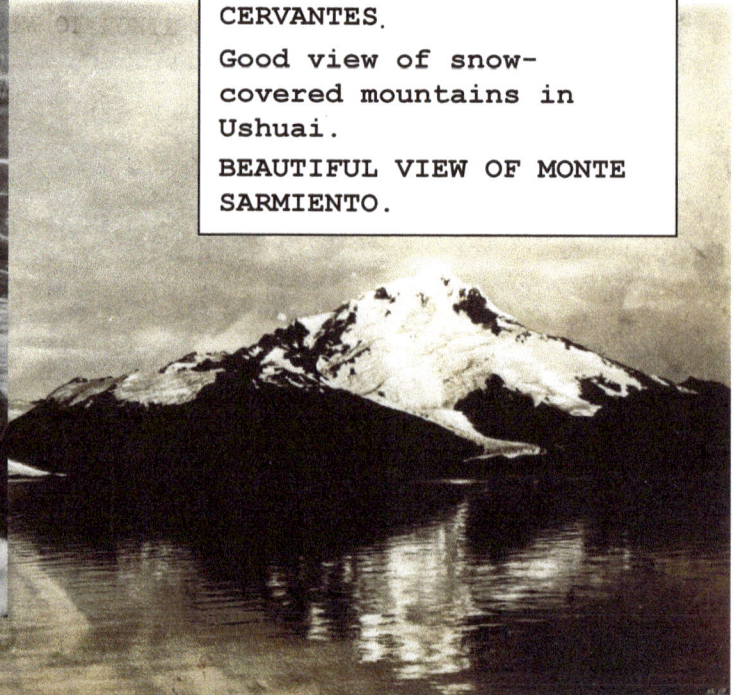

Shipwreck

A traumatic event, particularly one as dramatic and life-threatening as a shipwreck, can leave an indelible mark on a young person's psyche. The experience can fundamentally alter their worldview, their emotional landscape, and their trajectory in life. While the immediate physical and emotional shock may subside, the psychological scars can linger, influencing their behavior, relationships, and overall well-being for years to come.

This potential psychological impact did not appear to affect Dorothy off of Ushuaia on 22 January 1930, as she approached her 23rd birthday. On the contrary, from the photos, she is having a grand time. In her description to Kathie in her letter of February 1930, typed aboard the rescue ship, it was one more adventure. As Dorothy told her story, she walked around while others were scrambling; she took pictures and did not want to go to the lifeboats:

```
I walked around and watched the people scrambling for the
lifeboats and climbed up on a rail so I could see better.
Then I met a friend who had a camera and we took some pictures
of the people getting in the lifeboats. But finally an officer
made me get into a boat although I hated to because I really
felt much safer on the ship.
```

That hardly describes the actions of a traumatized passenger. Dorothy taped into her scrapbook some March 1930 magazine pages on the incident, most likely from her "friend who had a camera" as Dorothy's scrapbook includes some photos published in the article. The British company magazine is titled **NUMBER EIGHT** and pages 14-16 provided the following article with a detailed firsthand account of the incident by their employee, passenger E.N. Jones who is most likely that friend with the camera. His comments are accurate; the magazine's, a bit less:

THRILLS OF A REAL SHIPWRECK HIS
VACATION EXPERIENCE

Our readers at Head Office, as well as in South American Branches, will be particularly interested in the adventures and hardships experienced by E. N. Jones, of the Buenos Aires Branch, in a shipwreck off the coast of South America.

Mr. Jones, who for a number of years before being translated to South America, was employed in the Foreign Tellers Department at Head Office, left Buenos Aires on January 15 with 1,200 other tourist passengers and a crew of 302 on the Hamburg Sud American liner, "Monte Cervantes", for a cruise along the southern Argentina coast, expecting to return about the end of January.

The ship struck a rock at 1 PM January 22, in Beagle Channel, Strait of Magellan, at the extreme tip of the mainland, 9 miles from Ushuaia,

Tierra del Fuego, and sank after all the passengers and crew, with the exception of the Captain, who elected to go down with his boat, had been saved.

Mr. Jones had the presence of mind and coolness to make use of a pocket-camera during the launching of lifeboats and the resulting snapshots we are able to publish herewith, together with Mr. Jones description of the shipwreck, taken from a letter he wrote to his brother in England while on his way back to Buenos Aires on board the relief ship, "Monte Sarmiento."

"We arrived at Ushuaia from Magallanes (Punta Arenas) on the evening of January 21, and left at noon January 22, bound for Bahia Garabaldi, where the program called for a tour in small boats through the ice, etc. Being some

1,200 passengers aboard necessitated to take turns at meal times and my turn was second, at the country is bleak and mountainous (laden with ice and snow) I had had my breakfast at 7 a. m. (little thinking that it would be the last square meal I would have for a week) and a moment before 12:45 I was on the way down below to wash up before going into the dining room. In fact, the steward just had the bugle to his mouth to announce 'second sitting.' I was passing one of the dining room doors when there was a terrible grinding and the ship went over to an angle of 40 degrees to 45 degrees, with the resulting crashing of glass and plates, etc. I would say she remained that way some two minutes. Then, owing to what eventually proved to have been a skillful move by the Captain, she partly righted herself. I realized whatever had happened was very serious, but never for a moment thought we would have to take to the boats. We were only eight or nine miles from Ushuaia, in the Beagle Channel.

"You can imagine what might have happened in a panic with 1,200 on board. All this entered my head and in order to do my bit in preventing such a situation, I told all who were near me that there was no danger. However, I learned afterwards that the S.O.S. had already gone out. The boats were getting slung out, and I realized when I saw some of the officers appear with their life-belts on that it was more serious than I thought. I saw the ropes of one boat break while being slung out, but luckily, no one was in it—only two of the crew, who were both saved as one hung on to a rope, and the other was picked out of the water. I had no life-belt—in fact, never thought of it. A young American girl whom I knew by sight in B. A.[1] and an English woman asked if they could stay with me, so I said "yes." I went down below with the idea of getting a roll of film to take some pictures of the boats, etc., and also with the idea of getting these people life-belts, but found my door locked and was promptly ordered up to take to the boats. Then I realized how bad things were, as the ship was well down at the bow. I still had some unused films in my camera and so used them.

---

[1] Dorothy.

"Once up on up on the boat deck I met the chief officer. I told him I did not want to leave but there was nothing doing. I was bundled into a boat and the American girl and English woman with me, together with some sixty others. Then there was the suspense of waiting to be lowered and the spectre of what I had seen of the rope breaking when slinging out the empty boat.

"Well, we were lowered safely, and after a little difficulty the boat got away from the 'Monte Cervantes.' Even then I never thought the ship would go down, although the water was nearly up to the name in the bow. I will never forget the next four and a half hours in that boat in the cold and, at times, rough water, infested with morsa (sea lions).

"The wind was biting and it looked bad at times. Furthermore, you must understand that we never had an officer in the boat and language difficulty had to be overcome. I shared an oar with one of the crew, only a boy who came up

"This remarkable picture of the lowering of the life-boat was snapped by Mr. Jones."   Dorothy has typed caption upper left: A MARVELLOUS PICTURE OF LOWERING OF LIFE BOATS. Note odd-numbers to indicate starboard side boats: 3A, 5A, 7A, 9A.

from the galley, and suffered from the cold. Luckily I had woolen underwear on and that Donegal Tweed suit from Hopes and my Burberry and my camera was in the pocket when it happened. I lost everything else, including passport and cédula[2]—went down with the ship next night. The American girl just had what she stood in, so I handed her my Burberry.

"The boats got scattered and pretty soon we seemed to be all on our own. The hills which seemed so near when aboard the 'Monte Cervantes' now seemed miles away. Trouble arose in the boat—some wanting to go to the shore—others not wanting to go as we would find no landing place, and get battered against the rocks, with which I agreed. Then at times the sea whipped up and we shipped a wave or two. Nearly everyone was sea-sick, and I probably would have been too if I had had my lunch—I had had nothing since 7 a. m.

"I got soaked, and although I kept on pulling, I knew there was no strength in the pulls and I started to feel the cold. Then a launch (motor) appeared. It was one of the 'Monte Cervantes' launches slowly pulling three full lifeboats and it passed us up, saying it could not take us in tow. Bad sign, this. The next item was the most impressive to me. You have seen a picture of a walrus bobbing up out of the water. Well, a sea lion bobbed up, accompanied by a smaller one, and the big one apparently looked at us 20 or 30 seconds with big eyes and before going under it opened its big mouth. That was a fine 'future' after being passed up by a motor launch. Half an hour later we were taken in tow by another of the ship's launches, which already had three boats in tow. With such a load against wind and seas no progress was made and we started rowing even though in tow.

"Then the 'Vicente Fidel López' (old English coaster) which fortunately was in Ushuaia, hove in sight and spirits grew brighter. This is a Argentine Government boat which got the wireless and it was lucky for us that it did.

"It lowered a motor boat and took our boat alone in tow. The worst was not yet over, as we had to be taken to the 'Vicente Fidel López,'

---

[2] a national ID card used in several Latin American countries

where we got battered against the side. We left the 'Monte Cervantes' 1:10 p. m. and boarded the 'López' at 5:45 p. m.

"The 'López' already had picked up a few hundred and I think we were next to the last lifeboat to be picked up. It cruised around a bit and then smoke was sighted on land, for which 13 of the life-boats had headed. The launch went over and returned, saying that they were all empty and smashed, so we went on and after seeing the smoke people could be seen through the binoculars struggling along the so-called road or track.

"It turned out afterwards the people had been walking from four to six hours. The 'López' launch got them by taking a lifeboat load at a time. It was very cold and windy waiting on the 'López' and it is a good job it was daylight until about 10 p. m. Well we finally got back to Ushuaia about 1 a. m. and I was ashore half an hour later. The 'López' must have had about 800 aboard if not more. Altogether, with crew the "Monte Cervantes" had some 1,500 on board.

"Now I must tell you about Ushuaia. In the first place, the worst criminals in Argentina are sent there as the national prison is there. The civilian population cannot be more than 200 or 300, so you can imagine what it meant to have 1,500 extra dumped there. We just had to do the best we could. The prison came in useful as the prisoners (we were told) offered to go on half rations and I, with the majority, ate at the prison. The food was not so bad—tin plates etc., which served for soup, meat and dessert, were of course used. As it is surrounded by mountains there was plenty of drinking water so we were all right in that respect. For sleeping quarters, I slept with seven others in the house of the agent for the Minister of Marine (Anglo Argentine) and did not fare so badly, but some of the others were hard hit. The poor crew and even some of the officers had a hard time. The climate in Ushuaia merits comment. The wind changes about five or six times a day and is cold and strong and whips up the dust. The sun is strong and practically everybody came away with chapped lips and faces peeling. I got more than my share as I was already sunburnt in the 'Monte Cervantes' and after being splashed in the lifeboat with salt-water, and washing in the open, with the cold mountain water, which runs continually, it got worse. It is improving now, however. I never shaved for a week (lost razor, etc.) likewise the majority. Some 200 passengers spent the night on the land and the 'López' launch got them the next morning.

"The Monte Cervantes was visible from the shore and some passengers went back in a hired launch, but it was dangerous—so much so that she went down less than twelve hours later with the captain, Teodoro Dreyer, on her. The 'López' brought some luggage back which was somehow or other transferred but my two bags were not amongst it. All I recovered was that pair of rubber soled shoes and the sports coat, found amongst the pile. Picture the confusion—1,200 people looking for belongings. I would say seventy-five per cent of the passengers lost everything.

"If it had not been for the prison and the generosity of the people (who are very poor) goodness knows what would have happened. The 'Monte Sarmiento', sent for us, was en route to

E.N. Jones is standing, smiling at the right, wearing his oft-mentioned Burberry which he loaned to Dorothy who was wearing it outside the Billiard Hall. The Minister of Maritime, his host, is at left.

Europe but discharged her passengers in Montevideo and came down to pick us up. She arrived at six a. m., January 28 (six days after accident) and we left Ushuaia at four p. m. direct to Buenos Aires, not through the Straits of Magellan again as the program called for. We passed what was left of the 'Monte Cervantes', viz., about ten feet of the stern and one propeller sticking up. I forgot to say that if by chance anyone had got into the water the water was so cold that within five minutes they would have been dead.

"How the captain saved us all is as follows: When the ship hit and reeled over, a rip of over thirty feet (or thirty metres) was made on the ship's bottom on the left, which caused the list. Had the ship run on she would have been ripped all the way along, and as the water was some 300 metres deep just over the rock the ship would have gone down and probably nobody saved. The captain, it appears, immediately reversed the engines to keep the ship resting on the rock. The anchor was dropped and to give you an idea of the depth it went right down and the chain with it. In other words the anchor was lost as the water was too deep—mind you we were resting on a rock in one part while a tremendous depth was at the bow of the ship.

"The ship was going maybe 12 knots at the time. The ship was double skinned as the majority of the new German ships are, so this will give you some idea with which it must have hit.

"I have, no doubt, left out a lot of details but in conclusion it is only fair to say that generally speaking the people behaved very well, under the circumstances, and considering no lives were lost the crew did very well.

"It was a long and miserable six days we all spent in Ushuaia where the sanitation is abominable (I was all right myself with the Minister of Marine). There are only two shops and a drug store there and you can imagine the business they did. I bought the only sixteen shirt they had in the place, which is a terrible thing as regards color, but I will have to land in it as the only one I had on at the time is dirty and they won't do any washing on this ship. I have a blanket from the 'Monte Cervantes' which I will keep as a souvenir and it will serve to carry my sports coat and Burberry ashore as it will be hot when we arrive at Buenos Aires."

Messersmith & Einstein

Dorothy worked well with George Messersmith during his two years as General Consul at Buenos Aires, to include his transcontinental inspection tours to Santiago and Valparaiso, Chile. He had requested that she transfer with him when he was reassigned to the head of the Consulate in Berlin in 1931, a most interesting time in Germany. But the timing wasn't right for Dorothy for several reasons. She wanted the Far East, but she would continue to correspond with Messersmith. In December of 1932, she sent him one of her 'wooden Christmas cards' from Japan, and the General Consul replied with a very cordial letter as well as a personal note. He had been in the international news earlier that month, and it wasn't favorable press. Two snippets from the New York Times articles of December 5 and 8, 1932, provide context:

Einstein's Ultimatum Brings a Quick Visa

Our Consul Angered Him by Political Quiz

EINSTEIN ANGERED BY TEST FOR VISA

BERLIN, Dec. 5 — Professor Albert Einstein was so angered today by forty-five minutes of questioning at the United States Consulate General, as to his fitness to visit America that he refused to submit to further interrogation and returned home.

THE EINSTEIN EPISODE.

The Law Rather Than the Administrator Is Blamed.

To the Editor of The New York Times: The facts concerning the consular inquisition to which Professor Einstein was subjected when he applied for a visa are extremely annoying. I believe that the majority of Americans heartily resent the attitude adopted by Consul General Messersmith, because it places American officialdom in a very bad light.

AMERICAN CONSULAR SERVICE
Berlin, Germany, December 21, 1932.

Personal

Dear Miss Forrant:

It was very good of you to send us a card and I appreciate particularly your note. If you are proud to have worked for me I am equally happy that you were with me during those days in Buenos-Aires when we really had hectic times and long hours and where it would have been impossible for me to do many of the things which we were able to accomplish without your efficient and generous assistance. I am afraid you are too modest and you will never know how helpful you were to me when I was writing those long reports to the Department which required hours of continuous dictation and when I was making those long and difficult inspection reports. I was able to work rapidly and well because you were so efficient and so willing. I am really most grateful to you.

It is very nice to hear a few flattering things about myself because the newspapers have recently not been so kind and have said all manner of things about me in connection with the Einstein visa case. You will probably get repercussions of this even out in Japan and I am not going into the details because when you do hear about it you will know enough of me and of my work to know that Mr. Einstein could not have been badly treated by us. He is a

-2-

philosopher with his head in the clouds, but Mrs. Einstein is a silly woman with her ear very close to the ground, and the whole Einstein incident is due to her publicity seeking instincts. The story was that when he asked for a visa here we asked him all sorts of silly questions as to whether he was a polygamist or had been in an insane asylum, etc., when of course all this was pure imagination, but it was too good for the newspapers. It looked for a while as though the personal criticism which was widely spread might do me some harm, but fortunately all my friends came to the rescue.

I saw from the papers the other day that Junius Wood was in the Far East, and of course I remember Mr. Johnson and Mr. Wilson. It is very kind of them to speak so generously. I am tremendously impressed by your having learnt to talk Japanese at all, and I am afraid that if you get much wiser no man will be brave enough to marry you in spite of your other attractions! I am sure you must like the Far East because it has a charm of its own. My wife of course loves it and would only be too happy to go out there again but I am afraid that that is not likely.

If you ever see Mr. Grew (the Ambassador) I wish you would tell him that the moving picture machine which I told him on the boat going home last summer I would send him, turned out not to be as satisfactory as I thought and I am sure that it would not have met his needs, so I did not send him one as I had promised. If he is interested, however, in getting a fairly cheap projection machine I shall be very glad to look around here and I think I can get one, but it would not be quite as cheap as the one I had previously mentioned.

We keep very busy here because there is really a lot to do and our personal lives are very full here also, in fact just a little bit too full. I want to tell you again how much I appreciate your note and hope that we may have an opportunity of meeting in Washington when we will be both home on leave. My wife joins me in every good wish.

Always
Cordially and sincerely yours,

Messersmith

It was awfully nice of you to write me. Perhaps when I am finally a minister in some nice place, you will come as my secretary if you have not married some nice man by that time.

GM

Copies of the following relevant documents were included with Consul General Messersmith's letter to Dorothy:

The Consulate General at Berlin has received the following telegram from the Secretary of State dated December 10, 2 p.m.:

For the Consulate General: I explained to the Press this morning (December 10) that you were absent from Berlin at the time Einstein called that in accordance with instructions given by you he was received by your staff with the utmost courtesy and consideration and given the examination required by our laws to be given all persons seeking visas and as a result of that examination a visa was granted. It was made clear that the duty imposed upon Consuls by law was in your absence performed by your staff with commendable tact and discretion and the action has the Department's complete approval.

STIMSON.

Frank Kellogg (left) and Henry L. Stimson at the State Department building, 25 July 1929.

Herbert Hoover had appointed Henry L. Stimson as Secretary of State in 1929; he later became Secretary of War under Roosevelt. It is so welcome when your boss supports you!

And Messersmith was certainly right about "friends" coming to his rescue:

FOR CABLE RELEASE TO THE AMERICAN SUNDAY MORNING NEWSPAPERS.

The American colony in Berlin has been intensely disturbed and shocked by the unjust statements which have reached the American and international press in connection with Professor Einstein's experience at the American Consulate in Berlin.

The reports made in the press are based on misconception of facts when it is stated that Professor Einstein was subjected to an unnecessary and gruelling questioning by the American Consul.

Actually every foreigner who wishes to obtain a visa for entry into the United States is required by law to appear in person before an American Consul and this is unavoidable. Although every fairness and courtesy is extended to all who have business with the American Consulate in Berlin, such special consideration was given to Professor Einstein as is due to a man of his international reputation.

His examination was conducted not only in conformity with legal requirements but also with a view to assist Professor Einstein's smooth and undisturbed entry into the United States.

We know the official, Consul Raymond H. Geist, who questioned Professor Einstein, to be too efficient and courteous to have subjected Professor Einstein to any but the most necessary routine, or to have caused him any unnecessary inconvenience.

The inexactness of the statements in the press is evident from the fact that Consul General Geo. Messersmith, against whom personal criticism is made of his supposed examination of Professor Einstein, was absent from town on official business when Professor Einstein visited the Consulate.

Americans in Berlin find in Consul General Messersmith not only a most efficient official but also a warm friend, who has instilled into the consular office here a spirit of fairness and courtesy.

In justice to all concerned, the American Women's Club, the American Chamber of Commerce in Germany, and the American Club, have sent the following cable to the Secretary of State in Washington:

                                        Berlin, December, 10, 1932.

To the
     Honorable Secretary of State,
          Washington, D. C.

In view of the misunderstandings which have arisen
                              -2-
in connection with the visa case of Professor Einstein and particularly in view of the statements which have appeared in the press with regard to the manner in which it has been represented that Professor Einstein was received and questioned at the Consulate General in Berlin, the governing boards of the American Chamber of Commerce in Germany, of the American Women's Club, and of the American Club, these organizations representing the entire American colony in Germany, feel it necessary to bring the following facts to your attention:

1. There are certain formalities which, it is well known, all persons other than American citizens have to comply with before proceeding to the United States, and we knew that the Consulate General in Berlin received Professor Einstein with the courtesy due to one of his international reputation, and that it carried

out these unavoidable legal formalities with every consideration. Aside from our positive knowledge, of the considerate treatment accorded Professor Einstein, it is inconceivable to us that an exception could have been made in his case from the invariable courtesy extended to all persons - Americans and others - calling at the Consulate General.

2. The misunderstandings which have characterized the public accounts of the incident and which misled certain American associations are best illustrated by the fact that the particular object of criticism, Consul General George Messersmith, has never met Professor Einstein. Professor Einstein applied for his visa on Monday morning, December 5th, when Mr. Messersmith was absent on an inspection tour to the Consulate at Breslau, in consequence of instructions from the State Department. Thus, all criticism of Mr. Messersmith's alleged conduct of the interrogation of Mr. Einstein is obviously baseless.

It has been the invariable experience of the American residents in Berlin that the American Consulate General under Mr. Messersmith has provided the public with a service that can only be described as exemplary, not only in efficiency, but in courtesy. The American colony of Berlin wishes particularly to emphasize its high opinion of the character and conduct of Mr. Messersmith, who during his period of service in Germany has enjoyed a literally unparalleled prestige and popularity. It is singularly unfortunate that Mr. Messersmith should have been depicted as a bureaucrat who questioned Mr. Einstein like a school boy. Of all men in the American foreign service with whom we Americans have had contact, Mr. Messersmith is distinguished particularly by his elimination of bureaucratic methods, and would be the last conceivable person to have employed them in the case of Professor Einstein. We feel, therefore, all the more keenly the injustice of the criticism that has been levelled at Mr. Messersmith and are convinced that correction of the misapprehensions upon which the criticism was based is necessary and will be welcomed by those misled through

-3-

faulty information.

GOVERNING BOARD OF AMERICAN CHAMBER
OF COMMERCE
H. B. Peirce, President
AMERICAN WOMEN'S CLUB OF BERLIN
Mrs. Claire Schandein Best, President
AMERICAN CLUB OF BERLIN
Frederick Wirth, President.

Nineteen thirty-two was hardly Einstein's first visa experience or even his first visit to the United States (1921); he toured the Far East in 1922, Spain in 1923, and South America in 1925. However, Adolf Hitler was elected Chancellor of Germany in January 1933, and this would be the deciding factor in Einstein's decision to remain in America.

-2-

philosopher with his head in the clouds, but
Mrs. Einstein is a silly woman with her ear very
close to the ground, and the whole Einstein incident
is due to her publicity seeking instincts. The story
was that when he asked for a visa here we asked him
all sorts of silly questions as to whether he was a
polygamist or had been in an insane asylum, etc.,
when of course all this was pure imagination, but
it was too good for the newspapers. It looked for a
while as though the personal criticism which was
widely spread might do me some harm, but fortunately all my friends came to the rescue.

I saw from the papers the other day that Junius
Wood was in the Far East, and of course I remember
Mr. Johnson and Mr. Wilson. It is very kind of them
to speak so generously. I am tremendously impressed
by your having learnt to talk Japanese at all, and
I am afraid that if you get much wiser no man will
be brave enough to marry you in spite of your other
attractions! I am sure you must like the Far East
because it has a charm of its own. My wife of course
loves it and would only be too happy to go out there
again but I am afraid that that is not likely.

If you ever see Mr. Grew (the Ambassador) I
wish you would tell him that the moving picture
machine which I told him on the boat going home last
summer I would send him, turned out not to be as
satisfactory as I thought and I am sure that it would
not have met his needs, so I did not send him one as
I had promised. If he is interested, however, in
getting a fairly cheap projection machine I shall be
very glad to look around here and I think I can get
one, but it would not be quite as cheap as the one
I had previously mentioned.

We keep very busy here because there is really a
lot to do and our personal lives are very full here
also, in fact just a little bit too full.   I want to
tell you again how much I appreciate your note and
hope that we may have an opportunity of meeting in
Washington when we will be both home on leave. My
wife joins me in every good wish.

                                        Always

                        Cordially and sincerely yours,

Tokio[1]

Dorothy was poised to begin her Far East adventures. The 1931 transfer to Tokio would usher in Dorothy's greatest adventures. The 24-year-old had to have been excited about this upcoming posting as she returned to Ware in the spring for a long-anticipated two months' holiday. She borrowed money from her Aunt Kathie and Roger, recognizing the need for some extra funds: The Department paid for her ticket and transport but from her Buenos Aires experience, Dorothy knew a nest egg would come in more than handy for helping her establish herself in a new country. The transfer was exciting in itself, and to top it off, Dorothy was destined to meet the 'nicest lieutenant' on the ship over — after only recently being freed from her engagement to Bill Denker.

Dorothy's social life in Buenos Aires was quite full, thanks to her swimming and tennis pursuits and her interactions with her Argentine host family; however, as we will see, her social life in Tokyo was positively exotic, ranging from skiing and camel riding in Japan to Club Chefoo in China. Her letters home capture much of this. And her Foreign Service career was to end here — with her marriage to Lt. Blackledge at the Tokyo Consulate in April of 1934.

Once more, her serendipitous timing, particularly with regard to Japan and Germany, stands out. Recall that Dorothy had done well in Ware in 1926, which led to a clerk/stenographer position with the State Department. Moving to D.C. placed her in a prime location to accept work with the Sixth Pan-American Conference, which was a once-a-decade opportunity. Kudos from her work at the conference greased the skids with Mr. Messersmith and led to a consular assignment in Buenos Aires. Then Dorothy was asked to accompany Mr. Messersmith to his new position in Germany – in 1931. Critical times! Instead, Dorothy passed both on a potential

---

[1]This chapter on Dorothy's Japanese adventures is titled *Tokio* versus Tokyo. This now-quaint spelling of the capital city was more common in the 1870s and 1880s but had been overtaken by *Tokyo* by the 1890s. Dorothy would use Tokyo. However, as we will see, Dorothy's hometown paper, the *Ware River News,* would use the old-school spelling in their reporting of Dorothy's adventures.

spouse and that transfer to Germany ("anything but Europe!") to accept a position in Japan — and on the trip over she meets her future husband.

Yes, it was en route to her Tokyo station that she met my father, described in her very first Tokyo letter as the nicest Navy lieutenant. He was also a widower with a five-year-old daughter — and all of those variables figured into the marriage equation, as we shall see.

In the letter Dorothy says Allan had invited her to vacation in Shanghai, but the letters indicate that they had their adventure in Chefoo, China, the summer port for the Asiatic Fleet. (Quite a difference, as Chefoo was about one-fifth the size of Shanghai.) The chapter following will provide information on Club Chefoo, the city of Chefoo, and life in the Asiatic station in the 1930s in general. Dorothy and the lieutenant were married in the American consul in Tokyo in April of 1934. But first, the letter from the outbound trip — and the invitation to share a vacation. So many adventures at once!

AMERICAN CONSULAR SERVICE
American Consulate General, Tokyo, Japan.

July 25, 1931.

Dearest Kathie:

It sure was a pleasant surprise to find your thoughtful letter waiting for me and thanks very much. I don't know where to begin to tell you about Tokyo. I'm absolutely wild about it. I think it must be the most interesting and beautiful place in the world.

First I will tell you about the trip coming over. I met the nicest Lieutenant in the Navy. He has just come back from teaching two years at Annapolis Naval Academy and will have three years Duty in China. Well, we were together all during the trip and he sure is a peach. Very good looking and as nice as he is good looking. When we arrived at Honolulu he brought me to another naval officer's house to have tea there and they sure showed us Honolulu. They took us down to the boat and threw garlands of flowers around our necks like you see in the movies, real flowers too. On board I had a great time because Allan of course knew all the naval officers and their wives and they invited me to all the little stateroom parties.

When I got to Tokyo a nice young Vice Consul, an American girl working in the Consulate, a Consul and Consul's wife all met me and gave me a royal welcome. I sure am glad I chose this place instead of Germany, because everyone is extra nice to you here on account of it being way out of the beaten path and so few Americans. The first day I was here I had lunch and dinner with the Lieutenant who stopped over a day on his way to China, the second day the Consul's wife invited me to lunch, the third day two of the Vice Consuls took me to the movies (we saw Skippy, you must see it) and to dinner. The next day I was invited down to the beach, about an hour's ride from Tokyo, where both of them stayed during the winter, to play tennis in the afternoon, have dinner, and at night I was invited to a party, and one of the hosts was Mr. Titus, who is Mr. Brown in the Post Office's cousin in Ware. Someone asked me where I was from, and I said a little town nobody heard of, Ware. And Mr. Titus, said, why I know Ware well. I was born in Northampton and have quite a few relatives around there, one being Mr. Brown in the Post Office. He is a Trade Commissioner in the Commercial Attache's office.

Well, Saturday I was invited for lunch to another Vice Consul's house. This one is the son of Senator Bingham. He lives in a real Japanese house, where the floors are all covered with straw matting and at the door you have to take off your shoes and put on little healess slippers. All the walls are made of sliding doors, so you can slide all the doors together and you are practically living outdoors in a lovely garden.

- 3 -

But wait till I tell you about the new quarters! They won't be ready for a couple of months more but they are going to have a private swimming pool, ballroom, etc. They will be made up of little apartments, four girls to an apartment, but each one having her private bedroom, steam heat, modern washbowl in each room, all furnished, etc. but with a common dining room to each apartment, also a telephone. There are garages for ten autos, in case we happen to have one. The offices will be right next door so we just pop out of bed into the office. Now wait till I tell you our hours -- be prepared for a shock -- in the summer we work from 8 to 2, stopping to have a sandwich and coffee about 12. In the winter we have awful hard hours -- 9 to 4. *hour for lunch.* Also there is a swimming pool in the Y.W.C.A. here so what more can I want. These quarters are absolutely free. I didn't tell Mother about them, do you think I ought to? She might find out and feel pretty bad about it. On the other hand, she would think I was a millionaire and you should send home more money.

You know Kathie, when I arrived here I realized what a mistake it was to take out that $2,000 endowment because I have an idea I probably won't stay single all my life and I can't burden anyone just starting in with $42.00 a month for insurance. They

- 4 -

just wouldn't stand for it, particularly when I have to see that Mother has coal, taxes paid, etc. as she looks to me and not to Arthur because she knows he never contributes anything. Of course he can't, but he could have if he tried to study a little. And the first letter I got from her was that any extra money I had she could use--of course she is quite right and I would rather send it to her then pay insurance, but <u>I can't do both</u>. Because Kathie, this is a chance of a lifetime. I'm with nice people who don't treat you like a stenographer, but like one of them, and I was asked to spend my vacation in Shangai by Allan. I have never known anyone as nice as he is and I'm not going to risk any chance of losing developing this friendship just because my insurance premiums are so high I won't have enough saved by the time summer comes. One of the Lieutenant-Commanders wives ask me to spend a vacation with her in Manila, Philippine Islands, and repeated it two or three times. They all seemed to like me quite well on the boat. So I sent Arthur the money for one month's premium ($18.), I had already paid $3 for doctor's examination, and sent him $10 for himself to make up for the $7 commission he will lose. I am keeping up the .45 insurance on Mother, however, but I do think I have a right to drop the other if I want to. They will all be mad as blazes, especially

- 5 -

Sally who will tell all the neighbors, etc. but I am going to be very selfish this time as it might mean my whole future.

This place is the most colorful imaginable. All the natives wear beautifully colored kimonas with very wide silk sashes with a big bow behind of a contrasting color, and no stockings but little white socks and a piece of wood on each foot held on by a little strap over the toes which clatter all the time they walk.

Sunday I was invited down to the beach again with the Consul General and his wife and three of the Vice Consuls. We all went in swimming together, had lunch, and then went for tea to the top of a high mountain where you have a beautiful view of the city. We had a small earthquake yesterday, although I didn't notice it as I was about an hour's ride from Tokio and in an auto at the time and thought it was just a bump in the road, but the people in Tokio ran out of the houses into the street as that is the safest place.

Well, Kathie, I will write again soon. I love it here, especially the idea of having a swimming pool in the backyard, and one at the Y.W.C.A. for the winter.

Lots of love, Dorothy. XX

P.S. I am enclosing a check for $100. and you will keep on getting it regularly. Don't tell Mother about the Lieutenant as she will put it in the news. *(over)*

- 6 -

I appreciate more and more you and Roger letting me take the money because I wouldn't have this wonderful place to work in, etc., if you didn't let me. Thank you both a million times and I'll see you get it soon.

P.S. How much is coal a ton in Ware. When I can I will send a check to Anderson and have him put in some for Mother but don't want to send her the money direct.

Thus reads the very first Tokio letter. In Dorothy's next letter, a month later (note that letters often coincide with pay dates: the 1st and the 15th of the month), Dorothy's love affair with foreign lands continues.

AMERICAN CONSULAR SERVICE
American Consulate General

Tokyo, Japan,
August 16, 1931.

Dearest Kathie:

I had planned to send you a check this pay day but had to send it home instead. Mother has been writing me like this: She owes $65. for coal, $33.80 for taxes, is paying Rose Woods $1. a week for some things she got from her and how would I like that, and this time sent me this little clipping about being put out if taxes were not paid so I sent her a check for $33.80 for taxes and she also sent me a letter from the collection department of Gilchrists[2] for the radio batteries for $6.90 I sent her a check for that and some money for that insurance I took out (the .45 one) from Arthur. Well, that settles the $2000. policy one--he can say what he wants, I just <u>can't</u> keep it up. Well, I took care to make out the check for the taxes to the Ware Trust Co. and the other check to the Gilchrist Co. so to be sure it would be sent there, but Kathie, she told that Co. I would send the check and if they ever write a letter here with the return address as it was in the letter "Collection Department" or write to the Consul General, I'll just die. Anyhow, I'll send you a check next payday, as I had to send besides $34. to my own insurance company. She said not to tell you so don't say anything about it.

I sure wish you and Roger could come hero for a visit. Maybe you can someday when Roger retires. You can come on one of the freight boats that take a very few passengers quite cheap. It is perfectly fascinating. Did I tell you the men wear panama hats, kimonas like the ladies only don't have such a wide sash, carry a cane and wear wooden shoes. Everyone here has been very nice to me. I've been invited down to the beach every Sunday so far and next week am invited to a buffet supper which will be formal for the ladies. I understand they have quite a social life here and as girls are scarce I suppose I'll be in on all of it.

---

[2] Gilchrist's was a Boston department store, dating from the late 1800s and one of the big three stores (along with Filene's and Jordan Marsh) that dominated Boston's shopping district for years. Already in 1900, the building was referred to as "the daylight store" because of its large windows, and a well from the roof to the ground floor, that took advantage of natural light. It closed in 1977 due to bankruptcy.

-2-

I am going to wear the coral colored chiffon dress and am going to buy a black velvet ribbon belt for it to go with my moire slippers. The other night, three Vice Consuls took me to the movies and to dinner afterwards. They have real good talkies here, and a Japanese man explains them all in Japanese to the ones who can't understand English. They are making me a member of the american club now, and that has a dance every week during the winter, and is also a good place to eat, as you can get real American food there quite reasonably. They also have a splendid library and that is something in a foreign country as in B.A, you had to buy all the books you wanted to read.

It sure is wonderful to off at 2 in the afternoon. I am taking Japanese lessons 3 times a week and find it quite easy. I think when you know one language it helps you a lot in studying another. There are four ways of saying everything though --1, inferiors--2, familiar form-- 3. polite form-- 4. very polite. Some job!

Watakushi no heya wa hyaku roku ju nana ban des -- means my room is 167. I go swimming to the Y.W. about 4 times a week. They have a wonderful pool. We will move into the new building in about another month.

I hope Roger's mother is either better or has ended her sufferings. It must be an awful strain on the both of you. I'm awfully glad you have decided to sell the other house. Mother just can't get along with anyone. Would an auction do any good? How much will her taxes be if she stays in the cottage and you keep the other house? It would be best to make some arrangement so you could have separate interests because that Mrs. Potter business is bound to increase. I'm awfully sorry she's like that.

                    Goodbye for now.   Write soon.

                         Love, Dorothy

Soon, in September 1931, the conflict between Japan and China will have begun when Japan invades Manchuria. This would affect Dorothy's duties.

Much of Dorothy's service occurred during the Great Depression. She remarks on its impact from time to time — one could argue that an underlying theme of all of her letters is economic: paying taxes and insurance, sending money home, the cost of items — and the Depression did hit everyone. During the Great Depression, government economizing led to the suspension of promotions, a 15 percent reduction in salaries, abolition of representational and living allowances, elimination of paid home leave, and suspension of recruiting for four years. The result was a 10 percent reduction in the size of the Foreign Service between July 1932 and

December 1934[3] — which coincided with Dorothy's time in Japan and which will be touched on in her 1933 letter.

The following is the next letter available after the July description of the transpacific passage to Japan via San Francisco — and it relates another crossing of Dorothy's path with Charles Lindbergh's. But the real news is the culture change and her new offices under construction — plus the promise of a duty-free package.

AMERICAN CONSULAR SERVICE

Sept 1, 1931.
Tokyo, Japan.

Dearest Kathie:

It seems as though I haven't got a letter from you for an age. Maybe Roger's mother has taken a turn for the worse or something. I do hope you both are getting a little rest.

This is certainly a most interesting and peaceful place to live. Everyone has been most kind to me. I am now a member of the American Club which has a good library and where you can get good American meals. Last week on Wednesday, I was invited to a buffet supper which was outdoors and the whole garden decorated with Japanese lanterns. Thursday night the Commercial Attache and his wife invited me to their home, where they had a dinner party of ten people and Friday I went to the Lindbergh reception. Mrs. Lindbergh sure made a hit here. She's very tiney and cute and rather shy, which was a surprise to every one. And on Sunday I was invited down to the beach where some of the office bunch live in Japanese cottages for the summer.

I went up to see the new Embassy buildings and the offices are like big palaces, with fireplaces and huge windows, steam heat, with the building trimmed in mosaic and eagles painted on it, etc. The grounds where we are to live are right beside the offices and are beautiful, with a rock garden and a darling swimming pool, and a reflecting pool where they are going to put all kinds of gold fishes and water lilies. There are millions of crickets singing in the trees. You know the crickets here sing almost like birds, or whip-poor-wills. The people sell them in tiney little wicker cages where they live for about two months on sugar and water.

We have an earthquake scheduled for tomorrow. Maybe it is only a scare though. We have had two or three tremors since I've been here. You can feel them when you're sitting down and verify the earthquake by looking at the chandeliers which swing back and forth and our office clock always stops so we can always time just exactly time it happened

I am enclosing a draft for $50. and will send some more

---

[3] See history.state.gov/departmenthistory/short-history/rogers As a side note, back in 1924, the Rogers Act had fundamentally reformed the foreign services by establishing a career organization based on competitive examination (for officers) and merit promotion.

next pay day. Say, Kathie, I wonder if you would mind

.-2-

doing me a favor. One of the fellows in our office is

AMERICAN CONSULAR SERVICE

Sept. 1, 1931
Tokyo, Japan.

Dearest Kathie:

It seems as though I haven't got a letter from you
for an age. Maybe Roger's mother has taken a turn for
the worse or something. I do hope you both are getting
a little rest.

This is certainly a most interesting and peaceful
place to live. Everyone has been most kind to me. I
am now a member of the American Club which has a good
library and where you can get good American meals.
Last week on Wednesday I was invited to a buffet supper
which was outdoors and the whole garden decorated with
Japanese laterns. Thursday night the Commercial Attache
and his wife invited me to their home,where they had
a dinner party of ten people and Friday I went to the
Lindbergh reception. Mrs. Lindbergh sure made a hit here.
She's very tiney and cute and rather shy, which was a
surprise to every one. And on Sunday I was invited down
to the beach where some of the office bunch live in
Japanese cottages for the summer.

I went up to see the new Embassy buildings and
the offices are like big palaces, with fireplaces and
huge windows, steam heat, with the building trimmed
in mosaic and eagles painted on it, etc. The grounds
where we are to live are right beside the offices
and are beautiful, with a rock garden and a darling
swimming pool, and a reflecting pool where they are
going to put all kinds of gold fishes and water lilies.
There are millions of crickets singing in the trees.
You know the crickets here sing almost like birds,
or whip-poor-wills. The people sell them in tiney little
wicker cages where they live for about two months on
sugar and water.

We have an earthquake scheduled for tomorrow. Maybe
it is only a scare though. We have had two or three
tremors since I've been here. You can feel them when
you're sitting down and verify the earthquake by looking
at the chandeliers which swing back and forth and
our office clock always stops so we can always time just
exactly time it happened.

Senator Bingham's son and he promised to take a small package
back to Tokyo for me if you wouldn't mind getting the things
together and sending them to his address which will be:

> Hiram Bingham, Jr.,
> c/o Woodbridge Bingham,
> 1921 Capistrano Avenue,
> Berkley, California.

He will leave for Tokyo about November 6 and if you could
get them there before the end of October I think it would be
better. Now, Kathie, this week I'm not going to send the
money for things, as I think you might need two weeks to
scout around for them, as I prefer that you put the whole of
this $50. on my debt to you. So I will send the money next
payday for the things, if you wouldn't mind getting them for
me.

Two pair black kid gloves, size *6 ½ or 7*
Gauntlet style as the snaps always
come off, and long enough to be
about two or three inches above wrist.

two sleeveless blouses to wear with
my black suit, both white and the kind
you wear outside the skirt, that you
don't tuck under the belt I mean.
I saw these in that chain store where
I tried on the cheap blue suit in New York
with you. I can't think of the name, but
they have very pretty ones. Maybe one
lace one (that new eyelet lace) and one
white crepe. If they have got short
sleeves, all right, but prefer them without.

two velvet hats, small, toque kind. One
black and one color of enclosed sample
or lighter. I saw some darling ones in
San Francisco before I left, of chiffon velvet, all shirred,
and about $4. They were very chic. If you get the kind that
flop more on one side, I wear the kind that flop to the
right. If you can get kind that don't show up my long neck
too much, it would be a good thing. However, most any hats
look good on me, so don't worry about them, the ones here
look like farmer sunbonnets. Small, Frenchy looking ones that
can be worn with a coat with a big high collar. I don't want
to get any more dresses, but I have been thinking of the
winter for work and what a

-3-

lack of dresses I have for the office. I have only one, a
dark blue one I had dyed, that has long sleeves. I was just
thinking of that cute black dress May and I saw with the red,
white and blue crisscrossing across the front for about $2.50

in Filenes basement[4]. If you <u>could</u> get something like that or if that were still there, maybe it wouldn't make the package too big to squeeze it in. Something dark and serviceable for the office. I think silk would be better than woolen because you might catch cold changing from one to the other, either dark red or dark green, black with a touch of color that wouldn't have to be cleaned all the time would be fine.

I know this is a lot of trouble, but I will never get this chance again to get this stuff in duty free so would you mind doing it for me? Please buy nice hats and gloves, because I hate cheap looking things. I don't mind things that are cheap because they are marked down but I've found it doesn't pay to economize too much, as the stuff wears out more quickly, and the dye runs, too. So I will enclose about $20. for these things next payday (the 15th) with a check also for my debt to you and Roger. You sure were a peach to lend me the money and I'll see you get the interest you lost too.

Gee, Kathie, I had another awful letter from mother. She says something about having to pay $400. for the work Roger did on the other house if the house is sold and about having a lawyer, and everything, (Please don't let on I told you), It makes me so worried I don't know what to do. Please straighten things as best you can, won't you? It would be awful if she started having lawyers and every body in town knew her business. She doesn't seem to think of that at all. Is Mrs. Potter paying her rent all right? What a mess, isn't it? Please write me all about it.

It has just started getting a little cooler here so I suppose we will start working till 4 again. As soon as I can talk a little more Japanese I am going to send you a few little things that are real cheap here and there won't be any duty on but first I want to know just where to buy the best because the tourists naturally always get stung.

Please write soon. Love to Roger.

Dorothy x x

(over)

Kathie, if you see any cloth exactly like this, would you send me enough for sleeves & I could wear this in the winter too.

In Dorothy's next letter— her 'postscript' comes first, as she types above the printed header on Department stationery — we learn that Dorothy is quickly learning about Japan. Having the opportunity to have a package delivered to her duty free is not to be taken lightly.

---

[4] Filene's Basement, also known as the "Bargain Basement," was a chain of department stores in Massachusetts (though none in Ware), founded by Edward Filene about the same time as Dorothy: 1909. Their flagship store was in Boston.

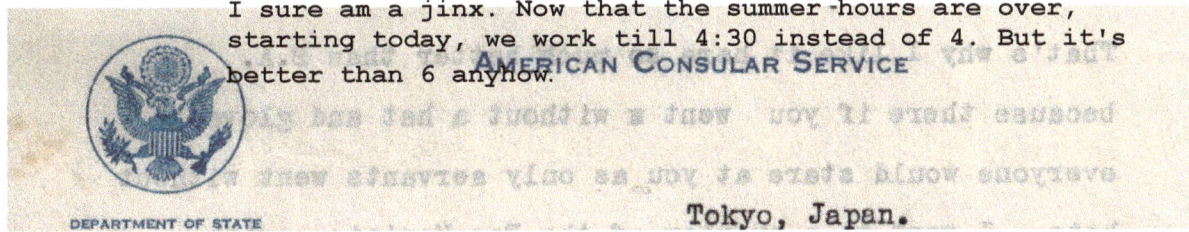

I sure am a jinx. Now that the summer hours are over, starting today, we work till 4:30 instead of 4. But it's better than 6 anyhow.

AMERICAN CONSULAR SERVICE

DEPARTMENT OF STATE

Tokyo, Japan.

Sept. 15, 1931.

Dearest Kathie:

It was sure nice to get your interesting letter. Yes, my trunk did come on the Munson liner Western World. Those boats never have accidents, so you can't tell when to expect them nowadays. I met your Miss Sullivan, and she leaving for the States next week for good, as she doesn't like it very well here. She seems very nice, but older than I. I told her someone in Marlboro had said some nice things about her, a school teacher, but couldn't remember the name. I bought Margaret Myhr a lovely Japanese painting on silk about 6 feet long which you hang on the wall. They tell me I may be able to send it by mail. If so, and it gets through all right, I shall send you one sometime if you like. They do some marvellous hand painting and are extremely artistic.

The girls here don't have pocketbooks but when they have little things carry them in the sleeves of their kimonas and carry big things done in colored cloth to match the sash on their kimonas with parasol and straps on their shoes to match too. They never wear hats you know, and have lovely hair. I haven't worn a hat for a long time. That's why I like it here so much better than B.A. because there if you went without a hat and gloves everyone would stare at you as only servants went without hats. I went to a preview of the Fox Movietone with the manager and the fliers Paghorn and Herndon were with us. They saw me sitting in the lobby the other evening and asked me to have dinner with them but I had another date. I think they will try the hop to the States if the Japanese ever give them the permit to go. They are very nice and don't talk about their flight here. I bet they won't fly over war zones again, though. So many people here knew Moyle and Allen personally and felt terrible when they found they must have been killed.[5]

Saturday I was invited down to the Beach but no more because everyone is moving back to Tokyo for the winter. Sunday I went with the Third Sec. of the Embassy and his wife to see off the Manager of the Fox Movietone who left for

---

[5] Four days after Dorothy's letter, the flyers were relocated after being missing for about 10 days. From the UPI Archives: "TOKYO, Sept.19, 1931 (UP) -- While silence shrouded the movements of Don Moyle and Cecil Allen, unsuccessful transpacific flyers, tonight, Col. and Mrs. Charles A. Lindbergh were in China and two other American aviators, Clyde Pangborn and Hugh Herndon Jr., were contemplating a non-stop flight from Tokyo to Seattle. Moyle and Allen apparently were still at Cape Navarin where they were taken by a Russian ship after being forced down on an uninhabited island. They landed while en route from Tokyo to Seattle when their fuel supply gave out."

China on the President Hoover, the new $8,000,000 new liner of the Dollar Line. It's a nice boat but now to [sic] luxurious as some German liners I've seen. All the Ameri-cans in Japan were down at the soda fountain which is a special feature of the boat, and they had to keep locking the door after the place got filled so they could orders out.

Last night was a good-bye party at the beach for one of the Consuls who is leaving Japan. I think I will ask to take Margaret's present if I think I will have to pay duty on it.

-3-

Tomorrow night I am invited to the Third. Sec.'s house for dinner. So you see I haven't had time to get lonesome yet. The Embassy building won't be ready till Nov. now. Just as I thought, Gov. red tape. It was supposed to be ready for March and the contractors have to pay $500. a month forfeit, so they are losing plenty. But it sure will be great when we do get there as there will be people around all the time to go places with, and I understand they are thinking of taking over some more land for a tennis court--at least renting some that is next door.

Kathie, I am enclosing $30. on my bill and $20. for the things I asked you to send if it isn't too much trouble. One blouse will be enough--a good quality slik [sic] crepe one, latest style, rather low neck, and made so you can wear it outside the skirt. Here's the list again.

> two velvet hats (one black, one color of sample or lighter)
> one serviceable silk or very light wool crepe
> sport dress for work (nothing kiddish)
> two pair black kid gloves, good quality, gauntlet style, long enough to go about 2 inches over wrist

Please make it as small a bundle as possible as when I asked him to bring me something I said it would be small and I don't want to impose on him as he will have plenty himself. Roll the things up and the velvet hats will be soft anyhow and maybe tissue paper inside of them will keep them looking nice. I don't like those new little felt hats very well, and you see plenty of felt here anyhow.

-4-

If there is any money left, please apply it to my bill, but don't buy anything cheap looking because it doesn't pay. Thank you a thousand times.

I hope Roger is feeling well. Isn't it a shame I couldn't have seen more of you both as long as Roger's mother is still all right? But that's the luck, I guess.

Well, goodbye for now, and I'll write again soon. With

```
loads of love to you both,
```

Dorothy xx

Mr. Hiram Bingham, Jr.
c/o Woodbridge Bingham,
1921 Capistrano Ave.
Berkley, California
He leaves there Nov. 6 so if you could send them right away I would appreciate it.

Dorothy must have been feeling her luck was strong to take a run at the Irish Steeplechase lottery. Perhaps it was the upcoming concert with Heifetz that encouraged her – or that her luck was strong even with earthquakes:

AMERICAN CONSULAR SERVICE

```
                              Tokyo, Japan.
                              September 26, 1931.
```

```
Dearest Kathie:

   I sure would like a ticket on the Irish Steeplechase, if
it isn't too late, just take it out of my last check. I'll
give you a percentage commission if I win a million.

   We had a nice little earthquake a couple of days ago. We
were all in the office (it's on the third floor) and you
could feel the building swaying. The pictures fell off the
walls and the chandeliers were swinging wildly. There were 14
people killed but none in Tokyo. I'm enclosing a newspaper
clipping. Our building is supposed to be earthquake proof
anyhow, but there were plenty of cracks around the base of it
and the sidewalk was torn up some in front of it. We have had
several tremors since I've been here but this has been the
worst.
```
(Don't tell Mother)

```
   There is lots of excitement here now with the Japanese-
Chinese trouble. Every other hour a new extra comes out and
they make plenty of noise, because coolies announce an extra
yelling as though they were having their teeth taken out and
ringing a little cowbell all over the town.

   I am invited to a concert tonight by a nice English boy
who stays in the hotel. It is Heifetz who is a famous
violinst. Thursday (the 24) was a holiday and the other girl
in the office and I were invited by two of the Kodak boys to
go to Mianoshita, which is considered the prettiest place
around Japan. It was a three hours trip in automobile, and
there are natural swimming pools of mineral water to swim in,
coming up from the ground just tepid so you can swim all the
year around. The mountains are gorgeous around there as it is
way down in a valley and yet about 8000 feet in the air.
Inside the hotel, it is built around a Hot Springs pool and
```

is called the dream pool. The ceiling is made of glass and as up above is a large goldfish aquarium, you can see the goldfish swimming up above. They have lovely goldfish here, as it is their specialty. White ones with just a red nose and red tale, black, white and red ones, etc. and all big enough for a whole meal.

Well, write soon, won't you, Kathie, and I hope you and Roger are well.

Lots of love,

Dorothy X X

Dorothy (at left) and her office-mate Eleanor Shields pose in front of the famous Fujiya Hotel, Miano-shita, Japan, 24 September 1931. Almost certainly this photo was taken by 'the Kodak boys' with whom the girls were traveling.

This next undated letter, one of Dorothy's longest, was typed in October 1931. Note that Dorothy indicates she is still living in a Tokio hotel, is taking tap-dancing lessons at the local YWCA and has already begun shopping for Christmas presents to send home. Plus: the promise of the new Government apartments.

Dearest Kathie:

I've been holding off this letter so I could put a check in it for you, but I just now remember that tomorrow, when we are paid, the banks will be closed so I won't be able to catch this boat anyhow. So in my next letter I will enclose $50.

I'm sorry I bothered you about Mother's letter and I might have known she got everything wrong per usual, and I'm sure she should be very grateful to you and Roger for everything but you know she is so jealous she sees everything upside down. I sent her $5. last month and $10. this month and will send her about $25. for Christmas. After I get on my feet I can send her $20. a month quite easily, with my rent being paid for me, but it's only right now everything comes at once. This payday I'm going to send $38. to Ben Rowe for my watch so that will clear up all the Ware gang, thank good-ness. It has come in awfully handy, though, and I'd have

missed lots of trains without it. And I'm awfully glad I got
a Waltham, although it isn't as pretty as the Swiss watch he
showed me for the same price, because a lady on the boat had
one of those Swiss watches and it did everything but run. I
wish I'd told you to get the cute felt hats, as everyone is
wearing them here, and to get a woolen dress instead of a
silk. I'm invited lots of places where I need a woolen dress
instead of a silk one, for instance the picnic I went on a
couple of weeks ago, where a silk dress looks out of place.

We are having the lovliest October weather. Everybody
waits all year for these autumn months here because it is
just right --not too hot or too cold. I went to a Japanese
play the other night and they last six hours! It was the
funniest thing, you should hear them sing--absolute different
from ours as they sing all in the minor key and to us it
sounds like cats on a backyard fence. I will try and get you
a record, if I can get a celluloid one, so you can try it
out. I sent you some pamphlets we keep at the office on
Japan, so maybe you can get a better idea of it. I'm almost
afraid to send things to you, as a boy here sent a necklace
home costing .75 and his mother had to pay $1.50 duty on it.
But I think I can for Christmas, as I will write a nice
letter to the Customs Inspector, who are always more lenient
at Christmas time. Now don't bother sending me anything as I
will probably have to pay duty on it and I don't need
anything anyhow, besides you could save it like you did last
time until I get home. Those beads with the pearl grapes I
wear almost everyplace and everybody asks me about them. I
get a letter yesterday from the Tokyo Amateur Dramatic Club
asking me if I wanted to be in a play they were going to have
Christmas, but nothing doing! You know how I hate appearing
in front of audiences. The Rotary Club was an awful ordeal
for me.

-2-

I must write on both sides of the paper as it is getting
near the end of the year, and we are running out of everything at the Consulate.

I am still living at the Hotel, but the finishing touches
are being put on the apartments. They are all nicely furnished with the very latest Simons beds, electric refrigerator, electric stove, each one having telephone (apartment I
mean) sunken bath, another room for a shower and the toilet
in another alcove. We each one have running water in our
rooms, hot and cold, so they are sure we will be on time for
work. How could we help it anyhow, when the office is right
opposite the apartment. The buildings are all white and I
think they will take pictures of them, and if so I will send
you some. Tomorrow night I am invited to a dinner party at
the home of the Asst. Commissioner, and it is sure a good

thing I loaded up on evening clothes, because nobody wears anything but that here. Tonight I am going with a man who works in the Embassy to a real Japanese home, the people being friends of his.

The ball players came last night, and I thought it was a wedding, confetti being strewn all along the sidewalk outside, and just millions of people all around. There are plenty of them, and the tickets to the game are costing $5. each, and are all sold out. Tomorrow, I am also going to lunch at the home of the Consul's wife. I am also taking tap dancing lessons at the Y.W. and it's lots of fun.

Tell May I am going to write to her very soon and will send her a nice Christmas present, but don't let anyone send me anything as I might have to pay duty on it, 1 don't want anything anyhow. Mother says the taxes this year are $131.68. Gee, that seems awfully high. She mentions them in every letter, but I can't lay any more golden eggs right now. We have until the end of what year to pay them?

I've been trying to be economic but I don't think it pays. I need a woolen sports dress so badly so I went to a tailor to see about making one, and he said he would charge $22.50 (supply the cloth, etc.) but I couldn't see that when I only paid $6.90 for my most expensive evening gown. So I had a dress made by a dressmaker, and it looks like a salvation army habit. They are so used to making kimonas that they make dresses the same way.

- 3 -

So Kathie, I am going to ask you to send me two tailored dresses for the office. It seems to be the only thing I didn't stock up on as I have enough of everything else. As I didn't get my pay check in time to buy a draft, I will enclose the money in my next letter. But Kathie, I have decided that it doesn't pay to be too economic, so please don't pay any less than $10. each for them or $15. Because, cheap things don't last long and look it. Now, in the case of the dresses I bought for $6. that was all right, because they were marked down from $15., every one. So, if you can find a marked down rack of light-weight winter dresses, why I don't mind having cheap ones. I've seen some darling ones in the fashion books, and the pattern I picked out for the dressmaker was so pretty, but you'd never recognize it.

So Kathie, I know you are very busy now, but Cummings in Marlboro have very nice things, and everything from the States is different here, so don't mind if there are six more like it on the same rack. The only color I don't want is brown or dark red. A nice powder blue or pretty green or orchid, would be nice. But I know you have such good taste I will like anything you get. I may only send the money for one dress now, but would you please send it right away? And I could get the other one later. Do you mind buying them for me? You see, perhaps around December I will go on a skiing party for the weekend as we have 5 days holiday then, and everybody here does that, and there is also skating, an artificial ice pond about half an hour's ride from here. And they would last me until I got home again. I like plain, tailored ones best, nothing kiddish. You know I will be 25 soon. Also, would you please send me some more of that "Luxuria" tissue you gave me for wiping off the cold cream. I can't get any here and two or three boxes without the wrappings could be flattened out real small.

   The other girl in the office just got a package from home of two very pretty winter dresses, very light weight wool, very tailored, and they sure stood out among the home-made things, and besides they were very cheap. Well, Kathie, I'll be writing you and Roger again soon and in the mean time will be looking around for some Christmas presents for you.

        Lots of love,

        Dorothy.

   Amazingly, Dorothy took to Japanese as easily as to the Romance languages. As we see in this November 11 letter of her first few months, she is already signed up for instruction in Japanese.

AMERICAN CONSULAR SERVICE
American Consulate General

                           Tokyo, Japan.
                           November 11, 1931.

Dearest Kathie:

   You can't imagine how pleased I was with the box. Everything is just what I wanted, I am wearing the black toque and black gloves and blouse and cuff protectors and beads right this minute, so you see how handy they came in. I sure like these cuff protectors. I have been pinning tissue paper on my sleeves every day and these look pretty classy. And I must write and tell May how much I liked the beads.

   The wool beret is something I have always wanted, and it looks swell on me. I hope to go ice skating here soon (they have an artificial rink about 30 minutes from Tokyo) and it will look like a million dollars. The blue velvet hat is a little big so I will just have a tuck taken in it, but the black one fits perfectly. It way over on one ear and looks very chic. The dress is just as cute as it can be, and the best part of it is, with the orange trimming, I can wear brown perfectly. It looks very nice. The blouses are a little big but after washing you know how they shrink so I am very glad they are not any smaller, and they are just what I wanted. I like the gloves a lot, and I think they will wear for two years at least, they are such good quality. I can't imagine how you bought everything for $20. I hope you haven't cheated yourself. Now don't forget to take the postage out of my last check (I sent you a check for $65. in the last mail) I certainly appreciate all the trouble you went to, and believe me those things sure looked good to me. I guess that keeps me stocked up for another year at least. As I said in my last letter, I can get along without another office dress, as the one I had made looks good enough, and you know how quickly the styles change.

I have already had an invitation for Thanksgiving dinner which will be on Thanksgiving Eve at the home of the Third Sec. of the Embassy and wife. They just got married about 3 months ago. And on the 24th I am invited to a housewarming and on Thanksgiving I think there will be another house-warming for the opening of the new Embassy. We expect to move in any day now, but something happened to the boiler. It sure looks like a million dollars.

- 2 -

I went to another Japanese show Sunday night, and this one too lasted six hours. Just in front of us sat the American ball players--or were supposed to sit. So they had about twenty little Geisha girls, (they are professional Japanese entertainers) all dressed up in new kimonas and with all kinds of flowers in their hair but the ballplayers didn't come in till the show was almost over. But when they arrive they had to keep busy autographing balls, handkerchiefs, and one little girl (some of them are only 13 years old) had her pocketbook, kimona sleeve, handkerchief and I don't know how many things with signatures.

I'm getting on pretty well with my Japanese. My teacher told me if I can master Japanese, any other language will be a cinch as it is supposed to be awfully difficult. But I don't think it's half bad. The pronunciation is very easy. Atsui kara, mado wo akete oku ho ga iidesho--means--as it is hot you had better open the window. And it is pronounced just as it looks.

I went to the chrysanthemum show the other night and it was a marvellous thing. Some of the plants had over 120 large blossoms on them, and grew all the same height. They had made them grow in the shapes of aeroplanes, automobiles, etc., by wiring them, and they were still growing although in those shapes. It was really wonderful. They even had figures of women and men with clothes made of flowers. But these had to be changed every week, as they were not still in the soil.

We are having lovely weather here. It is fall, but very balmy, and the leaves are falling just as at home. It gets very cold next month, though.

   Well, Kathie, I want you to know how much I appreciated
all your trouble. Those things mean so much here too, where
it is almost impossible to get them.

Lots of love to you both,

Dorothy

Finally, in late November, Dorothy was able to move out of her temporary quarters in the hotel and into that long-promised government apartment in Tokio.

AMERICAN CONSULAR SERVICE

                            December 17, 1931.
                            Tokyo, Japan.

Dearest Kathie:

   I'm just crazy about our new apartment. There are we three
girls in it and each one has a separate bedroom, with
dressing table, bureau, desk etc. all to match. Mine is in
dark green, and I have flowered glazed chintz curtains and
also thin beige ones underneath and they have silk cords so
that you can pull them shut with a jerk. And venetian blinds
in every room, and great big window and the latest kind of
screen that is just pulled down when needed. Mine looks out
on the swimming pool, which has a little summer house at the
head of it, and outside each window is a windowbox of ever-
green. And lovely steamheat and latest washstand with hot
running water and a big looking glass that sets in the wall
and opens and you can put all your toilet things inside and
no one see them. And the mattresses are big thick Simmons
ones. We had to buy our own bed linen and I was glad I had
that Bolivian blanket with me, although we did get furnished
one very nice white wool one. And a reading lamp. The
electric lights are in the shape of candles, two on each side
of the mirror. The other girls rooms are:
Eleanors: light grey with grey curtains with big pink roses
in it and a pink rose overstuffed chair to match. Alice:
Light yellow with apricot colored curtains and apricot
colored arm chair. Spare room: Light green with dark rose
curtains. (I am going to get the spare room furniture after
wards I think, but now they won't let us swap furniture.)
In the living room (dining room combined) we have a lovely
fireplace with andirons and everything (screen, etc.) and <u>it
works</u>. And as you know the latest fad is to have overstuffed
furniture all of different colors, but blending, so we have a
green soft rug and big green overstuffed sofa, two old rose
over stuffed chairs, and one golden brown velvet one, and
golden brown velvet curtains that touch the floor with
underdrapes of beige. And besides some small chairs of
various colored seats. And a gateleg table and another long

one that fits along the wall for buffet suppers.

And the lights are those candle looking ones again, and highboy (old fashioned) sort of desk and bookcase combined. And a small table for serving coffee and putting cigarettes on and two reading lamps on each side of the divan, electricity, heat, telephone, all furnished free. A lovely white tub, and in another section a lovely very modern shower so there is never anyone waiting for a bath, and two white toilets. Also a maid's room, and the latest kitchen equipment, including electric refrigerator and white gas range and beautiful glass closets. There are closets everywhere and downstairs we have a private store room and drying room. And also a private garage which we have nothing to put in. We have a cook and a chamber maid, but the two of them together only cost $40. a month.

Say, Kathie, the mail is going now, but I will certainly say I appreciate you and Roger lending me that money and making it possible for me to come.

Love, Dorothy

I am enclosing $52. Please use $50. towards my debt and give $2. to Arthur for the insurance money he paid for me. It was cheaper to send it all together. I now only owe $110., don't I (not counting the interest).

By year's end, Dorothy is well situated and has more activities than she can handle, skiing and holiday parties being the top attractions — well, besides Allan.

AMERICAN CONSULAR SERVICE
American Consulate General

Tokyo, Japan.
December 31, 1931.

Dear Kathie and Roger:

Happy New Year! Well, this is the last day I work for five days--Japanese holidays--at least 4 are and Mr. Garrels threw the other one in for good measure because I am going skiing with a bunch of girls I met at the gym class at the Y.W. We are going to the Japanese Alps, a place called Akakura (you can probably read all about it in those pamphlets I sent you--that's a good idea isn't it--every time I make a trip I can tell you the name of it and you can tell what it is going to be like). Anyhow, it is supposed to be wonderful skiing and every year mobs of people go up from all around Japan. We five girls are going to stay in a Japanese inn--and sleep on the floor all in the same room. That's the way the Japanese do, you know. I gave myself a skiing outfit for Christmas. It wasn't very expensive and I can have it all my life. I got

skii pants, hat, (I had my big red sweater from High School
days) stockings, big cowhide shoes and skiis. We are each
going to take some food with us as you can't get foreign food
up there and some of the girls can't bear Japanese food
although I like it. I am bringing pork and beans, coffee and
milk and the cook made me a whole batch of ginger snaps. Say,
it's swell having a cook of your own.

I just got the box you sent, Kathie and it was certainly
lovely. That is the nicest cleansing tissue. You can't get it
for love nor money here and the brassiere were lovely. Thank
you so much for sending them. The beads were really exquisite
and especially those pink ones which I am going to wear with
a green satin evening gown. And the Consul General's wife had
a pair of pink satin evening slippers made in China which
don't fit her and I'll wear those too with the green dress
(She gave them to me and they are just right) I expect to be
able to send you about $50. on the 15th, if the exchange
isn't too low. You see the Yen has gone down to 35 cents to a
U.S. dollar instead of 50 cents which it is usually. Of
course that makes it just grand for us as last pay day we got
50 yen extra just on account of the low exchange but when you
try to change it into dollars you sure get an awful gyp. I
had a very good time Christmas. Christmas eve I went to a
costume dance in Yokohama and to four eggnog parties there
Christmas day. That is the custom here. Everyone visits their
friends and

- 2 -

has eggnogs. And I just got home in time to go to the
Ambassador's dinner party--in fact the party was at 7:30 and
I reach home at 7:35. The people upstairs were outside
waiting for a taxi when I arrived and I dressed so fast that
I got up to the Embassy at the same time they did. Which is
saying something. Thank goodness they hadn't gone in for
dinner.

I got six lovely hand made handerchiefs with my initials
on from Allan in a beautiful hand embroidered handerchief
case. It came from the Philippines. I am going to take some
pictures skiing and will send you some. Talk about your
parties this time of the year. I got three invitations to the
New Years dance tonight in Yokohama (but I am leaving on my
skiing trip) went to a party night before last, have to go to
the Ambassador's at home at 4:30 this afternoon, was invited
to the Consul General's home to a party the 3rd and to
another the 4th but I won't get back till the 5th. And last
Sunday went to a dance at the home of one of the girls with
whom I am going skiing, I like this place much better than
B.A. The other girl in B.A. is trying to get a job out here
too, but they are as scarce as hen's teeth because the girls
are just waiting in line to get into the Embassy or Consulate
as our new apartment looks pretty good.

I hope you both had a nice Christmas and got your presents all right. That was a stunning Christmas card you sent. Some class with the names printed on and everything. Oh yes, I got a Christmas telegram from the doctor who operated on me for appendicits in B.A. and one from Bee and Marg. Marg's address is Mrs. Gene Sheeley, 39 Cascade Avenue, Lowell, Mass. I got a box of honey from one of the Consuls, chocolates from another, and the Consul General sent us some tea from Formosa.

                        Love,

                            Dorothy

                        Thanx again for the box.

P.S. I don't get any more stamps as I don't open the mail. Mr. Garrels keeps them for himself.

January 1932: Skiing in the Japanese Alps (Akakura). Dorothy (24) is 2nd from left.

As 1932 begins, we find that Dorothy is comfortably immersed in skating, skiing, and the social life of the Consulate staff in Tokyo. Mr. Messersmith's letter [see chapter following] has been sent to Allan to "read first" – Allan is definitely in her thoughts and her life.

P.S. Did you get the book I sent you?
AMERICAN CONSULAR SERVICE

January 12, 1932.

please send these home afterword

Dearest Roger and Kathie:

You can't imagine how pleased and thrilled I was when I saw your big Christmas box. I hadn't of course expected anything as I told you I didn't want anything and as it just arrived two days ago (I suppose on account of the Christmas rush it was delayed) I naturally thought Christmas was all over for me. You certainly thought of everything I could ever need. The dress is darling and I just needed something like that to wear on Friday nights for skating. As for the rubber overshoes, the ones you gave me when I went away had just about worn out and we have plenty of rain here so you can believe they were welcome.

The hat just fitted exactly and I have a black crepe dress which it will look lovely with for cocktail parties. I have been wanting a tape measure for a long time as the Japanese ones are all in their own measure which is different from ours and it's an awfully cute one. As for the kleenex, I was on the point of asking you to send me some as what I received before is just about gone. I never saw such unusual handkerchiefs—the little applique is very pretty and the other linen ones are lovely. The cleaner was also a happy thought and I've had an opportunity to try it out already. And the little puffs I can use when we have guests. The lingerie support is great and especially useful for evening dresses. It was certainly nice of you to send me so many things. I am keeping the manicure set for weekends as it slips into the bag so nicely.

Thank you both very, very much. I certainly had a grand time opening the box. I shall send another letter to May thanking her for the lovely pearls. They look grand with a white lace evening dress I have.

I'm certainly having a wonderful time out here. We are having a holiday on Monday afternoon on account of services for Coolidge but I'm going to use it for tennis. After all our 5 holidays for the new year we are getting plenty of rest. But you need it out here as there are so many parties. I've been invited out every day this week, most of them being formal dinners, so I got plenty of chance for evening clothes. I'm enclosing some of my invitations, but those are a very small part of them as most come by telephone, but you can see how hospitable the people are here. We have some wonderful parties.

I have a marvellous letter from Mr. Messersmith, and I'm sure I can go back to work for him any time I get tired of the Far East. I shall send it to you soon but I'm sending it to Allan to read first. I also got a letter from Allan saying he is going to try and get leave the latter part of this month to come up to Tokyo from Manila to see me. I hope he can but it's very difficult as he is next to the Commander on the his destroyer and when they are operating it is almost impossible to get leave. He sent me a lovely Chinese kimono and a balibuntal hat from Manila, a large one.

We had a wonderful 5 days skiing. I have gotten much better than last year and enjoyed it so much more as we had plenty of snow and it snowed almost every day we were up there. There was a big crowd of foreigners from Tokyo and Yokohama.

Say, Kathie, please let me know how Mother is getting along for money. I send her $20. regularly every month except Christmas month, when I sent $30. Do you think this is enough? I would like to save a little if I can still I don't want her to starve to death and her letters always sound that way. How is the work in Ware, do you know? She said Arthur and Sally gave her a box of chocolates for her birthday and I didn't give her anything, and all the time I send her money and she never thinks of that but takes it for granted whereas a box of chocolates from Arthur is something to write about. You'll tell me what you think about it all, won't you Kathie?

Many, many thanks again to you both for the lovely box. I was feeling rather sorry for myself as I had received no Christmas presents (Allan's didn't arrive until after Christmas either). I didn't have to pay any duty as they are quite lenient about Xmas gifts. I hope Roger's foot is quite well now and that you aren't both too tired with taking care of your patient.

Much love,

Dorothy X X

Dorothy's invitations for cocktails within the diplomatic community often used calling cards.

AMERICAN CONSULAR SERVICE
American Consulate General

Tokyo, Japan.
January 15, 1932.

Dearest Kathie:

Time goes by fast, all right doesn't it? Did you get a lot of Christmas presents? I'm enclosing a check for $60. You and Roger must be awfully tired of this long-drawn payment, but now I only owe $50., don't I (excluding interest of course). I got a letter from Ann Hennion in New York and it seems she is now connected with some purchasing agency (she is the girl I lived with in B.A. and who sent me the telegram when she heard I had appendicitis) and she didn't like my not seeing her in New York but I told her we tried but only had an old address. I also got a letter from Dr. Murray and he thinks he is going to Alaska, and his love affair is all off but he doesn't seem to worry much about it. I also got a letter from the Consul in B.A. and he says the other AM. clerk who I lived with wants very much to come to the Orient but nobody out here wants to swap jobs with her after my telling them how much harder we worked down there. No one here has ever heard from the girl whose place I took here so I'm just taking it for granted it isn't all she wanted.

-2-

We had a wonderful time skiing and I got as tanned as a berry by the snow. We are going to try and go again before the winter is over. I will send you some pictures of the skiing trip in my next letter. It was sure great.

Monday evening we all went to the Ambassador's for dinner and had a wonderful time. Sunday I am going on a hike with a group of people from Yokohama.

I'll have more news next time maybe, so will say good-bye for now. Hope you and Roger will be able to have your little house in the Spring.

                    Love, Dorothy
                         xx

AMERICAN CONSULAR SERVICE
American Consulate General

Tokyo, Japan.
February 1, 1932.

Dearest Kathie:

I'm so glad you liked your Xmas present and Roger too.

They weren't very much but when I come back to the States I will bring you something nicer. I'm glad I didn't try to send you a coolie coat because one of the other girls sent one and they collected $3.50 at the other end, just because it was silk, I guess. Did you find out if May or Freda had to pay duty? Please tell me if they did. That was certainly a good picture of Wilbur Marcil. If Arthur had had more spunk he could have gotten that job, and be sure of it the rest of his days and a nice vacation every year besides. Well, he's old enough to look out for himself by now, isn't he?

The Japanese people wear the wooden shoes with the stilts underneath for rainy weather and it is really quite a good idea. You had better start the fad in the states, as those wooden shoes last forever. You ask me if there are any Catholic churches here. There are all right. The place is full of both Catholic and Protestant missionaries.

I just got a letter from Mother this morning asking me to pay the taxes. I just sent her $10. and if you write me what the entire taxes are, her share, next month I will try to get them off in installments. I'm enclosing $25. on my debt to you and Roger which makes just $25. more and I shall send that, together with interest, which I figure will be about $30--well, I will (write) a check for $55. to you next month and that will about square things for us, won't it? I want to finish paying you & Roger before starting on the taxes. I certainly appreciate more than I can say your lending me it. I hope I'll be able to do the same for you some day.

- 2 -

I have been skating quite a lot lately. I like Japan very much because I've met some very nice girls who like sports too and we go quite a lot of places together and I have been invited to quite a few parties.

The trouble between China and Japan is getting worse but it doesn't affect us at all as it is all over in China. I wish I were in the Shanghai Consulate. They will probably get sent home at Gov. expense until it's over, or else get a winter in Manila. Just my luck to be here in Tokyo.

I would send you the money for the taxes when I got some together, but you know she would have a cat fit, and I don't want to make it out to Mr. Dupont because I know quite a few boys in the bank here and I don't want anyone to know my business.

Well, Kathie, I'll be writing again soon. Hope you get this check for $25. all right.

Love,

Dorothy

P.S. I got a nice letter from Albenia[6] and she says Agnes Shea is working in a bookstore in Boston for $12. a week! And Margaret Inglesby just got notice to look around for a job as her firm is closing down, so I guess I'm pretty lucky after all. Albenia has another little girl.

She says her father got fired from the Otis Co.[7] after 24 years of service, but found work as a manager of a garage in Springfield. Poor Ware must be going to pieces all right. Although with the new dam being built, you might get a chance to sell the other house. I hope so. Did you read my piece in the paper? I hope they threw it in the waste basket.[8]

AMERICAN CONSULAR SERVICE
American Consulate General

Tokyo, Japan.
February 16, 1932.

Dearest Kathie and Roger:

This is certainly a day for celebration for me and I bet for you too, because here's a draft for $54.-- $25. I still owed you and $30. interest (I want you to take the $1. I have in the Marlboro Savings bank to make it $30.) Now if $30. interest doesn't make up for what you have lost by taking the money out of the bank when it was just due to get interest and my having it so long--please tell me, however, if you think it is a little over don't tell me, because I refuse to take a cent back. You don't know how much I have appreciated your trusting me with so much money and I wouldn't have been able to come at all without it, as you well know. I wish I could have paid it back sooner but you know how it is. I appreciate it very, very much and if I can ever do the same for you please let me know.

I just got a letter from a girl I worked with in Washington and she says she has $2000. in the bank and her own car all paid for. Gosh, and I haven't got a red cent. But I have had lots more experience and that's worth a lot, I guess. I have been having such a good time here lately. I haven't been home for dinner one night for over two weeks. I've been doing quite a lot of skating as I have some new skating shoes and skates and they are wonderful because your ankles can't turn if you wanted them to. I'm going to try to do some fancy things next time. I have been going around with an awful nice bunch of Swedish boys and girls and they love sports so we get a lot of it. Thursday nite is a skating party and on George Washington's birthday the American community is having a big celebration and we have to dress up

---

[6] Albenia Elliott, Ware HS '25, had four children. See FindAGrave.com Memorial #230827319.
[7] Otis Co. Mill manufactured woven cotton fabric and was Ware's largest employer for almost 100 years.
[8] The Ware River News article on Dorothy's talk to the Rotary Club on her Adventures in South America.

in old-fashioned costumes and powder our hair. The next night the Ambassador is having a dance to which I am invited. He sure has a peach of a house--just like a palace. This week we have an inspector here so we are trying to get to work on time. It's a funny thing--down in B.A. I lived quite a long ways from the office and we were always there on the dot, but here where we have just to run across the yard we often don't get there till 9:15.

Say, Roger and Kathie, I just got your birthday card and it is the cutest one I ever saw. The others in the office thought so too. I never thought you'd remember my birthday as I had just about forgotten it myself, except that day the Consul and his wife came to call on me and he brought me a little book of poems and she brought me a little venetian purse. So that was very nice of them, wasn't it?

I told Mother beginning March 1, I would send her $20. a month for her taxes till they were paid. I just got a letter from her saying she felt sick with a bad cold. I hope she is better now. Thank you for all the clippings. They were certainly interesting. I sent the one about Miss Sullivan upstairs to a friend of hers in the Embassy and they were very glad to get it. The difference between the Embassy and the Consulate is that the Embassy takes care of the political side of things and the Consulate of commercial and personal services for Americans. That is why the Embassy is usually in the limelight as it has all the social side of it to look after, etc. But for clerks, it doesn't make any difference except the folks in the Embassy work till 11:00 some night and we always get out at 4:30, and they don't get a cent more money than we do. I haven't had a raise for ages but I guess I won't kick because everywhere they are giving cuts. Even the Dollar Line has cut the discount to Government employees to 15% instead 25%. We never use our fireplace though, because we have almost too much steam heat.

I think Tommy Flaven will be using his head if he goes into the Foreign Service. It would be impossible to start a law practice now in this depression and it costs plenty of money to get outfitted whereas the boys in the foreign service get six months of schooling after they take the exam free, and then get allowances which cover their rent, heat, light and for entertainment besides their salary and get transferred at least every three years with their way paid to their new post and have leave in the States every two years like we do. Lots of boys with training for the law enter the foreign service. Law training helps them a lot in their work and they can always use it. I'm awfully glad Roger hasn't got bumped off. When are you going to get that pension? It doesn't seem as though I've been here seven months, as I like it so much. I can't find that clipping about E. Shea to send back. I'm awfully sorry as I forgot you wanted to keep it. I hope you can get another.

Thank you and Roger again a thousand times. I am enclosing some seaweed which the Japanese are crazy about and eat it for breakfast, dinner and supper, --it's pretty good in soup, but they eat it on bread and everything.

Love, Dorothy.

Please don't forget to take that $1. out of the bank as I won't have any money to keep up an account at home. *Will keep it here if I get any as I mite need it in a hurry.*

AMERICAN CONSULAR SERVICE
American Consulate General

Tokyo, Japan.
March 24, 1932.

Dearest Kathie:

How the time does fly in this country! It always seems Saturday. I like it more and more every day. Thank you for all the clippings you sent me. Will Rogers came in the office and he looks rather old doesn't he.[9] I got a nice letter from Tommy and he threatens to drop in on me some day out here. Thanks for all the poems you enclosed too.

About the taxes, Kathie. I sent Mother $20. on the 15th of March and told her would send her $20. on the 15th of each month until paid, but would like a receipt from Dupont or would not send any more. I knew she would get mad if I made out the check to Dupont. I'm so glad the other tenement is rented and I hope it stays that way for a long time. Are the Potters paying their rent? I send all my invitations of any importance home so ask Mother to see them if you are interested. There is always something going on here. Apr. 1 I am invited to a fancy dress ball, March 30 to a dinner given by Lieutenant Melendy to all the navy officers attached to the Embassy, Apr. 2 to a cocktail party, April 14 to another, April 15 to a dinner with dancing, and April 17th to a buffet supper. In between I have little informal dates so you see I sure can use all the formal clothes I brought with me and then some. Me for a small post every time after this. I feel so sorry for the poor girl that drew B.A. as it is much harder to get acquainted in a big city. She has never written to her friends telling them how she likes it which probably means she doesn't.

I'm having some hard luck myself. I had some pajamas made of what I thought was cotton, because it is called challis or

---

[9] Editor: During 1931-1932, Will Rogers was on his second around-the-world trip, visiting Japan, China, Thailand, Greece, England and other countries. In 1932, he was 53 years old; he was to die in a plane crash in 1935.

something like that and is like woolen underwear. I guess the wool irritated my skin and the chemical in the dye finished it and I look like I had the measles and have been to the doctor every day getting injections for a week but expect it will be over soon. I'm not a bit sick but very uncomfortable. I just got a note from the gang that they are going skating tonight so I guess I will go as my face looks pretty good except for my arms etc, which won't show.

I am going to play in a tennis tournament a week from Sunday so have to get a new racquet. Swimming will be starting soon so I have had a piece put in my bathing suit which was too short. So I am all set. Now if the Government only appropriates some money for our swimming pool we can swim--if not we can only take sun baths. Did you get my last check for $54. I believe? It's so nice not to owe anything. I will look around for some of those lanterns you mean Kathie. The screen you mention is not a screen as you will see by reading on the back, but walls of a room in one of the Japanese mansions here. There are plenty of screens here, though, but dreadfully expensive. A plain gold coated one with a few clumps of trees on it is about $100. gold. However, I will try and find out what the cheaper ones are if there are any. If you think of anything you want I will buy it for you as a gift if you don't mind paying the duty. But I think they charge plenty of duty on Japanese art things but you could try anyhow if you want. Everything is so interesting here but we run around with English-speaking people so much we miss a lot. However, this summer there aren't so many social functions and I will have more time to look around. I think it is awfully nice your graduating from night school. Mother wouldn't think of making use of her time like that. I bet Roger is very proud of you. Well, Kathie, will write again soon. Write often as I enjoy hearing from you as Mother only writes to send some cloth for a silk dress for her and for Mrs. Richerson and for more money. I send her $5. and $10. besides the tax money every month. Love,

Dorothy xx

AMERICAN CONSULAR SERVICE

Tokyo, Japan.
May 7, 1932.

Dearest Kathie:

You would certainly love the Embassy grounds now. They have a lovely rock garden all covered with some kind of deep pink flowers in full bloom and all sorts of new trees are being added. They bring full grown trees and prop them up

compulsory month's vacation. Oh, well, it's a job anyway, and the apartments are still ours. Although they are even coming back for them, that is, charging for telephone service and window washing when they told us we would get them free at first.

I had an awfully nice time the Fourth of July. The Americans had a big field day in Yokohama which I went to and then to the dance at the Hotel in the evening. I am up in the Embassy now, but of course it's only up stairs so it doesn't make much difference. The only bad part is we have just started on summer hours, getting out at 3 o'clock and I have to work till five! But I suppose I should consider the glory.

I'm sorry Arthur has been sick. I just sent Mother $15. (Don't tell her you know or she'll have fits). I finished paying the taxes but only got a receipt for $20, Well, will write some more soon, and let you know whether I can make them take me with them to China. Fat chance, but you never can tell.

Lots of love to you and Roger,

Dorothy XX

The Tokyo social invitations continue even as the Inquiry work beckons in China.

June 9, 1932.

Dearest Kathie:

This has been quite a busy week for me. Friday they had a housewarming at the new Consular building in Yokohama, Saturday invited to lunch, then for a swim at the Yokohama boat club then to the tennis dinner and dance at yokohama, Sunday lunch at the Yokohama athletic club and then tea and swim at the Yoko. boat club--Monday, reception for the new Ambassador until 6:00, then at 6:30 a party celebrating the birthday of the people who live upstairs, Tuesday a tea, Wednesday a garden party for the new Ambass' daughter, tonight to Yokohama for a swim at the boat club and am invited to the Amateur Dramatic Club performance which is always formal, tomorrow night show, supper, dance, and Saturday a farewell luncheon. But that is the way it is all the time here. I always send my invitations to Mother to keep so any time you want to see them just ask her.

The new Ambassador is awfully good looking but very deaf.[11] His daughter is really beautiful, about 18, with very healthy complexion, dark blue eyes, dark hair and taller than I but

---

[11] Joseph C. Grew was the American ambassador to Japan from June 1932 until December 8, 1941. Grew was a career diplomat and Foreign Service officer who tried to prevent the slide to war with Japan. He faced many pressures in his role, including trying to convince Japan to stop its expansionist policies in the Far East.

very athletic looking.[12] So I suppose they will have plenty
of parties at the Embassy this winter. Everything here is
very formal--all the parties require evening dress for the
women and at least tuxedos for the men. However, beginning
about July the men wear white flannels usually and the women
chiffon or summery dresses as it is so very hot then. I am
hardly ever home for dinner.

The tea I went to Tuesday was for a new girl from the
States whose name is Dorothy Grow (quite a coincidence her
name being almost the same as the Ambassador's and coming on
the same boat). She is a Smith College grad. and about my age
and likes tennis and swimming so I guess we will have a lot
of fun together. I took her around and showed her where to
get her hair fixed, etc. and she was thrilled to death with
everything. After you are here awhile you get used to things
and think it's quite natural to see people walking around in
kimonas, etc. We will start getting out at 2 pretty soon so
expect to get plenty of swimming in.

*Will write again soon. Just sent Mother clipping about 50,000 people starving in Tokyo. I am getting docked
a month's pay!   Dorothy*

Have sent her $70.00 for taxes. Now wants $10. for new glasses.

This next letter provides a description of the lengthy time and travel involved that produced
the famous camel photo that leads off this chapter. Who knew that Japan has camels? A true
adventure for Dorothy.

AMERICAN CONSULAR SERVICE

Tokyo, Japan.
July 28, 1932.

Dearest Kathie:

You should feel some real heat. I can hardly type as my
fingers stick to the keys and all the locusts are singing so
that makes it seem hotter. However, I get out at 2:30 and
jump into the swimming pool, but even that is kind of warm.

I am sending you a box with some silkworm cocoons in it. I
didn't send them to Mother as she wouldn't care about them. I
thought you might be interested in seeing them. Inside you
can hear the dry shell rattle which belonged to the pupae as
it turned into a butterfly--at least I think that's the
explanation. The white ones are the cheapest, the light
yellow next, and the dark yellow have only been discovered

---

[12] This is Elizabeth Sturgis Grew, who the following year would marry the third secretary in Japan, Cecil B. Lyon.

recently by crossing certain kinds of silkworms. However, the customs officials might not let them by.

I had an awful good time over the weekend. About 18 of us went on a trip to a volcano. We took a boat for about 6 hours, leaving Tokyo at 9 p.m. and arriving at Oshima at 4:30. All the town was out to welcome us with banners, etc. Then about 7:30 we started to climb this big mountain and when we got to the top, about 2 hours and 45 minutes later, we came to a dessert which we rode across on camels. I had my picture taken on a camel. Then we climbed some more lava rocks until we got to the volcano which erupts every two or three minutes regularly with an awful noise and gives off sulphur gas which nearly suffocates you. One of the boys had a movie machine and next week they are all coming up to the Embassy to show the pictures. It was very interesting. We left there about 2 in the afternoon on Sunday arriving in Tokyo by boat about 8. We had the whole upper deck and brought along potatoe salad and fried chicken, etc. and had a wonderful time, getting very sunburned. There are lots of opportunities to take trips out here.

Well, Kathie, I hope you and Roger will have your little house soon so I can visit you when I go back and be living on your pension like kings and queens.

Lots of love,

Dorothy

I am starting to send mother $20 every month regularly. Don't tell her you know.

Lytton Commission

Recall that when Dorothy served as the private secretary for General McCoy in Tokyo as part of the Lytton Commission in China, she really wanted to be sent over there. She got her wish! The undated note shown at right was typed on a small slip of paper, no more than 3 ½ inches, and as Dorothy mentions, was written in a hurry. Dorothy's collection of letters contained no cables (telegrams) even though she requests that her mother save those "with the rest of my souvenirs." We know that the League of Nations Inquiry Commission arrived in China in April of 1932, and we know that Messersmith authored his letter to Dorothy in 1932 as well. Dorothy's snippet of a note was written circa 1 August 1932.

Dear Kathie:

Very rushed as just got this cable and am leaving tomorrow night for China. Am using my vacation time. As we don't get paid for a vacation this year, I thought this would be a good idea. If you give this cable to the Ware River News please cross out the amount of money I am being paid as it is very small, but I will get my hotel expenses paid too I think.

Dear Kathie:

Very rushed as just got this cable and am leaving tomorrow
night for China. Am using my vacation time. As we don't get
paid for a vacation this year, I thought this would be a good
idea. If you give this cable to the Ware River News please
cross out the amount of money I am being paid as it is very
small but I will get my hotel expenses paid too I think.

Please give it to Mother afterwards to keep carefully with
the rest of my souvenirs as it might be a very good
recommendation some day. Please keep it with letter from Mr.
Messersmith which I also sent you. Hurray for China!

                            Love,

                            Dorothy

It's the league of nations commission inquiry. Some class,?

Roland Sawyer is also over there now in same place

What was this League of Nations Inquiry? Well, it was rather involved and had been
ongoing for months – apparently Dorothy traveled to China as part of the Embassy group, but
once there, was able to visit Allan.

The League of Nations appointed the Lytton Commission in 1931 to investigate the cause of
Japan's invasion of Manchuria and to report on any circumstances that threatened to disrupt
peace between China and Japan. The five-member commission, led by British politician Victor
Bulwer-Lytton, arrived in China in April of 1932, but by then the Japanese army had already
established the puppet state of Manchukuo. The commission's report was issued in September
of 1932 and was unanimously adopted by the League of Nations General Assembly in February
of 1933.

In this letter dated 26 September (not on Department letterhead), Dorothy followed up that
quick note about leaving for China with a detailed missive. Twenty-four days – and time with
Allan!

Sept.26, 1932.

Dearest Kathie:

I had a wonderful
time in China. I
saw Roland Sawyer
one day at the
hotel just by
accident as he
thought I was still
in Tokyo. He was
only there one day
so I only saw him
after work, but we
had dinner together
on the roof garden
and danced and the

next morning I came early and he took my picture with his movie camera which he says he will show in Ware and then had breakfast and he left about 8:25 a.m.

I worked every day till about 7:30 so you see it wasn't any snap. At the boat the American Minister and his wife were meeting her mother who came to visit them from the States so they took me in charge too. They held up the train 40 minutes (an express) to wait for the boat. You land in Tangku[13] which is about 4 hours ride from Peiping. Gen. McCoy's aide met me at the station and took me to my hotel about 12:30 at night. He is a nice young man about 32 called Lieutenant Biddle. He took me out to dinner and dancing about every night until the last week (I was only there 24 days as I had only 30 days leave) when I got a cable from Allan who had managed to get emergency leave. He was in Tsingtao operating (he is Chief Executive Officer on a Destroyer) and it takes two days by train to get to Peiping so I thought he was pretty nice to come all the way up especially as Chinese trains are something fierce. So then I went out to dinner and had lunch with him every day, but he had only 4 days which isn't much after not seeing him for over a year. He gave me some pretty jade and pearl earrings. Lieutenant Biddle (Gen. McCoy's aide) gave me some crystals when he left Tokyo and when I left China gave me a lovely mandarin coat which I will use for an evening wrap. So there I was with the two Lieutenants which made it a little embarrassing but worked out all right I guess.

-2-

I also went to several parties in Peiping, including one given by Gen. McCoy at the temple of Heaven. They had four blind musicians playing Chinese music and just Chinese lanterns for light and it was very pretty sitting in the shade of the temple.

Also the Am. Minister gave a big dance for Admiral Taylor, head of the Asiatic Fleet, and I was invited to that. I really didn't have a minute to myself with the work and everything. I lived in an old temple turned into a glorified boarding house which was also very interesting. I didn't see much of Peiping except the hotel roof garden but I will go back some day and do it up fine. There are every so many fascinating things to see but it is dirty, terribly dirty. Everything is full of disease and germs. I was vacinatted and inocculated the first day I landed so I was all right. I didn't have time to take any pictures, however.

I wrote mother about not butting in, etc. I'm awfully sorry Kathie. Maybe I scared her this time. I can't understand her at all.

---

[13] Tanggu District was a district in the Tianjin municipality, now part of the Binhai New Area. It is on the Hai River where it enters the Bohai Sea, and is a port for Tianjin, which is about 48 km upriver.

Well, thanks for all the letters. Write again soon.

Love,

Dorothy X X

Bingham came early! That China-Japan conflict is a priority! No date on this next letter, but it must be early November 1932 from Bingham's updated travel plans (and back on Department letterhead).

AMERICAN CONSULAR SERVICE

Dearest Kathie:

This is just a little short note as I have to mail this letter right away to catch the boat. Mr. Bingham just came in and said he received the package for me two hours before the boat sailed. The Ambassador was called back here suddenly on account of the China-Japanese trouble and he had to come with him. So I sure appreciate your hurrying and getting the things to him. I haven't seen them yet as he hasn't unpacked but I know they will be just what I want. He got back here the 6th of Nov. instead of sailing the 6th as planned, so I was sure lucky

Say Kathie, that dress I had made looks good enough for this winter so don't bother getting me any. But I would like some of that luxuria tissue, and some ten cent chokers, as they don't have any here. If you get about 5 pair or so of 20 cent ones, all colors and any kind but crystal, I would sure appreciate it. You remember those pretty ones we saw in the windows of the five and ten. Mother broke the one pair I got, the big white ones with the blue beads in between. I am enclosing a check for $65., please use $60. twoards my debt, which means I now owe $160. I think, and the other $5.-- .$2.50 for my horse racing ticket, thank you so much for getting it, and the rest for postage, for both packages, and luxuria tissue and 20 cent chokers. Thank you a lot. I have to get back to work now or get fired and this job is such a cinch, I sure would miss it.

Will write you both a long letter soon. I am dieing to see what you sent me.

Love,

Dorothy

The following December 1932 letter is not on letterhead and the date is in an informal format. We learn about a disadvantage of her trip to China — and excitement about skiing in the new year!

Dec. 2/32

Dear Roger and Kathie:

How do you like my Christmas cards? They are made of wood. The mountain in the picture is the famous sacred mountain,

Mount Fuji, which I meant to climb last summer but had to go to Peiping. There are only two months in the year you can climb it, August and July, as otherwise it is too dangerous. It is an extinct volcano and has many crevices to fall in. A Japanese boy tried to climb it last Saturday and fell and was killed instantly.

We are having lovely fall weather here and are already making our plans to go to Akakura the first of next month, for 5 days of skiing. There is a big bunch going from Tokyo. We sleep on the floor Japanese style in Japanese inns. It is quite cold.

I am sorry Roger's ankle took so long to get better, but hope he is able to work now. You ought to be a trained nurse by now, Kathie. It is quite pretty around the house where you are now, isn't it? Plenty of grass and flowers.

They have foreigners night at the skating rink now so that makes it lots more interesting. I wonder if they will put through that 5 day week they are talking about. That would be great, wouldn't it?

Well, goodbye for now. I have 8 million Christmas cards to write. I sent one to Miss Shaughnessy.

Love,

Dorothy

And then two letters from March 1933. In the first one, Dorothy answers "Sure!" to an offer to move to a new post in Harbin, Manchuria – after all the love of the swimming pool, the great new quarters in Tokyo, would she really give it up so easily? Where is Harbin, Manchuria?

AMERICAN CONSULAR SERVICE
American Consulate General

Tokyo, Japan.
March 1, 1933.

Dearest Kathie and Roger:

I'm so sorry you have been sick and I hope by this time you have recovered from your fall. You were darned lucky not to break an arm or even worse. It was awfully nice of Roger to write instead as otherwise I would have been worried about not hearing. It must be nice to plan your house nearer Boston and I suppose Kathie is haunting all the sales buying curtains, rugs, etc. And now Mother won't have to worry about pestering you about your furniture. I hope you don't take her too seriously as you and Roger are really the only friends she has in the world and she would be in a fine fix if you got angry with her for good.

As for that typhoon we had here, it really wasn't bad at

all, at least in Tokyo proper. It just sounds worse in the newspaper. I sent some copies of TIME to Roger. I get it regularly now and if he wants I can send it to him after I get through, but if he gets it, or the news is too stale when I sent it, please tell me and I will throw them away.

Say, Kathie, you were pretty smart to win that refrigerator contest. I am sending you back the letter they sent you as you probably want to keep it. Some class to Ware being the coldest place in the whole of New England. But it is a dry cold so you don't mind it so much, whereas here it is damp and seems much colder sometimes.

Gee, this is some place for parties. I am enclosing a few invitations to send home, but they aren't an eighth of the ones I get as most of them come by telephone. I have been invited to the opera twice this week already (an Italian opera company is here for a week) and I am invited to six (6) farewell parties between the 4th and 13th of March, which is next week, one of them being a masquerade ball, and all being formal so you can see you have plenty of use for evening clothes here.

March 18, 1933.

Dear Dorothy -

Will you have suki yaki dinner with me at seven thirty Wednesday, march the twenty-second -

Jim has a dinner engagement and I am asking Dorothy Trow and miss Rummel.

I do hope you can come as we want you to know the way to our house for many future occasions Our address is
147 Aoyama Minamicho
6 chome, Akasaka -

Sincerely yours
Gertrude J. Rabbitt

right turn → first house (name in light)
left turn at end → 2nd police box
of street
x police box

Car line at foot of hill

↑ Kasumi cho

↑ Roppongi

The left turning is at 2nd police box after crossing car line

I love the things you sent in the Christmas box, and as it snowed here last week the overshoes came in very handy. I am sending you the pictures off of some of my Xmas cards as you may want to paste them in a book or something. If you don't, just throw them away.

It looks like we are going to have some trouble here between Japan and China but that is nothing new.

They have awfully cute little plants here. I have one on my window sill now, which cost about 25 cents gold and I

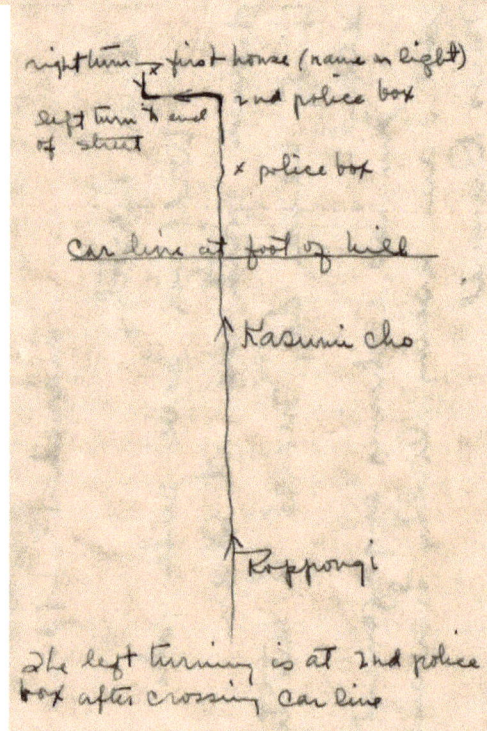

have had it almost 4 weeks. It has a little Japanese bamboo cate with a miniature pine tree behind it and big rocks and a plant with purple flowers, and miniature plum tree in it with pink blossoms, and they all grow just like the big ones. They do wonders making dwarf trees as you have probably read in some of the books I sent.

The Consul who used to be here, Mr. Coville, and who has been in Harbin, Manchuria, just came through here on his way home on leave and asked how I would like to work down there, so I said sure. Any old place, for a change. But that is really the most interesting place in the world right now. The women all carry guns when out shopping, not real ones but usually tear guns and someone is always getting kidnapped. I am enclosing the letter Mr. Messersmith sent me. Please send it home to be kept after you read it. I am also enclosing a picture of me in front of the big Buddha in Kamakura which you may keep if you want it.

The spring weather is just starting here and all the plum blossoms were out last week. They are white and look like apple blossoms.

Well, Kathie, hope you are much better and that you and Roger have a cute house by this time.

Lots of love,

Dorothy

And the second March letter, still so active in Japan:

AMERICAN CONSULAR SERVICE
American Consulate General

March 29, 1933.

Dearest Kathie:

It's certainly awfully hard trying to get any sleep around this town. Those six parties between the 4th and 13th developed into nine, some being cocktail parties. Last night I was invited to the Amateur Dramatic Club show, which is very formal, in Yokohama. Monday is a holiday so I am leaving with a crowd of people for a walking trip through the Izu Peninsula, which is the Florida of Japan, We are starting Saturday noon.

I just returned from my second skiing trip this year. We had a holiday on a Tuesday and the Con. General gave me Monday off, so we left on Saturday for Akakura. The snow was so high we had to bend down so as not to become entangled in the telephone wires and that was March 18th, so you see we have plenty of snow in Japan, though it took 9 hours train ride to reach it. That is the interesting part of Japan--this place where I am going this Saturday is about 4 hours ride and it is like down South in Florida, while at the same time you could take a train in another direction and in 8 hours be in a place like Alaska. Tokyo is sort of in between and we beginning to get a little spring weather here although last night we had a small frost.

Last week when I went skiing we had a blizzard on Tuesday when I was supposed to start back, and as the hotel is 7 ½ miles from the railroad station and you have to walk it, I had to stay another day so I had an extra day.

I just heard the good news that we get a 15% cut, starting April 1, which with the $52. Income tax I just paid makes about $625. cut I got in salary this year, counting the month without pay. Did you find out if Mother's taxes are paid? I suppose things are much cheaper in the States now.

I just bought a nice pair of walking shoes from the Con. Gen'l.'s wife. She paid $16. and sold them for $6. so I was in luck as they just fit.

Well, Kathie, hope to hear from you both soon. Will you send these invitations home when you look them over, together with the pictures of some of the people on the Lytton Commission which one of the delegates gave me.

I just got a letter from Dr. Murray who says New York is the swellest place in the world, and that he has a new aeroplane for $600, and goes up himself alone twice a week. He said my monkey had some little monkeys, the mother of which is a monkey in a Connecticut [zoo]. I would like to see the little ones. He also says he's not in love any more. Someone told me the other day he was trying to get back to Japan as he always liked it so much. I wish he would.

      Love,

Dorothy

Dorothy's letter from spring of 1933 has no mention of Allan although we know they are to marry one year in the future – rather, Dorothy is thinking of going home in July:

April 12, 1933.

Dearest Kathie:

I'm so glad you feeling better. That sure was an unlucky fall. I had a nice card from Miss Shaughnessy from Florida. Isn't she lucky to be able to spend the winter down there. Too bad she wouldn't let you live in her house while she is gone and sort of take care of it for her. Why don't you suggest that.

Thank you for the clippings, Kathie. I would never know about the work otherwise as Mother always says just the opposite. Well, anyhow, as long as she pays the taxes with the money I send I don't mind but hate to have her buying doctor's books, etc. which she doesn't need but always gets.

Yes, I did go skiing this year. I think I wrote you in my last letter I went twice this year, as we had a holiday on a Tuesday and I got Monday off and went on Saturday. Last week end I went on a swell three-day walking trip around the Fuji Lakes which you will see in your guide book and you could see old Mount Fuji from every angle. It looked like a big scoop of ice cream with chocolate sauce. I felt the recent earthquake even in our concrete apartment house so we knew it was a bad one as the beds shook back and forth. I was half asleep and thought the wind was blowing the bed, but when I heard the other girls talking outside, I knew it was an earthquake, but of course the damage was quite a ways from us, about 9 hours by train. When I do raise enough money to come home, I am due for home leave this July of course, I am planning to come home by ports, which means stopping at India, Africa, Singapore, Egypt, and Europe. It really cost about the same too, as you go on a slow short of half freer, which stops at all ports, going through the Suez Canal and ending up in New York. As you know, the big item is coming across the continent by train and it is much better to go by port and go all the way by ship. It takes about 2 1/2 months though, and I have a long time to think it over.
-2-
Well, people out here are getting fired right and left but I guess I'm pretty safe so I'm not worrying.

Thanks for all the clippings. Yes that was the place (Bolivia) where the hotel was like a bar. When are you moving to Boston? It will be lots more convenient, won't it? Will you please send these invitations home after looking them over?

Love, Dorothy XX
Sent you two more doilies.

Ah, but Allan was in the picture. We know Dorothy again got to go to China in July of 1933, as this handwritten note on Dollar Steamship Lines notepaper bears witness to her return trip. And this also refers to the time that Allan and Dorothy spent in Chefoo. (A mini-chapter on Chefoo follows this chapter.)

DOLLAR STEAMSHIP LINES
ORIENT AND ROUND THE WORLD

ON BOARD
July 25/33

Dear Kathie;

Well, I arrive in Tokyo today after a swell vacation. Everyone was so nice to me in Chefoo & invited Allan & I everywhere. I played tennis & swam every day. I came back

by way of Shanghai to get a look at the place but it looks too much like Buenos Aires to be interesting.

I am four days late going back to work & hope I don't get fired.

I just met Christine Mathewson, the son of the baseball player. He is an aviator & was married in Shanghai just 2 weeks when he went up to test a plane & had an accident which killed his bride. He has just gotten out of the hospital with a bad arm that hasn't mended yet & had his leg amputated about 2 weeks ago. The accident happened in January. The girl had come all the way from the States to marry him. He's only a young boy & very nice looking.

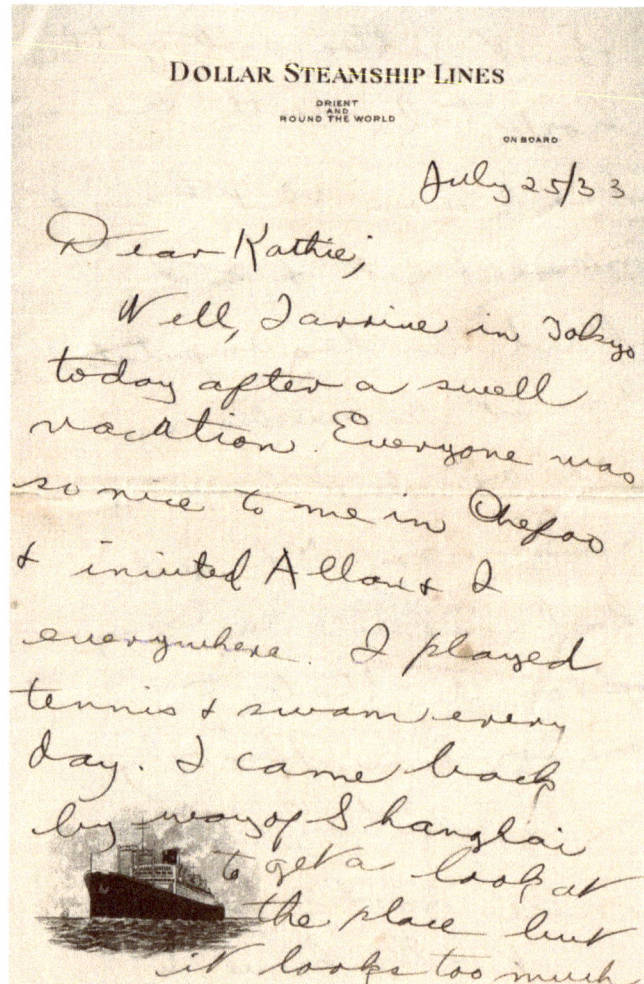

Well, have to pack now.

This is a wonderful ship.

Love,

Dorothy xx

Chefoo did its magic. The next month, Dorothy finally provides Allan's surname to her Aunt Kathie, and his two-year quest to visit Japan. No letterhead on this one, but a clipping pinned to the letter.

August 11, 1933.

Dearest Kathie:

How do you like the Prince of Sweden? I was invited to a dance Saturday night, he being in the party, and to swim on Sunday, also with him. He's certainly a good looking boy. The first Prince I've ever known.

I saw this in the Ware River News about the minimum wage and wonder if it will affect Mother? Please let me know as it would be quite a load off my mind, if it did, and she would never tell me.

We are certainly enjoying our swimming pool these days. I usually go in before

H.R.H. Prince Charles, Jr., of Sweden Visits Japan

H.R.H. Prince Charles, Jr., nephew of His Majesty King Gustavus V of Sweden, attended by Mr. H. Mamrin, representing Consul-General Axel Johnson of Stockholm, arrived in Japan on a round-the-world tour of inspection by the N.Y.K. California-Orient liner "Asama Maru" on June 22.

His Royal Highness and party left Sweden on May 16 by the Swedish American Line M.S. "Gripsholm," arriving at New York on May 25. Having travelled in America *incognito* as the "Count of Karlsborg," Prince Charles, who is particularly interested in the mechanical arts and steel industry, visited Detroit, Mich., and other American industrial cities. The Prince arrived in San Francisco by the San Francisco Overland Limited on June 6, and, on the morning of his arrival, paid a visit to the N.Y.K. San Francisco Office.

From the time of his embarkation on the "Asama Maru" from the Golden Gate port on June 8, Prince Charles was an official visitor to the Japanese Kingdom. During his trans-Pacific voyage His Royal Highness was fortunate enough to celebrate the birthday of the King of Sweden on June 16, on which occasion toasts to the King of Sweden and the Emperor of Japan were drunk. The table at dinner on that day was decorated with a huge sugar replica representing the old castle of Gripsholm, Sweden, which cake was made by the ship's baker and later presented to the Prince to be forwarded to his home country. His Royal Highness spent his morning hours in reading in the ship's special room on the port side, and, after lunch, took diversion in deck sports. One day the Prince inspected the ship's navigation bridge and her engine room, which seemed greatly to interest him.

Upon the ship's arrival at Yokohama on June 22, the Swedish Minister in Tokyo, members of the Japanese Imperial Board of Ceremonies, the Governor of Kanagawa Prefecture and other notables went to greet the distinguished visitor. Representing the N.Y.K. Board of Directors, Mr. Y. Shimidzu, Managing Director, went to Yokohama to bid a hearty welcome to the royal visitor, who graciously paid a return visit to the Head Office of the N.Y.K. Line and had an interview with President K. Kagami and Vice-President N. Ohtani on June 29. During his six weeks' sojourn in Japan His Royal Highness will travel throughout the country and study the source of Japanese culture, which will doubtless prove of much benefit to the promotion of friendship and goodwill between the two nations.

Photograph taken on Prince Charle's visit to the N.Y.K. San Francisco Office on June 6. Front row: Mr. S. Nahase, N.Y.K. Manager for San Francisco; Prince Charles of Sweden; and Mr. Harold Hamrin. Rear row: Fred L. Doelker, sub-manager of W. R. Grace & Co., and Mr. T. Kataoka, sub-manager of the N.Y.K. Line, San Francisco.

breakfast and also after work. We are on summer hours, and get off at 2 o'clock for the rest of the day about 3 times a week and Saturdays at 12. I have been going to the beach about every Sunday as it is only about 50 minutes by fast train, and have got a swell tan.

I sent you a couple of lanterns and if you want more just say, because they are very cheap here and I don't think you will have to pay any duty as they are so inexpensive. Please don't worry about paying for them as I wouldn't send them if you did. If you don't mind paying duty I could send you things from time to time if you let me know what you would like. One of them I sent you has a silk sort of lining. If it is torn when it gets there you can use one of the napkins I sent with the doilie sets to repair it.

Is there any chance of Roger getting his pension? Are you going to move nearer Boston soon? I am sorry you had such trouble over the memorial day flowers, Kathie. But you know that's just like her and I guess it's too late for her to change now. I threw the note you enclosed away as you said. Yes I got a <u>month</u> with pay and took 4 days extra and Mr. Garrels didn't say a thing, didn't even dock my pay. The folks in U.S. are the only ones who have been cut to 2 weeks. I sure had a wonderful time on my vacation. The girl I live with who got fired got a job in Kobe about a month later, which is about 9 hours from Tokyo by train, so she is all O.K. Oh, yes, we got the 15% cut all right. Roosevelt gives me a pain, telling everyone to raise wages and then cuts us and fires the rest.

Allan's last name is Blackledge. He said he would try and come to Japan in October but he has been trying for 2 years now, so I'm tot planning too much on it.

I wish Arthur and Sally would live with Mother. He has never done a thing for her. It isn't really fair. He really has more money than I because it costs almost nothing living in Ware compared with living in foreign countries or in a city in the States.

I go down to Yokohama 3 times a week for a tennis lesson and it is pretty hot this time of year. I have been going lots of places as there is always something doing in this place — too much so. Am going to the beach on a picnic this Sunday, and the Consul General and his wife have invited us on the roof of the Imperial Hotel for talkie movies and dinner. They have movies there every night, and I went on the roof in Yokohama night before last as they have dancing and dinner there.

On the 31st of this month I am making out the draft again to Dupont, which with the $26, Mother paid, will total $66. paid on the taxes. I wonder if that about covers it? Have you paid your 1933 taxes? Should I start sending every other check to Dupont for them, after finishing the 1932 ones? She was sore as the dickens about sending the draft for Dupont, but I don't care. She would just let them slide otherwise. Isn't there some bill we have owed Harrington for about 3 years or so, about $35? I seem to have a faint recollection of it.

Well, goodbye to you both. Probably will be seeing you about this time next year, if, I'm not fired before. But I guess I'm pretty safe.

Lots of love,

Dorothy

Though we know that Dorothy destroyed her 'love letters' with Allan, the next letter in the collection, from 22 April 1934, is from … Allan! (as typed by Dorothy):

Tokyo, Japan.
April 22, 1934.

Dear Folks, All:

As you see by the heading I am writing this letter in the American Consulate building, Tokyo, or rather I am dictating it to my future wife, thus starting a new phase in the proper manner, which she says she doesn't like. She is Miss Dorothy Forrant, whom you no doubt remember as the girl I met on the boat coming out here 3 years ago. Since that time I have seen her in Peiping, Chefoo and here in Japan. She is a very lovely girl whom I am sure you will all be proud to know and welcome. She originally hails from Massachusetts and has during the past eight years been in the foreign consular service acting as secretary in the State Department in Washington, In Cuba, in Buenos Aires, and Chile, and the past 3 years in the American Consulate in Tokyo. She is 27 years old, tall, slender, dark-complexioned, charming, intelligent, and has an excellent disposition. We are to be married here at the Consulate General Tuesday, the 24th, when I will leave immediately for Kobe with the destroyers where my ship remains for one week. Dorothy in the meantime will remain in Tokyo clearing up unfinished affairs, preparatory to joining me in Shanghai on the 6th or 7th of May where we intend to spend our honeymoon.

We are due to sail for Chefoo about the 16th of May and as yet I have no definite date of detachment. Should it be after that date she will come to Chefoo with me and we will start our homeward trek from there. I have requested permission to be returned to the United States via Suez and European ports --port of destination New York. Should this not go through we will be returned via Pacific landing in either San Francisco or Seattle. I have been informed unofficially and understand my orders are on the station detailing me to duty in Naval Operations, Navy Department, Washington, D.C. where we will be for the next two years.

To you, Dad, I will send a radio[14] when I learn when and where I will arrive in the States and leave it to you to disseminate this information to others concerned. I have

---

[14] Slang for radiogram, a formal written message transmitted by radio. Also known as a radio telegram or radio telegraphic message, Around 1906 industrial nations began building powerful transoceanic radiotelegraphy stations to communicate with other countries and their overseas colonies. By World War I these were integrated with landline telegraph networks, so citizens could go to a telegraph office and send a person-to-person telegraph message by radio to another country. This was written down on a standardized form called a *radiogram*.

ordered your p.j.'s here and will see what I can do about the rug in Shanghai. I've told her all about Babs and feel sure that they are going to be great friends. This will be a great change for all of us but we are looking forward with every confidence to a very happy life together.

                    Affectionately,

                        Allan

ADB/df

Remarks: The parties signed in my presence the notification required by Japanese law, which was witnessed by Carrie McMahon, residing c/o American Embassy, Tokyo, and C. A. Hutchinson, residing c/o American Consulate General, Tokyo. The notification above mentioned was on April 24, 1934 filed with and accepted by the Registrar of the Kojimachi Ward Office, Tokyo, Japan. This procedure is prescribed by Article 775 of the Civil Code of Japan.

WARE GIRL IS MARRIED AT TOKIO, JAPAN

Miss Dorothy Farrant Weds Lieut Blackledge of United States Navy

Ware, May 14—Mrs Mae Farrant of Eddy street announces the marriage of her daughter, Dorothy, to Lieut Allan Blackledge of the United States navy. The marriage took place at the United States consulate in Tokio, Japan, on April 24. Lieut Blackledge is an officer on the United States destroyer, Parrott. Miss Farant has been in the consulate service in Tokio for two years. She was also confidential stenographer to former Secretary of State Frank B. Kellogg and took the notes at the conference in Havana, Cuba. She also served two years in the United States consul's office in Buenos Aires, Argentine. She was graduated from Ware High school and the Northampton Commercial college, and entered the United States civil service and was assigned to the state department. Following her marriage, the United States consul general and Mrs Arthur Garrels gave a reception to the newlyweds at the Tokio consulate.

Certificate of Marriage
(See Revised Statutes of the United States, Section 4082)
AMERICAN CONSULAR SERVICE

American Consulate General, Tokyo, Japan

April 24, 1934

I, C. A. Hutchinson, Vice Consul of the United States of America at Tokyo, Japan, do hereby certify that on this twenty-fourth day of April A.D. 1934, at the Kojimachi Ward Office, in the city of Tokyo, Japan Allan Douglas Blackledge, a CITIZEN SUBJECT of the United States, aged thirty-seven years born in Culbertson, Nebraska, and now residing in Tokyo, Japan Dorothy Marita Farrant, a CITIZEN SUBJECT of the United States, aged twenty-seven years born in Salem, Massachusetts, and now residing in Tokyo, Japan were united in marriage before me, and in my presence.

In witness whereof, I have hereunto subscribed my name and affixed the seal of office at Tokyo, Japan, this twenty-fourth of April, A.D. 1934, and of the Independence United States the one hundred and fifty-eighth

C. A. Hutchinson, Vice Consul of the United States of

No. 11, One Dollar. To be issued in Quadruplicate.

1447

This little 9"x6" certificate marks the end of Dorothy's career in the Foreign Service, as well as her career as a typist/clerk. It signals the beginning of a new life – as a Navy wife and a mother of four, stepmother of one. The adventures will continue.

Chefoo, China, 8-8-26

Chefoo

In the opening to a mostly forgettable 1947 Orson Welles film *"The Lady from Shanghai,"* a blonde – yes, blonde – Rita Heyworth informs our hero that her parents were Russian – White Russian. And claims he'd never heard of the place where she comes from.

"I'll bet you a dollar that I've been to the place where you were born."

"Chefoo," says Rita.

"On the China coast, Chefoo." replies Orson. "The second most dangerous city in the world!"

Chefoo, now called **Yantai**, conjures up the lure of the Far East. It was opened as a treaty port by the British in 1862 and was a summer station for the U.S. Asiatic fleet between the world wars, primarily 1930-1940, with a population of about 30,000 year-round. The waterfront, an attraction for sailors on liberty, was once called the Brighton of China.

What was it about Chefoo in the 1930s? Pete Deutermann[1] provides the following anecdote:

---

[1] P.T. Deutermann is an American writer of mystery, police procedural and thriller novels, and 26-year veteran of the Navy, retiring with the rank of Captain. A classmate, US Naval Academy, Class of 1963.

"I got the impression that life in China amongst the expats was rather dissolute. I have a picture of my parents (engaged at the time) at the Chefoo Club in the company of two other naval officers, one of whom was married to a White Russian. My dad was USNA Class of '27 and met my mother, Dorothy Tinan, while on leave in Manila from his China Station assignment, a gunboat very similar to *USS San Pablo*. Mom was the daughter of P.W. Tinan, who was the principal Studebaker rep for southeast Asia, HQ in Manila.

"They were married in 1932; Mom and my (infant) brother, David, moved to Shanghai and lived there, until all Americans were ordered out of China due to war clouds gathering in 1933. She went back to Manila and then on to the States; my dad transferred to the *USS Preston*, a four-piper which remained on the China Station for another six months. I don't know any more about the Club Chefoo except that anytime they were reminiscing about those days they always shared a secret smile.

"When I went out to Manila in 1966 to take a Swiftboat MTT up into Manila Bay to train the Filipino Navy in Swift operations, I stayed at the Manila Yacht Club. Which was where my parents had honeymooned in 1932! Small damn world, eh what?

"Cheefoo, Tsingtao, Shanghai - all those names I used to hear around my house(s) as I was coming up. I still have a rug my folks brought back from Tsingtao. My mother grew up in Buenos Aires in the '20's when her father was the Studebaker rep for all of South America. He got fired when the company caught him with his claws in the petty cash till to support his horseracing habit over in Montevideo. He was subsequently 'banished' to Manila, P.I. where he became the Studebaker rep for the Philippines and points south. Which is where she met and married my father in 1932 and moved to Shanghai to join him on the China Station.

Chefoo, July 1931.

"The guy with the dark moustache on the right is my father, still a bachelor in 1931. There are a couple of so-called White Russian ladies in the picture, one of whom married Ed Dexter, a USNA grad who got out after his obligated time and went into the coffee business. He later became the head of the Coffee Exchange in NYC.

"My mother, whom Dad married in 1932 in Manila, was living there with her father who was the Studebaker rep for Asia at the time. This was after he got banished by the company for dipping into the petty cash funds at the Buenos Aires headquarters for his gambling in Montevideo. She told me that this picture was taken at the Chefoo Club, notorious for being the no-tell motel of east Asia for American naval officers. She said she'd asked Dad who the woman next to him was. His response was that he didn't know. People just tended to get together with whomever was there that night. Fun times in pre-war China. The Brits probably started the club."

In the 1933 photo above, the ship's party is at the Casanova Cabaret, one of the popular dance halls frequented by Asiatic Fleet sailors, and not far from the Club Chefoo. Dorothy's Allan, as Exec Officer of the *Parrott*, is pictured center, smiling into the eyes of a lady sitting on his lap and smiling back – but that is not Dorothy.

Pete Blackledge recalls his father Allan, a bit in his cups one evening, quoting the White Russian: "Oh, Allan, why you no marry me?" The cold answer was that Allan felt it would not be beneficial to his career.

In the Club Chefoo photo at the bottom of the page, we see Allan, again in the center and again with 'not Dorothy.'

Throughout the 1920s and 1930s, fighting between Chinese Nationalists and Communists often led to attacks on American lives and shipping. From 1925 to 1927, almost the entire Asiatic Fleet remained in Chinese waters to protect American interests. In 1928, upon the capture of Beijing by Nationalist forces, the Asiatic Fleet stationed 41 ships around northern Chinese ports to support the 3,000 Marines in Peking (Beijing) and Tientsin and protect nationals.

Part of the lure for our Asiatic Fleet may well have been Club Chefoo. Here is a description of this fabled destination as crafted by the Artificial Intelligence software Geni:

Stepping through the imposing arched doorway of Club Chefoo in the 1930s would transport a US Naval Officer into a world both familiar and exotic. Here's a glimpse of their experience:

Colonial grandeur: Imagine high-ceilinged rooms with polished wooden floors, adorned with Chinese tapestries and artifacts – a subtle air of colonial power softened by Eastern elegance.

Buzzing social hub: Laughter and lively chatter fill the air. Officers mingle with fellow servicemen, expatriate businessmen, and even the occasional glamorous socialite.

On shore on the China Station (Asiatic Fleet) circa 1931. Center: ADB with (possibly) the White Russian.

Entertainment: Tap your feet to the tunes of a live piano playing jazz or classical music. Catch a game of cricket or tennis on the club grounds. Attend a formal dinner or dance, indulging in exquisite cuisine and lively conversation.

Libations: The well-stocked bar offered a haven for weary sailors. Sample exotic Chinese liquors, local beers, or classic Western spirits. Engage in spirited discussions or lighthearted camaraderie over drinks.

Camaraderie: Club Chefoo served as a home away from home for US Naval Officers, fostering a strong sense of community and belonging.

Cultural exchange: Interact with Chinese staff and fellow patrons, gaining insights into local customs and traditions.

Social hierarchy: Though more relaxed than formal military settings, the club likely still reflected the social hierarchy of the time, with officers holding a higher social standing.

Whether seeking relaxation, camaraderie, or a taste of the exotic, Club Chefoo offered a unique experience for US Naval Officers in 1930s China. It was a microcosm of a bygone era, where East and West met in a setting of colonial privilege and cultural exchange.

Historic Background on Chefoo

Chefoo - Yantai - 烟台

Chefoo (now known as Yantai) is a seaport on the north coast of Shantung (Shandong) province. The city was traditionally known as Zhifu (Chefoo), which was the name of the island that protects Yantai's natural deep-water harbour, where a port has been located from early times. The name Yantai ("Beacon Tower") derives from a lookout beacon built on a hill overlooking the site as part of the 15th-century coastal defense system erected against Japanese pirates.

Later known as Dengzhou, until 1858, Chefoo became an international port - a 'treaty port' - in August 1861, with 17 nations establishing enclaves here; however, there were no formal concessions established.

Numerous foreign traders lived there, and a flourishing trade grew up in the late 19th century, consisting partly of exports of silk, beans, and local produce from Shantung and partly of imports from the West. During 1891–1901 the city's population almost doubled. Chefoo's commerce was, however, almost ruined by the development of Tsingtau (Qingdao) on the southern coast of the peninsula by the Germans after 1898. By 1904 a rail link connected Tsingtau with Tsinan (Jinan), after which the export trade of Shantung became concentrated at the better port of Tsingtau. As a result, Chefoo and the other ports of northern Shantung stagnated. This probably explains why Chefoo-based currency issues - especially by government and other major banks - diminished considerably after the 1920s.

Dashing Young Chinese War Lord Runs the Thriving City of Chefoo

Special Correspondence, THE NEW YORK TIMES.

CHEFOO, China, July 8.—The little city of Chefoo, which has a population of less than 30,000 persons for most of the year, has developed into one of the "free cities" of China. It is firmly held by General Liu Chien-nien, a young commander not yet 33 years of age, who maintains an independent State and conducts an almost continuous series of negotiations for alliances with various Chinese factions.

General Liu, of humble origin, is a dashing young warlord. He drinks only champagne or tea, and lives a life of contrasts—first of ease in his official yamen, then of hardship when he takes to the field at the head of his 25,000 troops.

Liu Chien-nien has been nominally a supporter of the Nanking Government for two years, but of late he has more than flirted with the rebellious Northern Coalition, which maintains a government at Peking. He has never seized the customs, so all collections made here go to Nanking's coffers, but he collects—and retains—all other taxes, and uses them for the maintenance of his army.

Chefoo is a prosperous and picturesque seaport, and the place of import and export for a large section of Shantung province, which has no rail or adequate highway connections with the rest of China. Taxation is high, but not extortionate, and business is less throttled here than in many other places.

Since the present civil war between Nanking and the Northern Coalition began last Spring General Liu Chien-nien has been assiduously courted by both sides. Nanking has sent him uniforms for his soldiers, munitions and money. The North has sent him money and munitions. So Liu's troops are paid up to date, and he has even had a cash surplus to invest in more munitions, sold to him from the Manchurian arsenal at Mukden.

Just now Chefoo is on the crest of prosperity. Many of the vessels of the American Asiatic fleet spend the Summer months here, and today on the streets of Chefoo there are almost as many white-uniformed American sailors as there are blue-gowned Chinese coolies. Chefoo is also a Summer resort held in high esteem by foreigners in China. The resort hotels are all open and every cottage on the long curving beach is rented.

Above: the quayside at Chefoo, c. 1900.

Above: a postcard view across the town, showing the numerous western buildings which soon dominated Chefoo. The stamp was issued by the German Post Offices in China - overprinted on a standard German stamp.

Below: A Chefoo issued local stamp of 1893.

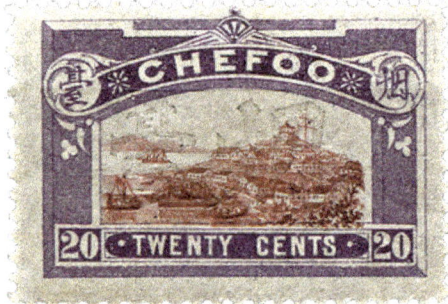

Chefoo was one of only five cities in which the first stamps of China, the Large Dragons, were issued. In terms of importance in a Local Post context, it ranked second only to Shanghai Local Post, which had a head-start of nearly 30 years, before Chefoo's Local Post's inception in June 1893.

China's Imperial Post began operation from 1897, at which point all other issuers were declared unlawful.

Below: Postcard of Chefoo Harbour in 1909, ½ cent stamp, French inscription.

Chefoo. *part a l'entrée au golfe au Petchili* · *Bau Dzin bydl and 1909*
L Roche

Since 1949, and especially after 1984, when Yantai was designated one of China's "open" cities as part of the effort to liberalize economic policy by inviting foreign trade and investment, the city has grown considerably. Industries producing textiles, processed foods, machinery, construction equipment, electronics, instruments and meters, metallurgical products, and auto parts have been established. Wines, tinned foods, wooden clocks, and locks are Yantai's traditional products, and gold trading and gold working are also important to the city.

Little information is readily available for the Bank of China's Chefoo branch. A limited number of series of 1918 notes were issued, followed much later by a now equally scarce issue of 1934 'Shantung' notes overprinted with 'Chefoo' in Chinese and English.

Above: A rare late Chinese branch issue of this British colonial bank; a $10 issued at Chefoo on September 1st 1922. A hand-signed note with a depiction of the bank's main offices on the back (not shown).

Following page: Two postcards, depicting:
1. St Jean Ermitage at Chefoo. Assumedly a French built residence. The postcard is unusual as it carries stamps of the German, French and Russian Post Offices in China, and an overprinted Chinese Empire stamp of the revolutionary period, and
2. the coastline of Chefoo.

Sources:

"The Lady From Shanghai" (1947). https://www.youtube.com/watch?v=NR9Nnq9q0-Y Accessed 18 March 2025.

https://asiamoney.weebly.com/towns-and-cities-chefoo.html retrieved 1 June 2024.

"Dashing Young Chinese Warlord Runs the Thriving City of Chefoo". New York Times, July 8, 1930 retrieved March 18, 2025.

CHEFOO.   Snt. Jean Ermitage

Chefoo.

Verlag von H. Sietas & Co., Chefoo China.

Woosung Fort[1]

In his later years, Allan Blackledge would remark that the movie "The Sand Pebbles" (1966) accurately depicted the US Navy situation within the Asiatic Fleet during his time. The movie is set in 1926 China on the Yangtze River, during a period of significant political unrest and warlord conflicts in the country; the main character is stationed on a U.S. Navy gunboat called the *USS San Pablo*. River gunboat duty in China in the early twentieth century was considered a desired assignment for a U.S. Navy sailor. American sailors were paid in U.S. dollars, which went a long way in China. American enlisted men were known to spend their disposable income at the bars and cabarets in ports such as Hankow or Shanghai or Chefoo.

In 1917, China had welcomed an influx of Russian, Polish, and Lithuanian refugees fleeing the Russian Empire as communism took hold. This led to an influx of Russian women, many of whom were former dancers and performers, at the Shanghai and Chefoo dance halls and clubs which American service members frequented.

Throughout the 1920s and 1930s, fighting between Chinese Nationalists and Communists often led to attacks on American lives and shipping. From 1925 to 1927, almost the entire Asiatic Fleet remained in Chinese waters to protect American interests. In 1928, upon the capture of Beijing by Nationalist forces, the Asiatic Fleet stationed 41 ships around northern Chinese ports to support the 3,000 Marines in Peking (Beijing) and Tientsin and protect nationals.

Allan arrived in July 1931. From 1930 to 1940, the Asiatic Fleet carried out patrols on the Yangtze River in South China, while also conducting training cruises to the Philippine Islands.

A primary part of protecting American interests was protecting the petroleum companies. By the 1930s, gasoline replaced kerosene as China's most important petroleum product. China relied on imports through the global oil companies Standard Oil, Asiatic Petroleum Company (APC)[2], and Texaco. Imports were stored at China's treaty ports (such as Chefoo) and delivered elsewhere by ship, mainly via the Yangtze river.

While Dorothy was working hard and playing hard in Tokio, Allan and the *Parrott* were

---

[1] The Alamy stock photo at the top of page is dated Jan. 28, 1932 and shows the Woosung Fort as captured by the Japanese.

[2] Asiatic Petroleum Company was a joint venture between the Shell and Royal Dutch oil companies founded in 1903. It operated in Asia in the early 20th century. The corporate headquarters were on The Bund in Shanghai.

observing and reporting the skirmishes with Japan planes and ships attacking Chinese sources. One of the more serious of these incursions occurred within sight and sound of the *Parrott*, over February 2-3, 1932. The *Parrott's* report follows, submitted by Allan as Executive Officer and complete with a navigation chart marked to show the hits and the ships involved. Researchers might compare this chart with the 1842 attack by the Brits.

The Woosung Fort was established at the entry to the Whangpoo River to protect the access to Shanghai by sea. The chart below lightly marks ship locations and artillery shell and bomb hits. Note that the direction North is to the left. Shanghai can be seen in lower right of the chart.

JAPANESE NAVAL AND AERIAL BOMBARDMENT OF WOOSUNG FORT AND VICINITY.

The first Japanese activity against Woosung Fort occurred at 0730 2 February 1932; by destroyers lying to the northwest Woosung Spit, firing from an approximate range of thirty-five hundred yards. It is believed these destroyers were of the 26th division. A total of seven salvos was fired. The weather was overcast and no planes were operating at this time. Towards noon the weather cleared and at 1135 six Japanese aircraft, bombers and observation planes, were sighted: heading toward Shanghai. No further activity occurred this day.

On 3 February, 1932, at 1128, destroyers probably of the 26th division, opened fire on the Woosung Fort and fired twenty-one minutes, during which time a Japanese plane was circling about in the vicinity of the fort at an altitude of about twenty-five hundred feet. The Fort returned an intermittent fire, no hits on Japanese ships were observed. The slowness and ineffectiveness of the Fort's fire made it apparent that either the material was in poor condition or that the personnel had little training.

At 1345 eleven Japanese aircraft, consisting of observation and, chiefly, bombing planes commenced an aerial bombardment of the fort, which lasted until 1500. The planes flew in sections of Vee's before maneuvering to drop bombs. The planes then broke formation and delivered a dive bombing attack in succession. Planes

-2-

dived at an angle of about forty-five degrees, pulling out and dropping at an altitude of from seven hundred to one thousand feet. The size of the bomb used is unknown, but it is estimated to be one hundred pounds. Whether or not any hits on the fort were made could not be seen, but the explosions occurred consistently within a small area. It appeared that the bombers carried only one bomb, as each plane would return toward the carrier after dropping one bomb. During the bombing, the planes were not under anti-aircraft fire, but may have been under machine gun fire.

On the whole, it is considered that the aircraft were capably handled. A good formation was kept and the bombs appeared to drop consistently in a small area.

At 1615 two Japanese planes were noticed flying near Lismore flats at an altitude of from two to three thousand feet.

At 1620 gunfire was heard and almost simultaneously a shell landed in the Whangpoo close to the bow of the PARROTT. By the time the officers reached the bridge several of the shells had landed close aboard and the sound of gunfire was continuous.

Officers were sent aloft to determine the source of fire and orders were given to single up lines and prepare to get underway. The officers in the foretop reported the firing was coming from two or three Japanese cruisers which appeared to be underway at steerageway and located approximately two miles bearing 115 from Lismore buoy.

-3-

Two of the cruisers were identified as the "NAGARA" type and the third of the "JINTSU" type.

The fire continued for about ten minutes when it ceased. It is estimated that about fifty rounds were fired.

No Chinese man of war, or troops, had been seen during the afternoon of this date.

What the fire was directed at, or its cause, is unknown. The diagram shows the approximate positions where shells were seen to fall.

When the firing ceased an inspection of the grounds nearby revealed the following damage sustained:

Shell through roof in Texaco compound, slight damage,

Dwelling struck by fragments of exploded shell in A.P.C. compound.

One shell struck the Customs Hulk which had moored in position indicated.

One shell struck and pierced two large gasoline stowage tanks in A.P.C. compound. This shell failed to explode and pierced the first tank above the floating roof and the second tank through the side, the floating roof and the bottom plate, burying itself in the earth beneath.

One shell struck the Shanghai Municipal Ferry at the landing indicated, resulting in slight damage and injuring one Chinese.

By observations of fall of shot, four shells landed in A.P.C. compound, two between A.P.C. and Texaco compound, three in Texaco compound, three to westward close to Texaco compound, thirteen in the Whangpoo from five to one hundred yards from the USS PARROTT, four in the shallows on the south bank and the others as indicated.

-4-

The map bears the handwritten annotation:

> Japanese Naval and Aerial
> Bombardment of Woosong Fort
> and Vicinity —
> Observations from U.S.S. Parrott
> 3-4 February 1932
> Lieut. A. D. Blackledge
> Executive Officer

During the greater part of the firing three gun salvos were

observed, the two ships firing alternately.

The salvo pattern in range was approximately two hundred yards and in deflection three hundred yards. As a whole the salvo patterns could not be considered good.

On the morning of 4 February 1932 four unexploded shells were recovered and were found to be armour piercing shells. These shells were measured and found to be 5:48 inches in diameter with the lands four times as wide as the grooves. The nose caps had been crimped to the shell and on inspection were found to be highly machined.

On 4 February 1932 at 0905 desultory firing was heard from the direction of Woosung, but it was not determined who had fired.

At 1050 four destroyers of the 30th division passed the USS PARROTT standing down river toward Woosung. The ships were fully cleared for action with ammunition laid out at the guns, the crews at "General quarters". It was noticed that hammocks were neatly lashed around the searchlights, bridge, rails surrounding the gun platforms and other exposed stations to protect the personnel from fragments and machine gun fire. The crews were neatly dressed in complete blue uniforms and made a good appearance.

At 1125 when these destroyers were in the vicinity of Fort Buoy they commenced firing. The fire was fairly rapid, and it appeared to be pointer fire. Just prior to opening fire these destroyers increased speed. The accuracy of the fire could not be clearly seen but the shells appeared to fall well scattered.

After passing the Fort the destroyers turned 180 in the

-5-

vicinity of Lismore Buoy and stood up the Whangpoo firing heavily.

When the 30th division was turning around in the vicinity of Lismore Buoy three Japanese destroyers, probably of the 26th division, maneuvering slowly to the northward opened fire on the Fort.

After the 30th division got squared away and was standing up the river three Japanese cruisers, maneuvering slowly about twenty-five hundred yards northeastward of Lismore Buoy opened fire with heavy salvos.

At this time the Fort was under fire from seven destroyers and three cruisers when the first shot was fired in return. The Fort fired a total of seven rounds. The firing interval was extremely slow. No hits were made but one shell appeared to fall close to a cruiser.

During the Japanese bombardment large pieces of material were seen to be thrown into the air, but the accuracy of the fire could not be judged.

The 30th division ceased firing between Woosung Creek and Fort Buoys but continued up the river at reduced speed selecting a place to turn, to head down stream. The division leader dropped an anchor just beyond Woosung Creek to swing to a flood tide but in this maneuver his stern went aground and required the assistance of two Japanese tugs to pull him clear. The next two destroyers dropped their anchors a little further up stream and successfully swung to a flood tide. The fourth destroyer stood up stream and when one hundred and fifty yards abreast the USS PARROTT dropped his anchor and swung to the flood tide.

This destroyer maneuvered here for ten minutes during which time his guns were trained point blank on the USS PARROTT. Shortly

-6-

before this this destroyer anchored and two guns were seen being loaded. No effort was made to train these guns clear of the USS PARROTT yet two officers were at the after guns and could clearly see that they were pointed at us.

The USS PARROTT made preparations to get underway and clear in event the destroyer close aboard would commence firing at the Fort from this anchorage. (Also went to general quarters just in case one of the Japanese guns should go off.) The destroyer eventually got underway and stood downstream to rejoin his division.

The three cruisers and three destroyers maneuvering in the Yangtze continued to fire until 1332. Shortly after the cessation of fire two Japanese planes flew over the Fort, probably to observe the effect of the gunfire.

At 1600 Japanese planes continued aerial bombardment of Woosung Fort but the effect could not be observed.

On 5 February 1932 at 1230 and again at 1345 eight Japanese bombed and machine-gunned Woosung Fort and adjoining territory.

Up to this time Chinese still hold the Fort at Woosung (10 February 1932).

Impression of the Japanese Navy gained by observation of their activities at Woosung Fort and vicinity is as follows:

   The aviators seem well trained and maintain good flight
      formation

   The bombing appeared accurate although this could not be
      definitely seen. The bombing height was low and no
      opposition was offered.

-7-

   The accuracy of gunfire did not appear good although the
      firing was done under excellent conditions.

   A very large percentage of their shells, probably 80% did
      not explode.

   The officers and crews appeared nervous and irresponsible in
      their actions.   OMF/EWA

Navy Wife

The newlyweds sailed from Shanghai on the *S.S. President Lincoln*, departing July 7, 1934, and arriving at San Pedro (the port of Los Angeles) on July 25. They had orders but no place to call home, and on the manifest listed as Allan's 'permanent address' the home of his father, Judge Lewis Blackledge: 2031 N. 55th St., Omaha, Nebraska.

They were headed for Washington, D.C. and would enjoy a few years of bliss, including much travel, before the world changed again. World War II would begin in September 1939 for Europe and December 1941 for Japan and the U.S., a full seven years after Dorothy and Allan returned from their respective Asian stations.

By March of 1937, Dorothy and Allan had completed three years of marriage, and the previous April, Dorothy had given birth to Patsy and Penny, her own set of twins, (Recall that both Dorothy's mother and Aunt Kathie were twins, as Julia Glancy had given birth to two sets of twins.) Allan was assigned to ordnance at Edgewood Arsenal in Maryland shortly after the twins were born, and as Dorothy reports to "Dad Blackledge" (Judge Lewis) and Allan's siblings, she and Allan are departing for their next duty station, Long Beach, CA:

March 23, 1937.

Dear Dad Blackledge, Gertrude and Floyd, Helen and Hobert:

I hope you don't mind if I make carbon copies of this letter as it is about leaving here. Although we haven't actually received Allan's orders, we have been told they are just waiting to be signed and expect them shortly. We probably leave Edgewood Arsenal about May 20th, and I know we shall also miss it very much indeed, to say nothing of our furnace man, gardener, the way our walks are immediately cleared off after a snowstorm--in short, all those little luxuries provided by Uncle Sam to keep the Army happy.

Right now it looks as though we could arrive in Omaha on the 5th day, Hastings on the 6th day, and after a few days with Dad Blackledge on to Kearney for a few hours stopover before continuing on to the West Coast. How we wish we could include Seattle in our itinerary! As it is, we feel more than guilty imposing our enormous family on anyone for an overnight stop, but Dad Blackledge has made us feel that we really won't be as much trouble as we know we really will be and says he is making plans for borrowed play-pens, etc., and the Darner's are very anxious to see Babs and to have her stay over a few days while we are in Hastings, there to meet us by train so she too can have a visit with her Grand Daddy. I, who have never had any of his scrambled eggs, am looking forward to sitting down and being waited

on while be prepares breakfast, as I heard that is quite a
Blackledge custom.

Patsy is now quite a young elephant, weighing close to 25
pounds, and Penny about to hit the scales at 23. Patsy's
hoped-for curls have turned into the kind collies have, and
are a light brown. Penny's are scarce but real and she is
very blond but tans. They are both standing and trying hard
to talk. Allan is now adding shaking hands to their reper-
toire of patty-cake, shaking bye-bye, etc.

Babs will unfortunately miss about a month of school, but
she is doing so well this year that I am sure she will pass
into

- 2 -

the seventh without any trouble. She loves school here and
has loads of friends. They are always having plays, dancing school, birthday parties, etc. They are having a big
dance recital in Baltimore in May.

Dad Blackledge, we are all so relieved that you weathered
the flu like a real sailor. I hope we didn't give you the
beginning of it here with the change of climate, etc.
Allan had a touch of it, and we kept Babs home from school
for about a week, but the rest of us were O.K. I guess it
takes your pep for a long time. The babies still love
their pink and blue robins, and were more than grateful to
have that nice cigar box you left for a pin box. Patsy
took a screw out of her crib the other day and had been
chewing on it for some time before I caught her. Penny is
still faithful to her thumbs.

Hobert and Helen, we want to thank you very much indeed
for the very clear and interesting snaps of your big snow-
storm. We certainly envied you your big snow fort, and the
coasting. We promised Babs a sled but didn't have enough
snow at one time to use one. I guess Spring is here for us
as we are awakened by woodpeckers every morning. According
to Allan, the expiration date of that very interesting
periodical LIFE, checks correctly. We certainly like it.
Even Babs has taken to perusing it!

It seems to be the custom on this Army Post, for everyone
to entertain everyone about once year, and as by now we are
indebted to about forty couples, we are having a dance on
April 2, for the whole Post. It's a good thing we're
moving because the poor Navy couldn't keep up this social
whirl much longer. We have bought sailor hats for the men,
as our idea of humor is to make the army wear them. In
each hat is the lady's name each man is expected to take in
to supper.

Gertrude, will you please tell Jean her letter reached us
O.K. We all enjoyed it as much as Barbara. I am glad
Phyllis and Doris enjoy skiing so much. That is my idea of

the sport. It always makes me a little homesick for Japan
when I hear about it. I wore the seat of one pair of skii
pants out entirely so you can imagine how good I was at it!

   Guess I'd better get the twins' baked potato on the stove
and their formula made up.

                    Our love,
                 Allan & Dorothy
                     (over)

Dear H & H:

   I'm so sorry not to have sent you the information you
asked for your records before. I sent my aunt after the
dates of my grandparents marriage, etc. but maybe she
forgot too. So I'll send you what I know, and the rest
when I get it.

My full maiden name: Dorothy Marita Forrant
Date and place of birth: February 7, 1907 at Salem, Mass.
My mother's maiden name: Mary Ann Glancy
My father's full name: Joseph Arthur Forrant
Date and place of birth of the twins: April 9, 1936 at
                                        Washington, D.C.

Even in a situation as relatively comfortable as a senior lieutenant's wife, finances were still a problem. One could always hope for a promotion. The following is the last letter in the collection in which Dorothy writes to her Aunt Kathie.

                                        May 16, 1938.

   Dear Kathie:

   Thank you for explaining about the checks Mother wants me
to send. It was certainly a shock to find she had borrowed
$225. and has no way of paying it. I wonder if any of it
has been paid? I don't see how she had the nerve to do a
thing like that. I certainly hated to let Allan in on all
these family squabbles, because he of course resents paying
when Arthur doesn't contribute a cent. I made the checks
out today --the one for $6.45 to the Ware Savings Bank, and
the one for $10. to the Ware trust Co, and put on each one
"To apply on interest due on Glancy Estate for Mrs. Forrant
which was due April 1938", and "To apply on loan made by
Mrs. Forrant in 1937", so she would not be able to use the
checks for anything else, and send another bill later,
which she has done.

   Well, Kathie, I feel pretty depressed about the whole
business, as if I was working, that would be different, but
to ask money from someone, even my own husband, is something which gets me down. I notice in that letter from the

bank, they say if the house isn't shingled they will be obliged to foreclose the mortgage--wouldn't she be justified in having it shingled if it kept them from foreclosing the mortgage? But I suppose that isn't so, or you and Roger would have agreed to pay half.

How much money are you asking for the cottage? And how much for the double house? What would they bring at auction? Is the double house always rented?

Allan had the week-end duty so won't be home till next Saturday. He is working very hard, and looks quite tired. It's no joke trying to get selected for Commander, as you only stand a 50-50 chance, but if he is we will be sitting pretty, unless there is a war.

I am glad Roger is able to go back to work, but am sorry he isn't feeling quite himself yet. Perhaps he shouldn't go back to work yet, but knowing Roger, I know how lost he feels in not working.

The babies are fine and get into everything. I have been trying to puzzle out that letter Sally sent you about a washing machine. I am glad she is going to help Mother, but usually she tries to get everything out of Allan and me for her, instead of trying to fix it so I won't buy a washing machine. Well, I haven't the money now anyway, so I guess everything is all right. I certainly hope Mother gets some State children, don't you?

Love,

Allan & Dorothy

Dorothy's mother, May Forrant, died in 1940. After receiving the news from Arthur, Dorothy asked Babs to take the twins out for a walk. Babs recalled the moment vividly, as it was the first and only time she had seen Dorothy crying.

Dorothy raised her family at the Naval Gun Factory (now the Washington Navy Yard) from 1940-1948, but was in Long Beach for the (April 8) 1940 Federal Census at 265 Orizaba Avenue, with the entire family: Allan is now a Lieutenant Commander, and Barbara is 15; Patricia and Penelope are 3. Son Mike would make his appearance in October 1941.

Dorothy used her typing and letter-writing skills to good advantage during these years, sending more than 225 letters (each numbered on the envelope) to Allan at his various combat posts. This March 1945 letter illustrates how Dorothy would forward Allan's letters to the family — by transcribing his handwritten epistles into her own family communications to Lewis (Dad), Hobert and Helen Blackledge (the H's), and Babs & Jack Tipton (the "Tees", who will marry in December 1946). It starts with a postscript, welcoming a young Army Air Force pilot Jack Tipton into the family as Babs' suitor. ("Go across" means getting sent overseas to combat duty.)

I wrote one full page to Babs of quotes from you all
regarding Jack, and she said you would even like him better
if you knew him. He called on Edna in Omaha and they liked
him a lot. Bob Darner is now training in Tucson. Jack is in
Iowa waiting to go across.

3807 Van Ness St., N. W.,
Washington (16), D. C.

I think Dick Darner has already gone across, and Bill
Minneker joined the merchant Marine sometime ago.

March 3, 1945.

Dear Dad, H's, and Tees:

I have some letters from Allan to report with messages
for you all so will start right out with them:

"I still have nothing more nor new on any change of duty
and am beginning to think it was flash in the pan or that
the Big Boy in Washington has put thumbs down on me. I did
receive word that Cincpac had again prodded Bupers on
giving me a combat command, so I am still wondering and
hoping - - And in the meantime, have started my 10th month
on this job. I hope I am not learning so much about this
type job to become one of the indispensable men! (joke for
Missy).

"Dad asked 'what is a BB'? For the edification of all,
the combat and types of men of war are (limited to those of
which I am personally available to command and desire:

BB	Fast battleship (the newest and latest)
CB	Large cruiser (practically same as BB)
CA	Heavy Cruiser (New Orleans type)
CL	Light Cruiser (differs mainly in armament)

> Anyone of the above classes will be
> more than OK by me. There is also
> the

OBB	Old battleship (Mississippi, West Va., Calif.),

etc.
They were, not so long ago our pride and joy and are still
plenty powerful and modernized. But I don't want one of
them for reasons too involved for this letter".

Speaking of the Mississippi, one of Allan's classmates,
Chick Hartman, has a young son, already a Naval Academy
graduate, serving on it. I think Dad probably remembers
him. Babs and Chick (I think she's getting a little past
the age for this nickname, but is still very attractive and
very nice) are the ones who had a little daughter the year
before Mike arrived. They always referred to her as "the
grandchild". By the same token, I think Allan has better
start changing my nickname, or rather his for me, to "Mrs."

One of Allan's classmates, Roger Brooks, called to ask
about Allan (he is in the Bureau of Ordinance and before
the war was on the retired list with a bad heart). I told
him about Allan almost getting the BB, and Roger said "So
that's where the chief of the detail office went in such a
hurry". Apparently he had fixed himself up with the job
Allan had been nominated for.

From another letter:

"The Xmas cards you spoke of--the Colberts--He is the
Captain paymaster who was on duty here with me, lost his
wife--is now at USNA--and who phoned you about me. Harry J
Carmichael is a big shot Canadian official with whom I did
business when in BuOrd. You remember my nice trip to
Canada.

- 2 -

"I have no more information on any change of duty, and am
beginning to think I am on some ones blacklist for some
reason or other. I am about resigned to being the forgotten
man lost on an Atoll in the vast reaches of the Pacific.
There continues to be <u>no</u> women on my island. Bawdy Esquire
which you so thoughtfully provided is my only contact. I
received my second copy (February) yesterday. They must
have a special mail set up."

Will you all please tell me if you have started to get
your magazines, or at least a notice saying they will
arrive eventually? You don't know how sorry I am and
chagrined that you should get your Christmas presents so
late. However, with the good news from Dad that he has had
a notice about his Navy Magazine, and Allan's Esquire,
which I subscribed to at the same time, maybe things will
begin to happen. The Magazine Lady has assured me she has
the file numbers of all my subscriptions and to let her
know if they haven't arrived.

From Allan:

"Your No. 184 arrived yesterday enclosing Mike's valentine to me which is very much appreciated. I still have
some difficulty in determining which side is "up" but I'm
sure Mike can straighten me out on that particular when we
get a chance.

"I continue with no further news on any change of duty.
I've written a few more influential friends and if nothing
comes of that I guess I am to assume I have run my professional course and will henceforth be just one of those old
senior captains.

"You know, I felt quite badly to learn of Sis losing her dog and knowing how Sis goes "all out" for anything or body she likes or dislikes, I know she feels this considerably.

"Let's you and I start a little postwar planning of our own and in an unhurried and "hobby" fashion survey where we would like to retire--near the water with a boat, a dog-- and a chance to direct, oversee and perhaps help the mental and physical development of my son."

If this letter seems a bit disjointed, it is because said son is enjoying one of his usual winter colds, and having him in bed, I am constantly called in with "I don't know what to do", where upon the crayons are taken away, and colored paper and scissors substituted--then when nothing holds his attention, he is allowed the "black bureau", a little miniature Japanese bureau which holds Mother's "jewels", which incidentally, Mother never wears. It's a good thing too, as they are pretty well mangled by this time, during the many sick periods when eyes could not be used for reading by the twins.

- 3 -

Allan writes:

"I still have no news on any change for me and as I wrote you last week I have about (not quite) become resigned as the Forgotten Man. I have started my 11th month on this job--worn out two admirals and the 3rd is due in about a week or ten days. No one seems to be concerned about the poor ole Chief of Staff -- except the C/S himself."

His last letter which arrived yesterday brings us up to date:

"No. 185 finally arrived about 3 weeks late and now I am complete through No. 188 which was mailed 16 Feb. and arrived the 23rd.

"Also has arrived is Rear Admiral W.K. Harrill, who is the new Commander Marshalls-Gilberts Area. This is my third Admiral I've run through as his Chief of Staff. I guess I must be pretty hard on them. He brought the news that I was to remain on here as Chief of Staff for another 2 months or so as they would not relieve the C/S and Admiral at same time. I was afraid of that and particularly since I missed by a hair getting command of a fast BB. I am afraid the parade has gone by me and I am not so happy.

"I hate to see Adm. "Slats" Sallada leave. He is tops in every way, and I like him very much. He is going to Washington as Chief of Bureau of Aeronautics which as you know is a No. 1 job--but he has no desire to go to Washington.

"I could use a little time in Washington right now. This continuation of duty here and what it forecasts has set me

down pretty hard. Particularly after being told I was to
get the finest job in the Navy. Someone has knifed me and
my spirits are about the level of a snake's belly."

The way I look at it is that if he has only two months
(perhaps) there, he will be here in May for 30 days leave,
which time we will use packing, and all can go together to
the West Coast, if his new duty is such that we are allowed
transportation, and he has made any contacts for a possible
place to live. I'm sure he will be getting some leave
within the next few months, and get to see Dad en route to
Washington, and maybe on the way back too! Anyhow, I, quite
selfishly, am so delighted he isn't at Iwo Jima right now.

Best love to you all,

Dorothy

P.S. to Dad:

Dad, I want to thank you for your letters of Jan. 22 and
Feb 15. Although I know you sent them to Allan too, I
think it would be a good idea if I also sent him the
carbons so that, in case the originals should not arrive,
he will not miss out on one of his chief pleasures--a
letter from his Dad of whom he is always so proud.

August 27, 1945.

Dear Dad, H's, and Tees:

I know, regardless of the fact that I haven't a bit of typing
paper in the house, you won't mind, because it means that I can
relay to you so much sooner Allan's two letters which arrived this
morning:

(August 19)

First I had better say that the last letter I received from
him was dated August 11, the day he arrived in San Francisco, and
he was leaving that night for Hawaii. He also said in that letter
how happy he had been to spend such a nice time with Dad in Chicago
on Monday, two days with Babs in Tucson, a day at Bill and Ann
McBride's in Los Angeles.

August 27, 1945.

Dear Dad, H's, and Tees:

I know, regardless of the fact that I haven't a bit of
typing paper in the house, you won't mind, because it means
that I can relay to you so much sooner Allan's two letters
which arrived this morning:

(August 19)

First I had better say that the last letter I received
from him was dated August 11, the day he arrived in San
Francisco, and he was leaving that night for Hawaii. He
also said in that letter how happy he had been to spend

such a nice time with Dad in Chicago on Monday, two days
with Babs in Tucson, a day at Bill and Ann McBride's in Los
Angeles.

"I have been here just one week today and expect to leave
for points west within the next few days—so from hereon
address me:

> USS BILOXI,
> c/o Fleet Post Office,
> San Francisco, California.

"Yes, I have finally actually been ordered to command a
first line combatant ship. The BILOXI is a light cruiser
(CL80)--one of our newest and most modern. She has been in
commission less than two years and I am her third command-
ing officer. Dan McGurl '19, put her in commission and I am
relieving a classmate, Paul Hineman. I am very pleased with
this assignment and although there have been peace
celebrations, I find the war is far from over.

"Isn't it strange, Missy--and I look upon as a good omen-
-that you should say you liked the sound of BILOXI so much
better when I told you I thought I was getting the MOBILE?

"Of course, I would have liked a fast battleship, but I
learned you are rarely if ever given one unless you have
already been picked for Admiral--and my chances for that
are practically nil--so all in all I am very happy to
report the Navy has seen fit to give me command of one of
its finest! It's been only a few months when I thought I
would never get anything better than an APA and now I have
at least made the varsity. So don't forget my new address--
my fine ship--and keep the letters coming!

"I think most of my mail has caught me. I have your Nos.
220, and 221 and your 224-5 and 6 written to me here. I
also received some letters from the twins written last May
and one from Babs written early in June.

"I've seen Bill Thayer who has just returned from Europe.
He has a squadron of destroyers and has put on considerable
weight. Dick is in S.F.

"It's good to know the small fry are having such a good
time on the farm and want to stay, and I'm sure you are
getting a much needed change--if not a rest.

"Did you deliver my IOU to Mr. Ettenger? I don't know how
I will arrange to pay him off--guess the best I can do will
be to send him a check". (Note: The Sunday morning Allan
and I left for Philadelphia, our very kind neighbors, the
Ettengers, invited us over for "brunch". The naval officer
bet the civilian two

- 2 -

quarts of whiskey that the war would not be over until
January 1947. I am sure, though, that in this instance he
is glad he lost the bet. He was so sure that he would win,
he made it a two to one bet. I guess the atom bomb was
justified--only I wish they hadn't used it on Nagasaki
too.)

"Will you please see that the entire family, and any
others who should know, get my new address--and it is a
Honey--USS BILOXI.

                    Honolulu, 22 August, 1945.

"Your No. 227 just arrived which as usual was more than
welcome and must have made some kind of a record in getting
here--only three days!

"Well, I'm off tomorrow at 2 p.m. in search of my ship--
my immediate itinerary is: Kwajalein--Guam--Okinawa, and
from the last place will probably ferry out to my ship or
start plotting a new search curve.

"Bob Ettenger's note was appreciated (Note: He had me
enclose a clever reply he had made to Allan's equally
clever I.O.U. to him) and should you find an opportunity to
purchase two quarts of good bourbon (Walkers de luxe--Old
Tayler--Seagrams, etc.) will you please do so and I will
reimburse you.

"I'm wondering how Patsy is making out and did you send
her back to the farm? It might be a good idea to have her
checked out again". (Note: on August 14th, I received a
telephone call from my farm lady to the effect that she
feared Miss Patsy had appendicitis as she had acute
adominal [sic] pains. Whereupon I hastened to take the
toonerville trolley that eventually gets you out to
Herndon, Virginia, and took Miss Patsy back with me. After
the Toonerville, one must take two more street cars to get
back to 3807, and while still on the train, peace was
declared. You can imagine my consternation when it seemed
as though we would never be able to get a car home--with
Patsy propped up against a post, on the curb, and holding
the necessary paper bag in her hands and looking about
ready to faint. It seems that when the streetcars passed
the White House, enthusiastic crowds boarded it to
celebrate, getting up on the roofs of the streetcars,
climbing in and out the windows, etc. Finally I made the
grade--hay was thrown through the windows, together with
various other articles. The next morning I took Patsy to
the doctor, only to have him give me a large bottle of
castor oil for the young lady, and in a few days she was
O.K. again. He asked her if she had been eating a lot of
corn--apparently eyes, as usual, were somewhat larger than
her stomach. In a week I delivered her back to her beloved
farm.)

"I hope you have given my new address to the family and I'll get a letter off to them the first opportunity. Please push out all the letters you can, and certainly not less than three per week, to the USS BILOXI, F.P.O., San Francisco, California."

And now, I want to thank one and all for various nice letters--Gertrude and Floyd's for theirs, two from H's dated August 7 and 19th, and one just received yesterday from Helen, and one Dad was kind enough to write from the Stevens. All that weren't sent to Allan, I am enclosing to him, which as I look them over, I guess mean all. It's a shame to bring up Christmas last year at this date, but do know H's, that if I don't get your NATIONAL GEOGRAPHIC to you soon,

- 3 -

I shall ask for a refund, and buy you something <u>I can mail myself</u>.

Wasn't it nice that everything worked out so nice for all of us,--Hobert's appointment as District Deputy Grand Exalted Ruler of the Elks for Nebraska West, was <u>certainly</u> exalted, and I know the change you did both a lot of good-- even though you did have to starve on victory day. I only wish Dad could have stayed away longer, but maybe he stayed away long enough to be glad to get back home--which is the principal reason for a vacation anyway. I do hope Gertrude and Floyd were able to take some sort of vacation somewhere.

The children are as happy as bugs. The farm lady is very nice--in fact, she asked before she would accept the children: "Do they use profanity", which rather startled Allan, who in his usual fatherly manner answered: "Not only do they not use profanity, but <u>I</u> think they are rather superior children". I found afterwards that one of the little girls had been prefacing her remarks with "God", at rather frequent intervals. However, Mrs. White, who, as Allan described her, has both feet on the ground, soon had that situation well in hand.

As for me, I am having a grand and glorious time, cleaning the house from top to bottom. After a period of three weeks, I have just finished the upstairs! However, there isn't a crack in the house that hasn't been scrubbed, even to the extent of removing the red wigs from Raggedy Ann (two) and Raggedy Andy, washing them and the ladies and gentleman plus their clothes. I must admit they look worse instead of better, but they sure are <u>clean</u>. Curtains have been renovated as I proceed on my snail-like pace, and best of all, when I get tired, I can <u>rest in peace</u>, all of which is novel and wonderful. The children too, are getting a

reprieve from Mother's too frequent do's and don'ts. Their
farm period has been extended to September 11 (they were
originally scheduled to arrive today), so here's hoping
I'll be able to accelerate things to the point where the
downstairs is finished on their return. All the time
though, the perfectly lovely khaki slacks and tops outfits,
which I was able to cut out of some of Allan's discards
during our week in Philadelphia, remain eyeing me reproach-
fully each time I pass the sewing machine. However, I find
one definitely needs a one-track mind--and boy, have I got
it!

    Babs left Tucson on August 12, after her summer school,
to spend the remainder of the time before the opening of
school with her Auntie Anne, and as her former roommate,
M.J. Campbell, also lives in Los Angeles now, she is really
making up for lost time and enjoying herself thoroughly.

    On Mondays and Fridays, I go downtown and do my "white-
collar work", that is, letters, shopping, dentists,
doctors, and what-not. In fact, I am thoroughly enjoying my
vacation, and with the very best wishes for the same to all
of you,

Dorothy

July 1948
Dorothy's children:
Penny (12); Mike (6)
holding Pete (1); and
Patsy (12).
On steps of Qtrs D,
Naval Gun Factory,
Washington, D.C.

"Babs," Allan's daughter Barbara, had been married the previous December to Army-Air
Force pilot Jack Tipton. Dorothy was enamored of being a Navy wife, and never shared with
her children her adventures in the U.S. Foreign Service. That was a previous life, and being a
mother/Navy wife was the current adventure: Total immersion.

Epilogue

In the summer of 1950, Allan retired as a Captain in the Navy and moved his family to Houston, Texas. He had accepted a position with Cameron Iron Works, a customer company and a natural extension of his munitions work at the Naval Ordnance Plant in Indianapolis. By this time, Babs and Jack were well into Jack's Air Force career. They had a daughter, Deborah, and were stationed in Alaska. Life's adventures continued for everyone.

Having never learned to drive, Dorothy continued to use local transportation as she attended the University of Houston to get her bachelor's degree in Romance languages at the same time that her twins graduated from Rice Institute: June of 1958.

Dorothy continued to love travel. Leaving Allan behind ("I've been to all those places!"), she would sail each summer to Europe as a passenger on a cargo ship. (Once, on a return trip, she reported that the cargo was all elephants and Volkswagens.) In the summer of 1961, Dorothy would travel to France and as part of her fun/learning objectives she would stay with a French family, immerse herself in the language, and take summer courses at the Sorbonne. This adventure would inspire her to enroll in Rice University in a Ph.D program in Romance Languages. As featured in the Houston Chronicle Magazine, Dorothy was at the top of her game.

MRS. ALLEN D. BLACKLEDGE
Student

She is working on a doctorate degree at Rice University, from which her twin daughters were recent graduates. She has a son in the Naval Academy and one in Pershing Junior High. In 1953, at 45, she enrolled as a college freshman. Years ago, she was a secretary in the foreign service, with a yen to study languages. Her B.A. and master's degrees were from University of Houston, where she majored in languages. Last summer she studied in Sorbonne in France, and plans a return trip this summer.

THE HOUSTON CHRONICLE MAGAZINE, TEXAS, SUNDAY, APRIL 23, 1961

But life intervened. In June, Dorothy suffered a heart attack that put her in the hospital, ending her Ph.D program before it began and cancelling her summer return to the Sorbonne. That incident also precipitated her teaching career at Lamar High School in Houston, where three of her children had graduated and the fourth, her youngest child Peter, was a student. Dorothy taught Spanish and German at Lamar, while Allan referred to himself as a go-getter: "My wife works and I go get her!"

Dorothy had succeeded in launching her four children, who were all off on their own adventures: the twins Patti and Penny had each graduated from Rice University (then Rice Institute), married, and entered the teaching profession. Patti had a son and her master's degree and was teaching reading skills in the Texas School System; Penny had two sons and was working as a legal secretary in Southern California.

Mike and Pete both graduated from the United States Naval Academy (Mike with the Class of 1963, Pete with the Class of 1969). Mike earned a master's in mathematics and was teaching at the U.S. Air Force Academy, and Pete was completing his service commitment.

Dorothy with son Michael and husband Allan at Plebe-Parents' Weekend, September 1959, in Memorial Hall, United States Naval Academy, Annapolis, Maryland.

Dorothy never stopped writing letters. Her 1967 Christmas thank-you letter to the family also reminds us that Dorothy never stopped her adventures.

2307 Gramercy Blvd.
Houston, Texas, 77025.

December 26, 1967

Dear Kathy; Gertrude and Floyd; Hobert and Helen; Babs and Jack;
    Patti and Chuck; Penny and Fred; Mike and Helen; Pete –
    and their respective nephews, nieces, sons, daughters, etc.:

It's the day after Xmas and all through the house not a creature is
stirring, not even a mouse. ADB is snoring peacefully in the other
twin bed, though it is only 2:45 PM. Alexander the Great is doing
the same in Uncle Pete's room, and Uncle Pete – as has been his ill-
luck all these holidays – is forced to do his napping in front of
the television set on the downstairs porch. Patti and Helen and Mike
have gone to spend their Xmas checks at Pier 1, where they sell
imports famous for being unusual and just the type young-marrieds
like to use in their self-decorated homes. Chuck is off, earning the
family bread.

However, ADB has good reason to snore away as he has a bit of flu,
plus the fact that he took Penny, Fred and Andy to the airport this
morning to see them off for Pampa, Texas – about 600 miles from here
– where they will spend all that remains of Xmas with Fred's Mom and
Pop and his grandmother aged 92.

It was a very nice, even though very hectic Xmas. Mike and Helen and
Pete will be with us until January 3, but now we have more or less
put everyone on their own, which they like as they can go to shows,
etc., at their own leisure. Annie came today, which was wonderful
for Pete, as he has at last gotten a room of his own (after
Alexander's naps) as Helen and Mike have been promoted to the guest
room, (appropriated by Penny, Fred, and Andy.)

Andy is not only most advanced for his age physically, but actually
stood up on the Davenport, and pointed to his mother's picture taken
at the swimming pool, about to embark on a swim race, which we have
in large size on the porch. He looked at the picture, looked at his
mother, and being only 15 months old could not say: "Hey, good-
looking, I didn't know you were a former beach beauty", but the
meaning was quite clear.

We loved the Xmas cards and letter from Gertrude's family and the
lovely portrait pictures of Helen and Hobert. We particularly were
fascinated by the lovely silhouette of Helen – how that up-hairdo
emphasizes her patrician features and the slimness of her neck –
throat contour – so rarely seen in our particular age group. We were
quick to recognize the white Blackledge sideburns (which we have
here in our own house) on Hobert's half humorous rather Mona Lisa
expression, but particularly regarded with appropriation the
sterling character and obvious integrity of the Judge himself in
this true likeness. In fact, one would refer to the photographer
rather as an artist, who knew how to capture the inner self of his
subjects. We do thank you both.

-2-

We thank Babs, Jack and Debbie for their Xmas towel, and we were particularly intrigued that they had come upon one of our most guarded secrets (the Cannon towel company, that is) - that old Turkish towels, (they say "terry") make the best dish towels. With a dishwasher, one doesn't need dish towels as often as heretofore, but when one does, the Blackledge ménage has lots of shorties cut down from old holey longies for that purpose - also good to take dishes out of the oven - oven mitts get holes when you aren't looking and always weld your skin to the hot object when you least expect it. We had always wanted a calendar linen towel for our kitchen. However, it is so good-looking, it is quite probable it will end up in the bedroom, where the whole year doesn't look so doleful outlined by little bows and cheerful flowers. The little I LIKE YOU book, says it most succinctly "I guess I don't know why I like you really; I guess I just like you, because I like you." But most of all, we liked talking to you on Xmas day and we were sorry we were busy pressing out the lumps of the gravy and didn't have more time to communicate.

Patti and Chuck hit below the belt by giving the ever-hungry mother some wonderful food items - two boxes of tulips in pots (excuse me, I just had some pot) bonbons from Holland, some Swiss nuts (sort of Nabisco shaped like cashew nuts, etc., with delicious chocolate inside) an old-fashioned plum pudding, and then - as if sorry for all this pro offered temptation - a huge box of rye reducing wafers. Chuck is making (and he brought one completed) a hand-made magazine rack - the holding compartment of the very finest suede, hand-scalloped - the standing compartment of the finest woodmanship. Allan received his favorite shirt present (which Pete immediately tried to make off with and failed) while Pete received one also, his being short sleeved, and the long sleeved being more to his taste that particular date night.

Penny and Fred, besides giving us this trip from California, brought a pair of hand-made candleholders, cut so intricately that one part fits exactly into the other, and burnished in old gold. Unfortunately, we were unable to use them, as we had no candles at the moment to fit, but shall look for them shortly. (However, we did use your Xmas tablecloth, Tiptons, as we have for several Xmases). Pete was happy to have a Charlie Brown Banner, to start his creative effort on his Naval Academy room when he goes back - making it all psychedelic (I don't know whether this is a Second-Class Privilege?) Dragging along Andy with them, was a most appreciated gift, as he weighs a ton, and had no highchair, although Patti kindly erected Alexander's old crib in their room. However, Andy sat most happily on the floor on the latest edition of the Houston Chronicle, eating everything that was good for him, and not good for him, with equal relish. He knew how to tell you he didn't have half enough, too.

Mike and Helen gave Patti and me twin mu-mus (although she called them burnooses), but Kathy, who has just returned from Hawaii, will certainly be able to visualize a mumu, just as we do, rather than a burnoose, which they actually are. Well, I'm off to India, if that's how comfortable the life is down there. When I tell you that Patti and I looked like twin sisters in our twin burnooses, you will understand why I like them particularly. I immediately put mine on, and Xmas day was one comfortable and decorative success after that for me. These too-generous people also gave me a subscription to QUINTO LINGO, which gives articles in five languages. I already had subscribed to it, and it had just run out, and I had decided to be economical this year, and didn't resubscribe, so you can imagine my delight with this gift. Allan thanks you for all his gifts, too, Mike and Helen, but because he is snoring, I am afraid to awaken him to inquire further.

(*note*: *Pages 3-4 are missing, but starting on page 5, Dorothy describes her summer travel*)

p. 5

I went to East Berlin twice and to East Germany once. So I have passed through CHECK-POINT CHARLEY three times. That's the American side; then you go through all the grilling, to get over into East Berlin. You have to confess how [much] money you have with you, down to the last dime. You have to give it to them in all the different currencies; they keep track of it, and each time, when you come back, they check to see if what you spent, and what you have left, tally. (We are now on the Soviet side, where all this checking is done). You cannot carry any East German marks. You might be carrying more money for a possible defectant. They look behind all the seats when you come back, to be sure he hasn't hidden on the bus.

East Berlin looks much poorer than West Berlin, which is hopping. Lots of night clubs, bright lights, and obviously making money. East Berlin seems to have more of the cultural monuments, and they make their money on them by getting the West Berliners to come on over (that is, the tourists in West Berlin)

In East Germany I went to Potsdam where they have this castle of Sanssouci, where the agreement that Roosevelt made with Stalin and Churchill in Yalta, was ratified by Truman, etc. All the Americans on the bus seem to be of the opinion that it was that agreement which was responsible for Berlin being cut in half by THE WALL. I didn't think the wall looked as formidable as I had imagined; however, it was well barbwired, and as any pictures are absolutely forbidden of it, perhaps well mined. I was about 2 1/2 weeks in Berlin, and liked it very much.

From there I went to Czechoslovakia — and had my first taste (besides Checkpoint Charlie) of how they check on you. Had to report our money again, and stay at a hotel under Russian Government Intourist jurisdiction. It was so brandnew, that the (excuse the expression) stink of mothballs was just overpowering. I didn't like the hotel being so far away from stores, little restaurants, etc. as I like to wander about, looking into things. I started wandering right after my arrival, and found a beauty parlor, very well filled, sort of lower middle class; found one lady who could speak German (no one could speak English), and got one of the best haircuts and manicures in my life. They were very very kind to me. So wandered out and was about to enter an old church when in the middle of the street what seemed to be a rubber ankle gave way. This has happened occasionally since I used to play basketball for a good old Ware High School, but this time it was different. Seem to be more of the arch was included; (so I sympathize thoroughly with Helen – how helpless one is without one's ankles). I hobbled back to the hotel, and found out I didn't like the restaurant at all. One had to eat there, it was all paid for, and if you were alone, they made you wait for the 3 or 4 tables they had for alone-people, whereas the people who came in groups (Barney will like to hear this) got excellent service with reserved tables with little flags of all different

p. 6

nations – well, I finally got a seat, but it was like that all the time I was in Czechoslovakia – and I wanted to eat Czech food, which is delicious – but they kept giving everyone the international cuisine – mostly French – to show how very sophisticated it all was, and of course, more expensive than wonderful chicken and *knedlings* (dumplings). So to top it off, the ankle-arch business had gotten to the point, where for the first time in my life, I realized I was incapacitated. At about 10 p.m. I asked them to call me a doctor – they said it would cost 250 korunas – plus his taxi fare – I said I would have to have a doctor that night or I wouldn't be able to finish my trip. So (although medicines and hospitals are free there as in Russia) they sent me a doctor – in fact two, one to chaperone the other. He (they) seemed most proficient, very dignified with long black beards. Put something on the offending member, bound it with elastic bandages, and gave me an address of the clinic – especially for foreigners – in Prague.

So next day, as I was allowed a car with guide, we went there. There was a beautiful lady doctor, who was most kind, took x-rays of the foot, nothing broken, but according to the interpreter "distorted". I'm not sure yet if that was what it meant in English. She bound my leg up in a most psychologically satisfying manner – from bottom of feet to kneecap. With first an inner gauze stocking, then with elastic, then sort of cemented, a semi-cast, I think. I was to keep it on for two weeks. She remarked she knew how Americans liked to have so many baths, but no bath for two weeks. I was delighted with my cast, and immediately started sight seeing but didn't have to do so much because of the cast, as she had told my guide not to let me. One can see just so many churches and chalices studded with diamonds and former kings crowns, and a paperback begins to take on new charm.

Anyhow, no one met me in Berlin (that is, he said he came, and I did hear my name paged, but he left before I got to the paging place). But a lovely university student (girl) met me in Prague. In fact, that was the ONLY PLACE someone actually met me and took me through the maze of customs, and directly to the hotel, etc. as they were supposed to do at each place. One woman alone doesn't mean enough profit, you see, whereas a whole group of tourist is money in the bank. Besides, everything was paid ahead (and probably spent ahead). When you leave Prague, you must turn in all your Czechoslovak currency, and I didn't pick up the receipt at the cashiers' stand, so I almost didn't get to Russia, because they were absolutely adamant about letting me through. I ran back and found it right there where the cashier had put it - outside his cage, where anyone could have gotten it.

When I got to Russia, complete with cast up to knee, NO ONE met me. Even worse, they said in a very gruff tone "Your name isn't even on the list", which is tantamount to saying off with your head. I sat there 3 hours while they phoned all around for a hotel. You can't go to just any hotel - must go to an in-tourist hotel, one presumably comfortably bugged (in more ways than one) by the government. Finally got a "de luxe" room in the Metropol - beautiful old-timey living room with the bed in a sequestered corner, shut off by orange drapes. Found straw on the floor next morning and finally decided it came from said bed's underpinnings. Water dripped all night. Had a beautiful tub, but couldn't use it on account of cast, and when I used the wash basin, it had a special personality - you had to turn it just right, or it would flood the room, and had to get the hot water just in time before it was shut off.

p. 7

I learned in Moscow to go to lunch or dinner at off-hours, as I had the same problem. "No, you can't sit there; it's for the group". Then you get a table, and sit and sit, and finally the waiter comes back from where he has been presumably cooking the entire dinner in the kitchen. The other waiters are standing around having fun mocking the customers, doing little dances, and take drinks out of the little ice box, open up cans of orange juice, etc. and sit down to get that load off their feet. So you don't tip them? Well, you better if you want to be waited on at all next time. They had an orchestra, all dressed up in sort of khaki jumpsuits - the music was good Russian music - but they certainly looked strange in what had evidently been a beautiful ball room during the days of the Czar.

Went to enough museums - but as there are about 40 in Leningrad, and about 50 in Moscow - couldn't make them all. Most interesting was the subway. For a guide I had a very nice young University student - told me his father was killed in World War II, and I reminded him we were friends then - he seemed to know. But the taxi driver was most astonished. This nice young student took me and my casted leg onto the subway; we got off at various stations, and each one was a separate art gallery, beautiful chandeliers, unusual murals, and always the sculpture of Lenin in some sort of new pose.

Took me to visit Lenin's Mausoleum, a beautiful monument of red granite (or marble). The foreigners were allowed access to the tomb of their hero before 11:30; from then on, until the shutting down time, streams of Russians from out of town on vacation - some with flowers – waited patiently their turn. They were broken-hearted when it was 4:30 and they weren't allowed inside that day… I must add that the subways had escalators so very long, that it was like climbing Mount Everest. I was really very surprised as I had never been on escalators like that, and didn't expect them in Russia.   I was right across from the Bolshoi Theatre, but they were giving their ballet at Canada's Expo this summer. However, I still almost got to see it; when I arrived at Kennedy airport, we were obliged to circle 2 1/2 hours above the city because of the fog. Then we got word we had to go to Canada, to get refueled (they didn't say that but it was easy to guess, one couldn't keep going around in circles forever). After about 4 hours in Canada, and we were kept cooped up in a little room, finally just made my flight back to Houston, much to my delight.

Oh, yes, I almost forgot Finland. Leningrad, the city of the Hermitage museum, and lots of others, including the Museum of Atheism – very interesting, somewhat depressing – was formerly St. Petersburg. My girl guide (also a university student), said the Czar moved to Moscow because of the danger from enemies just across the Bay. I went to Helsinki next, and while it was very expensive, it was such a pleasure to feel so free once more. Nobody made me write down that I had two rings on my fingers of platinum, etc., etc. They accepted tips with great and open pleasure, instead of waiting until the head man was outside, and then sticking out THE HAND. The Finns were very nice indeed, if somewhat money-minded. And aren't we all?

Love and a very merry Xmas from us-all to you-all.

Allan and Dorothy and Pete.

The Houston Blackledges

p. 8

That last paragraph on p. 4, which was to contain comment on my Russian trip, seems to have extended to a brown P.S. on page 8 – anyhow, I think it would be a shame not to show here how very nice people are all the world over (that is, the nice ones). When I was wandering in Prague, (this is after I had my cast on) I found a purse store. Now, in the Iron Curtain countries, luxury items are hard to find, so I went in there as I now saw one in the window (Penny has it), complete with shoulder strap, nice to have when lugging a 30 pound Andy around.

I was trying to decide between the one I purchased, and another, and a very nice looking woman with an 11 year old daughter, said: "May I help you", in sort of high school English, and together we compared the bags, etc.

I was beginning to have a cold, so I asked her where I could buy some tissues. She told me about a drug store not far away, and noticing my cast, gave me a certain amount of sympathy which I enjoyed immensely (it is nice to be an ambulant sick person, *nicht währ?*).   She left the store and I shortly afterwards to find my drugstore. As I sauntered up the street (very badly paved, half brick, half cobble stones, half broken cement), I now saw this same woman running toward me, all out of breath. She thrust a package in my hand, and said something about my injured leg. I saw that she had given me 4 large packages of lovely paper handkerchiefs, and as I started to fumble for my purse to pay for these wonderfully useful items, she said "No, No "- and ran lickety-split away - even crossing to the other side, so I couldn't possibly catch up with her. So, of course, I have never found her name, and can only thank her this way, by saying the Czechoslovakian people are certainly very nice.

I also had a good sampling of their young on the Czechoslovakian plane to Moscow - it was just my luck to have about 30 girl-scout type (but under Iron Curtain, called Young Pioneers, I believe), girls board the small plane with me, and in just my luck to have the one sitting next to me be plane sick. However, they were very nice little girls, and were on their way to the Russian "Young Pioneer" camp at Yalta, I believe, on the shores of the Black Sea. Occupying the other seat, on my right, was a bearded blonde artist-looking man who agreed very enthusiastically that the Czechoslovakian young ladies were much better looking than the Russian stewardesses (maybe I was on Aeroflot by this time, a Russian line). I could see that naturally the Czechoslovaks didn't love the Russians. And when I was [in] Finland, what did I see but a big Russian Destroyer in the harbor, on a "friendly visit." The Finns said many uncomplimentary things about the Russians when they found that I was an American.

However, the Russians too had their nice people, like this fine young brain-washed student from the University who showed me around Moscow. "Why is President Johnson killing all the poor Vietnam people who never did him any harm?" and referred to the Germans as socialists with a great deal of contempt. And in Leningrad, after visiting that Museum of Religion and Atheism, when I remarked to my very nice, rosy-cheeked girl guide from the University that now I knew the Russians were religious, although they were taught there was no God in the school - that they worshiped God in the form of Lenin, that's all, as he was their ideal of a generous man who had tried to help the Russian people. She was quite shocked that I should think the Russians should have some sort of belief in a Supreme Being, even though he might be Lenin - who, by the way, looked most life-like with his wax covered face beautifully tinted, and with a very Jesus-like smile on his face.

Enough for now, except to say you should have tasted Penny's confetti bread.

Dorothy and Allan were returning from a trip to Mexico in July 1971, and were relaxing in the hotel bar in Coronado, CA when Dorothy said, "Allan, I feel dizzy. I think we should go in to dinner now." Then Dorothy's head fell onto Allan's shoulder. He thought she was just being coy – so like her. But just that quickly, she was gone.

That Christmas following Dorothy's death was spent at Farrish Memorial Retreat at the Air Force Academy in Colorado Springs. Many members of the Blackledge family gathered, seeking solace and connection, a large family of all ages. During dinner, as Allan shared his life without Dorothy, his voice broke with emotion. In the ensuing quiet, their one-year-old grandson, Douglas, burst into laughter, a sound that eased the grief and restored the family's spirit. Life goes on.

Dorothy never spoke to any of her children about her life prior to marriage, nothing about her eight years in the U.S. Foreign Service. Yet she kept the letters. Her daughter Penn opined: "I think that Mother had the ability/understanding to live in the *now* and not in the past. I also think she did not want to brag about her past because she wanted to promote/ solidify her current married state and future with her husband. Mother's job, in her mind, at this married stage in her life, was to continually promote her husband."

Dorothy's life, a tapestry woven with threads of quiet determination amid unexpected turns, ultimately revealed a woman of remarkable resilience and depth. Her years in the Foreign Service during the Depression, a time of both personal and global hardship, instilled in her a sense of duty and a keen understanding of the world beyond her small-town beginnings. Those experiences, though seemingly just a stepping stone to a different life, shaped the woman she would become.

Marriage to her Navy lieutenant opened a new chapter, one filled with the joys and challenges of raising five children. It was a role she embraced wholeheartedly, pouring her energy and intelligence into nurturing their growth and development. Yet, even amidst the demands of motherhood, the flame of intellectual curiosity continued to flicker within her.

And so, with her children grown, Dorothy embarked on a journey that had been deferred but never forgotten. She pursued her college degree, a testament to her belief in lifelong learning and the power of personal growth. Her passion for languages, certainly sparked by her time abroad, found its outlet in teaching, where she shared her love of French and Spanish with generations of high school students.

Dorothy's life wasn't defined by a single path, but rather by the grace with which she navigated its various turns. From the steno pool in Washington to the classrooms of a high school, from the responsibilities of motherhood to the pursuit of higher education, she embraced each phase with quiet strength and an unwavering spirit. Her story as captured in her own letters is a reminder that fulfillment can be found not just in grand achievements, but in the courage to pursue one's dreams, no matter the season of life.

The Players

You can't tell the players without a scorecard. Every life of adventure involves many individuals, a few famous, most of anonymity; most in passing, some affecting history. Dorothy had several famous and near famous individuals come through her office and her life.

George S. Messersmith (1883 –1960): Dorothy's boss during his tenure as US Consul General in Buenos Aires, Argentina, from 1928 to 1930. In his later career, Messersmith was a United States ambassador to Austria, Cuba, Mexico, and Argentina. Messersmith also served as head of the consulate in Germany from 1930 to 1934, during the rise of the Nazi Party. As Dorothy relates in her letters, in 1930, Messersmith left his position in Argentina to accept the same position in Berlin and suggested Dorothy could transfer as well, thus keep her job.

Messersmith received significant notoriety in that position in late 1932 due to his controversial decision to issue a visa to **Albert Einstein** to travel to the United States. Much later when he returned to Argentina as Ambassador, he appeared on the cover of *Time Magazine* (Dec 2, 1946).

Messersmith in hindsight was most prescient in his reports back from Berlin in 1933. As America's consul general in Berlin in 1933, Messersmith wrote a dispatch to the State Department that dramatically contravened the popular view that Hitler had no consensus among the German people and would not remain in power:

> "I wish it were really possible to make our people at home understand how definitely this martial spirit is being developed in Germany. If this government remains in power for another year, and it carries on in the measure in this direction, it will go far toward making Germany a danger to world peace for years to come. With few exceptions, the men who are running the government are of a mentality that you and I cannot understand. Some of them are psychopathic cases and would ordinarily be receiving treatment somewhere."

Will Rogers (1879-1935): American vaudeville performer, actor, and humorous social commentator. He was born as a citizen of the Cherokee Nation, in the Indian Territory (now part of Oklahoma). By the mid-1930s, Rogers was hugely popular in the United States for his leading political wit and was the highest paid of Hollywood film stars. As an entertainer and humorist, he traveled around the world three times, made 71 films (50 silent films and 21 "talkies"), and wrote more than 4,000 nationally syndicated newspaper columns. Rogers traveled to Asia to perform in 1931, and it was on this trip that he came through Dorothy's office at the American Consulate in Tokyo. He died in 1935 with aviator Wiley Post when their small airplane crashed in northern Alaska.

Pangborn and Herndon: Clyde Pangborn and Hugh Herndon, Jr., were the two pilots who made the first non-stop flight across the Pacific Ocean. Their departure point of Misawa is some 700 miles north of Tokyo. The two had been unjustly held on unfounded suspicion of spying. Just a week after they asked Dorothy to join them for dinner in Tokyo, they finally received their permission from the Japanese government and departed in their 1931 Bellanca aircraft *Miss Veedol* from Misawa, Japan, on October 4, 1931. They landed in the hills near the present-day

Replica of *Miss Veedol* in the Misawa Aviation & Science Museum, Aomori, Japan.

town of East Wenatchee in Douglas County, Washington, some 41 hours later. The flight won the pair the 1931 Harmon Trophy in recognition of the greatest achievement in flight for that year. A 14-ft high basalt column memorial to them exists at that Washington location today. The two fliers previously had gained some notoriety as aviators and barnstormers who performed aerial stunts as a pilot/co-pilot team in the 1920s for the Gates Flying Circus.

Grandson of the Kaiser: More research is required to determine the grandson who walked into Dorothy's Buenos Aires office in early November 1930. Kaiser Wilhelm II had seven children, and a large number of grandchildren. His grandmother, Queen Victoria, had some 42 grandchildren, of which the Kaiser was the eldest.

From Dorothy's description, we only know this grandson was "very tall skinny guy and very plain." One possibility would be a grandson who was about the same age as Dorothy, as he also was born in 1907: **Prince Louis Ferdinand of Prussia** was the second son of Germany's Crown Prince Wilhelm. He travelled extensively and settled for some time in Detroit, where he befriended Henry Ford and became acquainted with Franklin D.

Prince Louis Ferdinand c. 1930

Roosevelt, among others. He held a great interest in engineering and worked as a mechanic for the Ford Motor Co. in Detroit during the 1930s. He later became first in the line of succession and head of the Hohenzollern family even though the German throne no longer existed.

Charles Lindbergh (1902-1974): Just five years older than Dorothy, Lindbergh had become a national hero on May 20-21, 1927, when he made the first nonstop flight from New York City to Paris, a distance of 3,600 miles, flying alone for 33.5 hours. The first time he ever sat in an airplane was 1922, just five years earlier. And four years later, Charles was working with Pan-American Airlines. In 1931, the company provided him with yet another chance to make history. He and wife Anne would attempt to chart a commercial air route from New York to Tokyo. All they'd have to do is fly 7,000 miles and end up at Ueno station. Their plane would be a black-and-red Lockheed Sirius, cutting edge at the time and custom-made for "Lucky Lindy"—a 575-horsepower, dual-controlled tandem cockpit, with the ability to land on water via pontoons.

Their trip, dubbed "the Great Circle route," began on July 27, 1931, the couple leaving behind their 13-month-old son, Charles Jr. At this stage in their life together, the Lindberghs seemed invincible to the general public, but three months after returning from the trip, Charles Jr. was kidnapped—pulled from his crib on the night of March 1, 1932.

But that was the horrific future. They almost didn't survive Japan. For this trip, their first encounter with Japan began on the "harborless," "uninhabited" and "volcanic" Ketoy Island. Back in 1931, Japan had control over the then-called Chishima (now the Russian-controlled Kuril) Islands, and as Charles and Anne flew toward the city of Nemuro on the eastern side of Hokkaido, they hit the remnants of a typhoon. Weather in this area during August was particularly difficult for flying. As Anne noted while checking her weather forecast notes, the Chishima islands tended to have heavy fog for 28 of 30 days.

Charles was able to land on the water and drop anchor close to the uninhabited island, but it was a struggle the whole way down: "My young wife and I lay braced against the fuselage walls while waves broke across our pontoons and wind howled through the cowlings," he wrote in his *Autobiography*. It should be noted that they were sleeping inside their luggage compartment, on top of their parachute packs and oar paddles, cans of baked beans and tomatoes around them.

Fortunately for Charles and Anne, the Japanese had been tracking their plane, and sent a ship, the *Shinshiru Maru*, to monitor their movement. The sailors aboard the ship braved the storm and managed to alert the couple by tapping an oar against the side of the plane. The ship pulled the Sirius to a safer location, and they handed Charles a formal message in an envelope, rain pouring and wind howling: "The Japanese people eagerly welcome you to Japan and await your safe arrival."

On Aug. 25, after 28 days and 7,132 miles, the Lindberghs landed their plane on Kasumigaura Bay, near the Kasumigaura Naval Airport. There they were greeted by thousands of Japanese residents waving flags of both Japan and America. Soon after, they boarded a train that took 90 minutes to reach Ueno station.

Charles and Anne remained in Tokyo from Aug. 26 to Sept. 13, traveling by car to Kyoto and Nara to take in the sights. The two had been together constantly throughout the trip, so this was a chance for each of them to follow what they desired. Charles, who'd perhaps rather continue exploring the world with Anne in the Sirius, instead attended to several diplomatic duties, since his reputation at the time was not just an employee of Pan-American Airlines but also an unofficial symbol of peace in the eyes of both Japan and America. This was when Dorothy attended the diplomatic dinner for Lindbergh.

Baseball Players: Some of The Players were actual players. Dorothy casually refers to 'the baseball players' in her 1931 letter to Kathie. In 1931, baseball players traveled to Japan as part of a tour that some say was the best baseball team to visit the country at the time. The tour featured Herb Hunter, who was considered "Baseball's Ambassador to Japan" by 1931. An oversized presentation photograph of the team on the deck of the ocean liner Tatsuta Maru is available on Christie's and is depicted below.

Baseball teams had previously toured Japan in 1908, 1913, 1920, and 1922, but the players on those tours had played against Japanese amateur or college teams.

From Christie's: Original oversized presentation photograph of members the 1931 Tour of Japan baseball team on the deck of the ocean liner *Tatsuta Maru* (which transported the team to Japan). Includes eighteen members of the team including Lou Gehrig, Frankie Frisch, Lefty Grove, Mickey Cochrane, Al Simmons, George Kelly, Lefty O'Doul and Rabbit Maranville.

We know the players were in Kobe, Japan on 22 November of 1931 from this photo snippet, taken at the entrance to the Oriental Hotel which was the same hotel at which the All-Stars stayed during their 1922-23 visit to Kobe. Lou Gehrig (center, back) is one of several well-

known players, but umpire "Beans" Reardon (left, front) and sportswriter Fred Lieb (two rows up from Beans) were celebrities in their own right.

Bank of Boston Building: As shown in the brochure she sent her Aunt Kathie, Dorothy's office in Buenos Aires was on the 2nd floor of the Bank of Boston Building on Florida Street, whereas her boss Mr. Allen was on the 1st floor. The emblematic Bank of Boston Building, facing Plazoleta Ciriaco Ortiz, and now Standard Bank, is a 1924 neocolonial structure with a gothic touch. It's noted for its huge 17-meter arched Plateresque-style doorway, meticulously carved from limestone.

The architects of the Bank of Boston were two notable Argentine immigrants, Englishman Paul Bell Chambers (1868-1930) and American Newbery Thomas who worked together on many other Buenos Aires' buildings including Harrods Buenos Aires. Due to the strict municipal design codes of the Diagonal Norte area, the architects had to submit several plans during a two-year period before being approved by the city government.

As with most of the buildings remaining from Argentina's golden era, no expense was spared in its construction. The skeleton of the building was built with 1,650 tons of steel shipped from the United States. The large doorway was made in England with four tons of bronze. Inside are huge columns, green Uruguayan porphyry detailing and marble-lined walls. The teller windows are framed with bronze and the high ornate ceiling is covered in a gold-colored casing.

Elinor Glyn (1864-1940): Dorothy was a bit star-struck at a party in Habana to shake hands with Elinor Glyn. Glyn was a British novelist and scriptwriter who specialized in romantic fiction, which was considered scandalous for its time, although her works are relatively tame by modern standards. In the 1920s, readers were all about her book *It*. Linguistics professor D.W. Maurer explains it: "*It* translated *sex appeal*, taboo at first but soon pounded into the cultural matrix by Hollywood." Pre-*It*, Maurer notes, Americans didn't have socially approved words with which to describe pregnancy or menstruation, let alone sex.

Jascha Heifetz (1901-1987): Jascha Heifetz was a Russian-American violinist, widely regarded as one of the greatest violinists of all time. Born in Vilnius, he was soon recognized as a child prodigy and was trained in the Russian classical violin style in St. Petersburg. Dorothy attended a Heifetz concert in Tokyo in 1932.

Fujiya Hotel, Mianoshita: *(at left)* Dorothy and Eleanor Shields sitting proudly in front of the Hotel in 1931; *(below)* the popular hotel as it appears today.

Calvin Coolidge (1872-1933): The 30th President of the United States (1923-1929), Coolidge and Dorothy intersected twice: in Habana where Dorothy got off work to watch the parade for Coolidge who had arrived in his 'fleet of ships' to kick off the Sixth Pan-American Conference (the only international trip Coolidge made during his six years as president), and in Tokyo where time off Consulate work was granted to honor Coolidge's death, January 5, 1933.

The boy friends: Just the ones that warranted named descriptive mention in Dorothy's letters:

Herbert Richer: (Habana) "a nice English boy here who teaches English in the University of Havana. He is 27, speaks Russian, German, French and Spanish like a native, has a college degree and also has a little importing business. He seems to like me very much and is a perfect gentleman. He is blond, very tall and nice looking. On my birthday he sent me eighteen <u>dozen</u> roses."

Mark Harris: (Buenos Aires) "That American boy, Mark Harris, has fallen head over heels in love with me. He isn't good looking but very nice. He couldn't be any nicer to me and has a wonderful future as he expects to go into business (exporting), himself before many years."

Bill Denker (1899-1967): (Buenos Aires – Dorothy's only fiancée) "Nice American chap. He is an assistant manager in the Dupont company here and from Boston. He has spent three years in Turkey and seven years in Europe in general, a graduate of Harvard, but not a bit conceited. He is 30 years old, has a moustache, tall but not good looking but very nice." William A. Denker remained overseas most of his career with Dupont and died in Mexico City, 1967.

Dr. Vance Murray (1887-1959): Dr. Murray was assigned to the Consulate at Buenos Aires and thus was the doctor who visited Dorothy with her ailments and her appendicitis after the German doctor had prescribed loading her up with cream. Dr Murray was one of the Consulate employees who made the ill-fated 1930 *Monte Cervantes* cruise, and appears with Dorothy in the Wikimedia Commons photo as they await their rescue ship in Ushuaia. They maintained corresponddence. In the Tokio letter of 1931, Dorothy mentions that Dr. Murray is no longer with his girlfriend; however, he finally married Muriel, some 18 years younger, and went on to travel extensively throughout a distinguished career in the US Public Health Service. Dr. Murray is buried in the National Cemetery in Santa Rosa, CA.

Samuel Walter Washington Jr. (1901-1978): Walter Washington was a Vice-Consul at Buenos Aires from 1927 through 1929, and took Dorothy boating on the Tigre River, as she reported to the Ware River News as of February 14, 1929. Walter was also to be married at the Tokyo Consulate, but in September 1933, months prior to Dorothy marrying Allan. Walter and his wife Simone Cecile Fleisher had one son, John Augustine, who was born in Istanbul, Turkey, in 1936 during Walter's posting there as a full US Consul.

Gen. Frank Ross McCoy (1874-1954): Dorothy worked as a private secretary for Gen. McCoy in Japan prior to his travel to China, which almost certainly accounted for her call to join the Lytton Commission in Peiping.

Burton Crane Jr. (1901-1963): Dorothy received an invitation from Mrs. Lewis Burton Crane Jr. for Wednesday, April 12, 1933 to a party to say farewell to two departing colleagues. The Cranes were stalwart American hosts in Tokyo; Consulate members came and went, but the Cranes had been there since 1924, and the couple remained there until 1936, when Burton moved to become a journalist for the New York Times.

The friends: Two that are mentioned frequently in Dorothy's letters.

Bee Comeau (1905-1993): Bee was one of Dorothy's good friends; they had met in Washington D.C. and became roommates and good friends, as both were from Massachusetts. Bee and Dorothy would exchange letters and gifts during Dorothy's Buenos Aires post. Bee had her own adventures as she was one of 15 women chosen to work on the 1930 London Naval Conference that was held from January 21 to April 22, 1930. Eventually, Bee was posted to Tokyo for six years, probably after hearing all the good things that Dorothy said about it, and in a way, taking Dorothy's place after Allan and Dorothy left in May 1934. However, Bee's adventures took a turn. She was stationed in Tokyo in December 1941 when the Japanese took the US consulate workers into custody after the attack on Pearl Harbor. All Allied diplomats in Japanese territory, including the US ambassador, Joseph Grew, were interned. The embassy personnel were held until June 1942, when they were sent to Portuguese East Africa for repatriation. At age 36, Bee eventually was brought back on the *M.S. Gripsholm*. That story is worth learning about. Bee lived for a while after her return with her father in Lexington, MA. She did marry late in life and moved with her husband Frederick H. Spengler to Manila, P.I.

Albenia Dorothy Elliott (1907-1936): Albenia was a Ware High School classmate and one of Dorothy's good friends; they were assistant editors on their school yearbook. Recall Dorothy went to Northampton Commercial College; Albenia went to the Commercial College in Boston and later married John Edmund Campbell. She moved to Chicago with him, and had at least four children. Albenia died quite early, at age 36 in Chicago, apparently shortly after the birth of her fourth child. Albenia's body was brought back to Ware by her parents who held a memorial service at the house and had her buried in Ware. John Edmund Campbell remarried.

Afterword

Dorothy's story has been captured and made available. But how did this book become a book? How did Dorothy's letters come into my hands, and how have I endeavored to safekeep them for future researcher? This Afterword addresses those questions, and provides some rules of engagement that the reader may have preferred to know up front.

Dorothy was a medal-winning typist but not perfect, especially when freestyling letters to family vice formal documents for the Consul General to sign. I realize the average reader is not interested in font details and compiler decisions. I credit my son David with providing a mantra to describe the clarity of my purpose, that I was working to capture family history, not recreate a work of art. The reader might want to know that Dorothy's typos were, by and large, left in the transcriptions to provide some ambience of authenticity. Thus, the town of Ushuaia remains spelled as Dorothy typed the story, as Ushuai. Minor typos like *washington* stay *washington*. Some missing words stay missing, some appear. In some cases, readability required correction, and thus like magic, trin became train. Readability, not art.

Dorothy's letters [to and from] found in the book have been painstakingly transcribed from the originals, placed chronologically, indented left and right, and reproduced using font Courier New 11 pt [bold] to contrast with the compiler's text and comments delivered in Times New Roman 12 point. Courier New font is so lightly printed – here is an example – that I felt the bold was needed: **Here is the bold Courier New, 11 pt.** Courier New is not as crude (or sometimes as stylish) as the Courier of those early 20th Century typewriters, but sufficiently close to lend a certain look of authenticity to the transcriptions – and bold since most of Dorothy's keystrokes are not lightly printed but hammered onto the State stationery with finality.

The curious reader might like to know how this book came into being. How indeed. Every day, I shake my head when I realize what a strong personality Dorothy had and maintained throughout her Life. As solid evidence, consider the path of the letters that form the basis for this book. The path from her Underwood typewriter to this book, and eventually, a permanent repository. Easily argued that Dorothy made it all possible.

To me, the role of primary driver for this book belongs to Dorothy Marita Forrant who created, typed, and somehow maintained and sequestered copies (or originals) of her own correspondence, especially when she was on her own at three foreign service posts during the 1926-1934 period. I can only guess at the chain of events that placed the set of 80 typed letters plus photos and archival objects into my hands, specifically into the Uncle Hobert Closet for Genealogy as maintained (quite informally) at 14321 Stalgren Ct NE, Albuquerque NM. Several times Dorothy makes a typed plea to Kathie to place the letters in a box at the Forrant family's house on Eddy St in Ware. We infer that the plea, as surely as specific requests for items to be purchased for Dorothy and sent through pouch mail (yes, Dorothy, keep it under five pounds!) was carried out by Kathie and Motherkat.

How did these letters come into *my* possession? It's another mystery. My sister Penn (Penelope Sue Blackledge Woods) thought I had acquired them, whereas I felt strongly that Penn must have brought them back as part of her 'spoils' during the time the five siblings gathered in Houston forty years ago at the A-11 condo of Dorothy's only spouse, our father Allan Douglas Blackledge. That activity took place in Houston Texas during Christmas break 1982 following Dad's unexpected death in Plano, TX earlier that month. The condo had been reluctantly purchased by Dad – he didn't want to own another property, as he felt that would complicate conditions for his children, and thus wanted only to rent. We convinced him: "the mortgage payment is equivalent to the rent, you are happy in the Condo, you don't want to move, so go ahead and stay with it." However, following the sale by Dad of 'the ancestral home' of 2307 Gramercy Blvd and Dad's death, Dad's trust lawyers, Sivley et al of Houston, were placing the condo on the market. Everything must go.

During those family gathering days, we siblings spent considerable time going through Dad's numerous, at times overwhelming, personal items, papers, artifacts – all that he had brought to the condo from 'the ancestral home' at 2307 Gramercy Blvd a few years prior, and that had somehow survived his contract with an estate sale/antique dealer who took so many special items, e.g., the little three-inch plastic Japanese people that had lived in our painted green heavy wooden bookcase. Such figurines, we were told by Mother/Dorothy, were used in doctor's offices in Japan, when kimono-clad women, too shy to talk about their ailments, would just point to a location on a figurine to communicate their personal pain or problem.

As we went through the condo, we had some discussion as to who wanted what – if multiple siblings wanted the same item, it was quickly resolved by mutual consent. I recall sitting on the floor, going through multiple boxes and items; after a long time, we began to burn out a bit with all the detritus and when someone would hold up something and say, "Does anyone want this?", the chorus would ring out, "*Throw it in the dumper!*" Sadly, that item was then promptly consigned to the garbage bin. Another story lost forever, perhaps.

Regardless, many items survived as treasures and were thus dispersed and taken back to the individual siblings' homes. I took some items of furniture, plus some of Dad's framed photos and documents (to include his Naval Academy diploma), and (after calling Helen) some Pyrex quart measuring pitchers (used by Dad to hold copious amounts of ice cream to be devoured in front of the TV). My brother Pete took Dad's USNA 1920 class ring and the Samurai Sword. Sister Patti took a family pocket watch and Dorothy's old typewriter. Penn took mother's little desk with all of mother's files, to include (I argue) her typed letters on American Consulate stationary. Babs took the eight-bell Seth Thomas Navy clock that would chime the quarter-hour

throughout our childhood, a clock that Allan would faithfully wind with its big brass key each Sunday evening.

One of the items that I thought had disappeared into the craw and almost certainly went with the antique dealer that was invited to have his way with the treasures of Gramercy Blvd was a WWI Japanese rifle with bayonet. To my relief, my brother Pete has that artifact and will pass it along to one of our nephews, along with a Samurai sword Dad received in September 1945 from RADM W.K. Harrill, Commander of the Marshall Gilberts Area. Pete's own tribute to our mother, featuring some of his trademark accolades and embellished story-telling was published in his 36-page program that accompanied a racing shell christening at the US Naval Academy, October 2019. An image from the program is on the next page.

From Pete, a specific memory: "I clearly recall Babs suggesting that we melt down Dad's USNA ring for the gold, to which I immediately and emotionally reacted "*No!!!!!!*" That ring meant so much to Dad and was such an iconic artifact; I strongly felt that "melting it down for the gold" would be terribly disrespectful of our father's memory and legacy. I currently have and revere that ring. Also, I have willed Dad's Navy sword to my nephew Alexander Price per his specific request to me."

Fortunately, Pete also acquired the NOPI tongue-in-cheek recognition of Dad's retirement as Commander, featuring a sultry lamppost corner girl and her come-on line, *"Hi ya, **Sailor**!"* Oh, wouldn't that make a great cover of yet another book!

Where are Dorothy's letters and artifacts today? A permanent collection was desired — I certainly did not want them forgotten in another closet, or worse, end up in a yard sale. Interest was expressed by two or three places, and it became a decision based on what might help future researchers.

The curator of the National Museum of American Diplomacy (https://diplomacy.state.gov/) in Washington, D.C. clarified that their museum is into physical displays vice providing a permanent repository of papers and reports available to researchers. Following the suggestion of Heidi Reed, I negotiated a Deed of Gift agreement with Massachusetts Historical Society (https://www.masshist.org/). I was delighted with the reaction of Interim President Brenda Lawson: "[T]hank you for bringing this to our attention. And a shipwreck?! Wow. It sounds very exciting! The MHS would absolutely be interested in adding these materials to our collection." Curator Stephanie Call cautioned me that the process of indexing the collection to prepare it for researchers would consume several months.

Lt. Blackledge's report to include the marked navigation chart showing the results of the Japanese raid on Woosung Fort have been accepted by the U.S. Naval Academy Museum.

Finally, the Young Men's Library Association (https://warelibrary.org/) of Ware, Massachusetts will house "Dorothy's Library," hardcover books for her self-education and inscribed from her time in Japan. Full circle: Dorothy started out from Ware, and her artifacts now return to Ware and Massachusetts. Dorothy would be pleased – everything in its place.

IN TRIBUTE TO "THE ALPHA-DOT" DOROTHY FORRANT BLACKLEDGE

References / Sources: "Blackledges In America" (First & Second Editions), Multiple News Articles, Historical Artifacts, Personal Photographs & Papers of Dorothy Forrant Blackledge, Personal Conversations Between Allan Douglas Blackledge and Peter Douglas Blackledge.

Dorothy "Dot" Forrant was born in 1907 in Salem, Massachusetts. At Ware High School (WHS), she excelled both academically and athletically, lettering in Varsity Basketball while also playing Tennis and Swimming, winning laurels in Theater productions, and being Assistant Editor of the WHS yearbook. After graduating from Northampton Commercial College, Dot joined the State Department so she could see the world — becoming one of the few women engaged in the U.S. Foreign Service at that time. Over the next years, she traveled widely during her postings and assignments in Havana, Buenos Aires, Valparaiso, Santiago, Tokyo, and Peiping — with her adventures including: horseback riding in Tokyo; tennis in Buenos Aires; skiing at Akakura and Ivahara; rowing for the Yokohama Boat Club; hiking through Kamakura; participating in costume balls in La Paz, Bolivia; crossing the Oshima Desert on a camel; ice skating at Mikko; "spar fighting" (pillow fighting on a greased pole above a water-filled ship's well, to the exhortations of fellow ship on-lookers) & experiencing "Neptune's Court" as she crossed the Equator in S.S. Southern Cross; dining with Congressmen, expat millionaires, Countesses and the Consul General; being escorted to her home by a U.S. armed guard force through rioters and machine gun fire during the Argentine Revolution; surviving earthquakes and typhoons, and being adrift for hours in a lifeboat after her ship Monte Cervantes sank in the Straits of Magellan (and watching the Cervantes' captain go down with his ship) during her vacation cruise to see the glaciers and snow-covered mountains of Ushaui (a southernmost city in the world), and then being marooned on a convict/prison island for weeks until Cervantes' sister ship could be sent for rescue.

During this time, working directly for Secretary Of State Kellogg, she was selected to be a junior diplomat as part of President Calvin Coolidge's team for his historic trip to Cuba aboard the battleship Texas, escorted by a dozen other naval vessels, to attend the Pan American Conference. While posted in Buenos Aires, she was personally asked by the Consul General to be part of his transcontinental train trip over the Andes to Chile for inspections of the American Embassy in Santiago & the Consulate General in Valparaiso. While stationed in Tokyo, Japan, in 1931, she was personally invited by the American Ambassador to attend a special reception honoring the 1927 "Spirit Of St. Louis" first solo non-stop transatlantic pilot Charles Lindbergh. During this period, she also served on the historic commission of the League of Nations in Peiping, China, which was investigating the Japanese and Chinese differences in Shanghai and Manchuria.

In 1931, while on a trans-Pacific liner to Japan, she met Naval officer Allan Douglas Blackledge who was en route to his ship in the China Sea. He was instantly smitten, pursuing her across the Orient, filling her rooms with hundreds of roses, until they were married by the Vice Consul in the American Consulate, Tokyo, Japan, in 1934, with their wedding reception hosted by the American Consul General in his home.

Over the next 2 decades, Dot raised 5 children—mostly on her own due to Allan's extensive sea duties, particularly during World War II. When her fifth child, Peter, entered elementary school, she went back to school—distinguishing herself in graduate work in Paris at the Sorbonne, earning her Bachelor Of Arts degree and graduating Summa Cum Laude in Romance Languages at University of Houston, and earning a scholarship to Rice University. At Rice, she earned her Master Of Arts degree and continued her scholarship into Rice's Ph.D. program. A fluent speaker in Spanish, French, and German, she made frequent trips to Spain, Mexico, and France to perfect her language skills. Despite experiencing her first heart attack at age 52, she went on to teach French, Spanish, and German at Hartman Junior High School and Lamar Senior High School in Houston, Texas, until dying instantly of her second heart attack within months of her retirement, at age 64.

Well done, Mom. You are now with the Angels, receiving a well-deserved rest. They are fortunate to have their "Dot" back in Heaven again, as we were so very fortunate to have you here on Earth. --- With love & admiration from your youngest child, Peter

26

Acknowledgements

The primary Acknowledgement for this book goes to the intrepid and talented **Dorothy Marita Forrant** who originated and somehow maintained and sequestered copies (or originals) of her own correspondence, especially when she was 'on her own' at three foreign service posts during the 1926-1934 period, in such a way that they were maintained as a collection into the 21st century.

Closely followed is an acknowledgement for **Celia Catherine Forrant Crotty**, the Aunt Kathie who was the recipient of 90% of all of Dorothy's letters in this book; thus, Aunt Kathy must have been instrumental in saving them. In the letters, we see Aunt Kathy as the sounding board and the shoulder to emote upon for Dorothy throughout her Foreign Service career, and a bit past. I must also acknowledge Dorothy's mother **May/Mary**. We never see a letter from these two sisters but we could easily reconstruct one from Dorothy's reactions.

As discussed in the Afterword, my sister **Penn** somehow gathered up and preserved all the typed letters and artifacts when all of us siblings went through my father's things in his condo in Houston following his death in December 1982. I shudder to think how easily the collection could have been left behind, discarded in the detritus of my father's closets or tossed 'into the dumper' as we consigned so many family items.

Naïvely, I thought this ***Letters from Dorothy*** project was going to be a lone wolf project, mine to mess up or glory in. However, as I was reminded again and again, any non-fiction book requires a team to produce. This perhaps more than most, as we instituted an assembly line.

The assembly line for transcribing Dorothy's letters into what would become this book consisted of the following: **Lea Elena** at the Stalgren Lenovo computer, scanning the letters one page at a time via the Brother printer/scanner. Lea would save the result in a PDF file using a file naming convention of yyyymmddLtr[twocharacterOriginator]2[two-character-Recipient]-OriginatingLocation.pdf and then request the software OCR (optical character recognition) translation into a .rtf (Rich Text Format) file and place the 'captured' letter into a brown manila envelope marked "Scanned!". **Cee Blackledge** would operate the HP laptop physically close enough to select a specific original letter which she would hand to me. I in turn would read the letter out loud quite rapidly as Cee would type the corrected text into a Word document, as OCR was never more than 80% accurate, and sometimes (on old faint print) 0%.

In transcribing Dorothy's letters, Cee and I had a few discussions as we captured each of the letters – do we correct obvious typos or put in a *[sic]* and keep the original? My primary editor Carla felt that authenticity should prevail, typos should remain, and the use of *[sic]* should be rare. My son **David** suggested we needed to decide if we're doing a work of art or a work of history as it relates to the 'accuracy' of the transcription. That was the decision template we needed, an excellent thought exercise. In general, we were capturing the history, but at times we wanted to 'preserve' a typo that added to the flavor of the letters. Each incident was treated separately.

Special recognition to **Heidi Reed**, Library Director for the Young Men's Library Association in Ware, Mass. I had contacted originally **Julie Bullock**, the President of the Ware Historical Society regarding the availability of the book the ***History of Ware Massachusetts 1911 - 1960*** by John and Dorothy Conkey, and was soon referred to Heidi. Heidi mailed me a copy of Conkey's book before I wrote a check. Heidi also went the extra mile: "As far as what I found, we don't have a lot on life in the textile factories in that time period – the age of employee newsletters came later. What I did find is that we have your mother's High School year book, if you don't have that. I could scan the whole thing or just her page. We have the commencement program from the year she graduated. We have a program for a play put on the by Senior class her year, though she is not listed in the cast. The other thing I have from that general time period is the Alligator magazine from Ware High School from 1928, which would give a flavor of the time, though not her actual graduation year. If any or all of this would be helpful, I can scan and send it to you." Which she did, also copying Penn, David, and Taylor Forrant-Sullivan, my Executrix for All Things Forrant.

My thanks to **Carla Genoni**, that intrepid "volunteer" who responded to my softly-worded request to review completed chapters and make suggestions. Every change she suggested improved my text. And Carla often made her deadline.

I was fortunate to be contacted by **Lindsay Henderson** of the State Department, currently stationed in Washington D.C., and her efforts in support of the National Museum of American Diplomacy (https:// diplomacy.state.gov/) and its collection of more than 10,000 items located in the Harry S. Truman building. Lindsay, building on a 22-year career with the Department, has been working with a few dedicated colleagues over the past five years as volunteers to document the lives of members of the Department in times past in a way that is accessible for future researchers. This effort includes gathering images, documents, and stories in both hard copy and electronic form to preserve and share. Beyond that, her personal focus is women in the Foreign Service and a current project on women who served as clerks – yes, Dorothy Marita Forrant represents that demographic. I strongly encourage Lindsay in her research and publication.

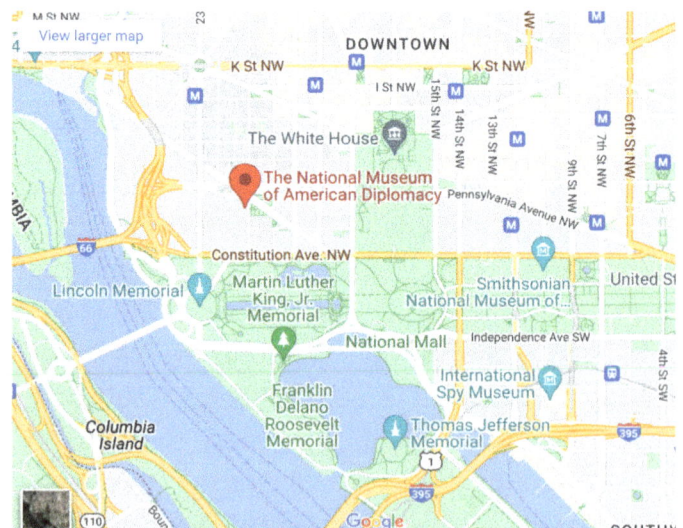

I recognize the support and strong interest from **Brenda Lawson** as Interim President of the Massachusetts Historical Society, and her very able colleague, Curator of Manuscripts **Stephanie Call**, who was my contact for details within the Society. Brenda's strong interest in adding the primary source material from Dorothy's life in adding these materials to the Society's collection stemmed from their primary collecting focus of personal papers—letters, diaries, etc.—of individuals from Massachusetts, thus right on target for Dorothy's records. The Society also collects photographs and can handle digital records. Stephanie, Brenda, and I worked up a Deed for Gift that we could all agree with, and Dorothy's letters are thus saved in perpetuity.

At the United States Naval Academy Museum, I thank **Tracie Logan** who worked with the Collections Committee to find a home for Lt Blackledge's 7-page report and marked navigation chart on the Japanese bombing of Woosung Fort, 3-4 February 1932.

My thanks to **John Dorroh** of Houston, a Lamar High School classmate of my brother Pete, and a former homeroom student of Dorothy's at Lamar, who is my 'go to' Latin guy – his tribute to Wahleah Tennyson, the Latin teacher at Lamar who later befriended Dorothy during her teaching career, is found in *Every Memory a Story*. I asked John's help with the Latin phrase that was Dorothy's Class Motto out of Ware High: *Faber est quisque suae fortunae* and it is John's opinion that wins the day in the Ware chapter.

My Naval Academy Class of 1963 classmate **Pete Deutermann**, author of ~ 30 novels of military adventure and intrigue, kindly shared with me his memories (and photo) of his parents in the Far East, and especially with the sly smile they exchanged when speaking of Club Chefoo. I appreciate that he had to descend into his basement and go through files "organized by gravity."

My Naval Academy Class of 1963 classmate **John Kelly** and his spouse CiCi Williamson, who used their photoshop skills to determine the engraving developer mark on Dorothy's (or was it E.N. Jones') photos of the shipwreck of the *M.V. Monte Cervantes*, 22 January 1930.

I was most fortunate to find **Dr Elda Maria Salmoral**, the past president of the Buenos Aires YWCA, who (beyond all rules for coincidence) was working on a book on the history of the Buenos Aires YWCA. She kindly researched (and found) Dorothy's name in the 1929 YWCA Register.

Chris Flebotte of the Massachusetts Cemeteries for his work at St Paul's Cemetery. On my behalf, but without my requesting it, Chris visited the cemetery to double check that no other stones existed for the Charles Forrant family in an eight-grave plot.

My first cousin and friend **Richard Forrant**, who kindly connected me to his granddaughter **Taylor** (now my Executrix for all Forrant Genealogy related artifacts) and with his "**Uncle Joe**" (Adelbert Swirk). Uncle Joe, himself a graduate of Ware High, as well as the Naval Stenography School (San Diego), and the Naval Intelligence School/Language Division (Washington, D.C.), accomplished some amazingly detailed research work on the Forrant, Glancy, Swirk, and Bouvier families during 1998-1999 which included trips to County Clerks, cemeteries, land records offices. Uncle Joe died in June of 2012 at age 89; like many of these volunteers, I never met him in person. Taylor will become the recipient of Uncle Joe's in-depth report, and I treasure the opportunity to recognize his efforts here, in a book that will feature some of his investigative efforts 'forever.'

As with so many of my books, I am most appreciative of **Michael Wilson**, the erstwhile webmaster for the Albuquerque Genealogical Society. Mike W. (I always feel I need to designate which Mike I am referring to) has conquered the IngramSpark steps for creating a book cover, as well as using his Adobe Pro skills to take my unvarnished Microsoft Word chapter files and PDF them at a higher resolution than Microsoft would accomplish, thus preserving the resolution of Dorothy's photos. IngramSpark requires one giant PDF file of the book's contents, and Mike W. creates that for us.

I gratefully acknowledge my 'current' wife **Bonnie Armes Nolan-Blackledge**, bravely marrying a late-60s widower after coyly asking, "May I read your genealogy book?" Once the 900+ pages were produced, Bonnie's question quickly morphed into "Is there perhaps a small chapter I can read?" For *this* book, Bonnie read the Dorothy letters with interest, and participated in the process by translating the fuzzy newspaper clippings as photographed through brother Pete's display glass cases into the text of the critical Ware River News articles on Dorothy's 1926-1932 adventures. Critical in that they had been spared the New England Hurricane (1938) which took the WRN archives forever.

Finally, I wish to thank all the unnamed and named folks that helped me gather up bits of history to create this book, and those that helped Dorothy along the path she chose from entering her senior year at Ware High School in 1924 right up until Vice-Consul Williamson performed the marriage ceremony in Tokyo in 1934. Included in this plethora of kind souls is the afore-mentioned semi-mysterious **E. N. Jones**, of which this book displays photographs with and without the Burberry coat he loaned Dorothy during those first 24 hours of being shipwrecked in Ushuaia. His/their photos will hopefully commemorate this great adventure for future researchers.

I thank you all.

Michael A. Blackledge
Albuquerque, New Mexico, USA
24 April 2025

Bibliography

Dorothy's Library

Dorothy's library consists of a small collection of books each inscribed by her on frontispiece [see image at right] that was part of her personal collection during her Foreign Service stint in Buenos Aires and Tokyo.

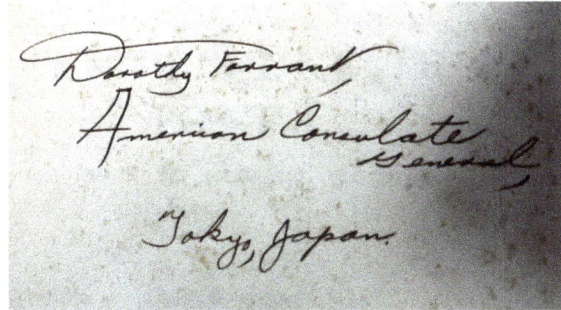

Gibbs, Sir Philip (Tenth Impression; original 1903). *Knowledge is Power: A Guide to Personal Culture*. London: Hutchinson & Company Ltd.[1]

Jones, Llewellyn (1927). *Gems of the World's Best Classics: A Collection of Complete Short Stories and Essays chosen from the Literatures of all Periods and Countries Written by Standard Authors.* Chicago: The Geographical Publishing Co.[2]

Tolstoy, Leo. *War and Peace.* Translated by Constance Garnett, Carlton House, J.J. Little & Ives Co., New York, 1904.

Black Diphtheria

Blackledge, Mary Ann Ryza; David W. Blackledge; and Michael A. Blackledge. *Blackledges in America: A Genealogy of Blackledge/Blacklidge Descendants with Roots in the United States of America*. Second Edition. Albuquerque, New Mexico: Blackledge Books, 2012.

Blackledge, Michael. "A Virtual Cemetery: Forrant Family." Find A Grave. Database. https://www.findagrave.com/virtual-cemetery/559851 : accessed 20 October 2024. Includes links to memorials for Julia Garde Glancy, Mary "May" Glancy Forrant, Arthur J. Forrant, and Dorothy M. *Forrant* Blackledge.

Ware

Chase, Arthur. History of Ware Massachusetts (1911). The University Press, Cambridge. https://archive.org/details/historywaremass00chasgoog (accessed 7 January 2025).

Conkey, John Houghton and Conkey, Dorothy Dunham. History of Ware Massachusetts 1911 -- 1960. (1961) Barre Gazette, Barre, Massachusetts.

Habana

Special Handbook for the Use of Delegates, Sixth International Conference of American States, Habana, Cuba, January 16, 1928, prepared by the Pan American Union (Washington, Government Printing Office, 1927).   https://catalog.hathitrust.org/Record/102031777 (accessed 13 March 2025).

Report of the delegates of the United States of America to the Sixth International Conference of American states held at Habana, Cuba, January 16 to February 20, 1928 / With appendices. United

---

[1] available online via Google Books.

[2] refurbished January 2025 by Pilgrim Bound Bibles, Albuquerque, NM.

States Government Printing Office, Washington
https://babel.hathitrust.org/cgi/pt?id=mdp.39015070220986&seq=7 (accessed 27 February 2025).

Buenos Aires

Memoria y Balances Anual de la Asociación Cristiana Femenina, Y.W.C.A. de Buenos Aires, Argentina desde 1 de Octubre de 1928 hasta el 30 de Septiembre de 1929, calle Sarmiento 652. Oficina General: U.T. 35 Libertad 3505. Oficina de Empleos: U.T. 35 Libertad 3513. Dirección Telegráfica "Emissarius", Archivos Y.W.C.A.

Smith, Gretchen. *"15 WOMEN CHOSEN FOR NAVAL PARLEY."* The Evening Star, Washington, D.C., Wednesday, December 18, 1929, p. 6.

Tokio

Blackledge, Michael. "A Virtual Cemetery: Lewis (H.) Blackledge Family." Find A Grave. Database. https://www.findagrave.com/virtual-cemetery/321169 : accessed 18 August 2020. Entries include Allan Douglas Blackledge, Irma Harriet *Ranney* Blackledge, Dorothy Marita "Missy" *Forrant* Blackledge, LTC Douglas Faust "Doug" Blackledge, Hobert Lee Blackledge.

Report: League of Nations, Situation in Manchuria: Report of the Lytton Commission of Inquiry, (1932). Appeal by the Chinese Government. Report of the Commission of Enquiry. https://www.loc.gov/item/2021666890/ Accessed 9 March 2025.

Meehan, John David. (2000). *From Ally to Menace: Canadian Attitudes and Policies Toward Japanese Imperialism, 1929-1939* [Doctoral dissertation, University of Toronto]. National Library of Canada. Includes reference to A. Keith Doull, Assistant Commercial Attache, Canadian Legation, Tokyo. Accessed 20 October 2024.

Navy Wife

Raytheon Analysis and Test Laboratory. *https://indyencyclopedia.org/raytheon-analysis-and-test-laboratory/ Accessed* 9 March 2025.

Epilogue

Blackledge Michael A. *Every Memory A Story: Anecdotes and Images Capturing Family History.* (2023). Albuquerque, New Mexico: Blackledge Books.

Blackledge Michael A. 2020. *Blackledge Stories: and other BS.* 1st ed. Albuquerque, New Mexico: Blackledge Books with LithExcel Ltd.

Index of Names